The Disability Reader

Social Science Perspectives

Edited by
Tom Shakespeare

CASSELL

London and New

D0293892

Cassell
Wellington House
125 Strand
London WC2R 0BB

370 Lexington Avenue
New York
NY 10017-6550

First published 1998

Reprinted 1999

British Library Cataloguing in Publication Data
A catalogue record for this book is available from the British Library.

ISBN 0–304–33975–X (hardback)
       0–304–33976–8 (paperback)

Library of Congress Cataloging-in-Publication Data
The disability reader: social science perspectives/edited by Tom Shakespeare.
      p.   cm.
    Includes bibliographical references (p.   ) and index.
    ISBN 0–304–33975–X (hardback: acid-free paper). – ISBN 0–304–33976–8 (paperback: acid-free paper)
      1. Disability studies – Great Britain.   2. Sociology of disability – Great Britain.   3. Handicapped – Great Britain – Social conditions.
    I. Shakespeare, Tom.
    HV1568.25.G7D57   1998
    362.4'0941 – dc21   97 – 43065
                                                                              CIP

Typeset by York House Typographic Ltd, London
Printed and bound in Great Britain by
Redwood Books, Trowbridge, Wilts

Contents

Notes on Contributors   v

Acknowledgements   ix

Introduction   1

PART ONE: From Activism to Academia

1   A Critical Condition   7
Paul Hunt

2   Independent Living and the Medical Model of Disability   20
Simon Brisenden

3   Emancipating Disability Studies   28
Vic Finkelstein

PART TWO: The Developing Discipline

4   Sociology, Disability Studies and Education: Some
Observations   53
Len Barton

5   The Social Model of Disability: A Sociological Phenomenon
Ignored by Sociologists?   65
Colin Barnes

6   The Spectre at the Feast: Disabled People and Social Theory   79
Paul Abberley

7   The Best Burgers? The Person with Learning Difficulties as
Worker   94
Stephen Baron, Sheila Riddell and Heather Wilkinson

8   Researching a Disabling Society: The Case of Employment
and New Technology   110
Alan Roulstone

9   Oppression, Disability and Access in the Built Environment   129
Rob Imrie

10   Enabling Identity: Disability, Self and Citizenship   147
Nicholas Watson

11   Body Battles: Bodies, Gender and Disability   163
Helen Meekosha

12 Understanding Cinematic Representations of Disability   181
    Paul Darke

PART THREE: Debates and Dialogues

13 Multiple Oppression and the Disabled People's Movement   201
    Ayesha Vernon
14 Still out in the Cold: People with Learning Difficulties and
    the Social Model of Disability   211
    Anne Louise Chappell
15 Disability Discourse in a Postmodern World   221
    Mairian Corker
16 The Sociology of Disability: Towards a Materialist
    Phenomenology   234
    Gareth Williams
17 Activists and Academics: Part of the Same or a World
    Apart?   245
    Penny Germon

    Afterword   256
    Bibliography   258
    Index   307

Notes on Contributors

Paul Abberley is a disabled writer and sociologist, formerly at the University of the West of England and the University of Bristol. He has published a number of articles on aspects of disability over the last ten years. He now lives on Dartmoor.

Colin Barnes is a disabled writer and researcher. He was the founder of the Disability Research Unit, University of Leeds, and is also the research director of BCODP. With Geof Mercer, he is the founder of the Disability Press at Leeds. His books include *The Cabbage Syndrome* and *Disabled People in Britain and Discrimination*.

Stephen Baron is currently Senior Lecturer in Education at the University of Glasgow, where he co-ordinates research in education and adult and continuing education. His research interests lie in cultural studies and the mechanism of reproduction of disadvantaged groups, especially people with learning difficulties.

Len Barton is Professor of Education at the University of Sheffield. He edits the international journal *Disability and Society*, and has been at the forefront of the development of disability studies in Britain. His books include *The Politics of Special Educational Needs* and *Disability and Society: Emerging Issues and Insights*.

Simon Brisenden was a disabled writer, and a leading member of the disability movement, particularly in his work with Hampshire Centre for Integrated Living. His work has been published widely in disability movement journals, and in two collections of his poems.

Anne Louise Chappell is Senior Lecturer in Social Policy at Buckinghamshire College. Her research interests centre on community care and the social model of disability, with particular reference to people with learning difficulties.

Mairian Corker is a deaf self-employed writer, editor, researcher and part-time counsellor. She is author of three books and numerous articles on deaf and disability issues as they relate to counselling, education, employment, cultural processes and social policy.

Paul Darke is a disabled researcher, writer and critic, and has published widely on issues of film, art and culture. Having studied for a doctorate at the University of Warwick, he now works as a freelance media consultant.

Vic Finkelstein achieved liberation from the world of the shoe-bound owing to a spinal injury while pole vaulting at school in South Africa. Following graduation from deprivation torture, ten months' imprisonment, and five years' banning for his opposition to apartheid, he emigrated to the United Kingdom in 1968, joining the Open University in 1975. He was a founder member of the Union of the Physically Impaired Against Segregation (UPIAS), London Disability Arts Forum and the British Council of Organisations of Disabled People (BCODP) of which he was the first chairperson, and represented the UK on the first World Council of the Disabled Peoples' International (DPI).

Penny Germon has been an activist in the disabled people's movement since 1989, initially as a management committee member for the West of England Coalition of Disabled People followed by seven years as a paid worker. She now works for the BCODP supporting the development of disabled people's organizations.

Paul Hunt was a founder member of the Union of the Physically Impaired Against Segregation, and a leading activist in the early years of the disability movement in Britain. Formerly resident in the LeCourt Cheshire Home in Hampshire, he edited *Stigma*, a pioneering collection of writings by disabled people, in 1966.

Rob Imrie is Reader in Human Geography, Royal Holloway College, University of London. He is author of *Disability and the City*. He has recently completed research on local authority policies and practice towards disabled people's access requirements, and is currently researching property markets, disability and access in Sweden and the United Kingdom.

Helen Meekosha is a Senior Lecturer in the School of Social Work at the University of New South Wales. She has worked as a community worker in the UK and Australia, and as a social policy consultant. Her political and academic activity attempts to cross boundaries of race, gender, disability and chronic illness. She co-founded and co-ordinates the Sydney Disability Research Network, which received Australian Research Council funding in 1997. She is author of *Body Battles: Disability, Representation and Participation* (forthcoming, Sage).

Sheila Riddell undertook a PhD at Bristol University on 'Gender, social class and subject option choice'. She subsequently worked as a Research Fellow at Edinburgh University, investigating the impact of the 1980 Education (Scotland) Act (as amended) on children with special educational needs. A move to the Department of Education, Stirling University followed, where Sheila taught and researched in the area of gender, special educational needs and disability. Following a period as Dean of Arts and Social Science at Napier University in Edinburgh, Sheila is currently working as Professor of Social Policy (Disability Studies) at Glasgow University.

Alan Roulstone lectures in disability studies at the University of Sunderland. He is the author of *Enabling Technology: Disabled People, Employment and New Technology* (forthcoming, Open University Press). He identifies as disabled, having a hidden impairment, and his research interests centre on this issue.

Ayesha Vernon was formerly part of the Disability Research Unit, University of Leeds, and has written widely on the interrelationship of disability, 'race' and gender. She currently works at the Social Policy Research Unit, University of York, and is active in the disability movement.

Nicholas Watson lectures in medical sociology in the Department of Nursing Studies, University of Edinburgh, and was formerly a health promotion officer in Scotland. His doctoral research explored disabled people's health experiences, and he is currently co-directing the ESRC-funded 'Life as a Disabled Child' project. He is active in the disability movement, and convenor of Accessibility Lothian.

Heather Wilkinson is Research Fellow on the ESRC project *The Meaning of the Learning Society for Adults with Learning Difficulties*, based at Napier, Glasgow and Stirling Universities. She is about to move to the Disability Research Centre, Glasgow University. Prior to this project Heather spent five years as a researcher in the Departments of Applied Social Science and Educational Research, Lancaster University where she undertook work on the integration of children with special educational needs, and community development and family support. Her PhD is on 'The process of parental choice for mothers of children with special needs'.

Gareth Williams is Professor of Sociology and Deputy Director of the Public Health Research and Resource Centre at the University of Salford. He has published widely in sociological and health journals on chronic illness and disability, lay knowledge of health and illness, and the NHS reforms. He is co-editor of *Challenging Medicine* and *Researching the People's Health* (both Routledge) and *Contracting for Health* (Oxford University Press) and co-author of *Understanding Rheumatoid Arthritis* (Routledge) and *Markets and Networks* (Open University Press).

Acknowledgements

Thanks are due to the following: Geoffrey Chapman, for the reprint of 'A critical condition' by the late Paul Hunt, from his edited collection, *Stigma* (1966); Carfax, the publishers of the journal *Disability and Society*, for permission to reprint 'Independent living and the medical model of disability' by the late Simon Brisenden; Paul Chapman Publishing, for permission to reproduce sections of *Disability and the City* by Rob Imrie.

Thanks also to Colin Barnes, who drew up the original bibliography from which the comprehensive list of references has been developed. Support, encouragement and advice from Colin Barnes, Len Barton, Mike Oliver, Mark Priestley, Nick Watson and numerous others is appreciated. Thanks to my editor, Roz Hopkins, for constructive feedback and ongoing support.

Dedicated to my mother, with love and thanks

Introduction

Although the disabled people's movement in Britain dates from the 1970s, the development of disability studies, as an academic discipline, really took off during the 1990s. While there had been previous accounts exploring the implications of the social model of disability, it was Mike Oliver's 1990 study, *The Politics of Disablement*, which established the intellectual credentials of this approach to defining and understanding disability. Jenny Morris's *Pride Against Prejudice* (1991), a more populist and feminist-focused book, developed the debate from a slightly different perspective, and since then there have been a steady stream of publications and courses, of which Colin Barnes's postgraduate programme at the University of Leeds is the most notable.

This Reader, however, is the first book which offers the student or researcher new to the field a broad introduction to disability studies, from a social science perspective. Unlike predecessors, the focus here is on theoretical development and empirical evidence, not on policy, practice or political action. There are certainly major practical and political implications of many of the arguments advanced in these chapters, and most of the authors write from a position of engagement, not the ivory-tower detachment of traditional academia. However, the theme of this book establishes disability as a major and neglected area of human social experience, to which it is essential and timely to devote scholarly attention. The dialogue of the collection is between the new researchers in disability studies; the political disability community; and the traditional academic approaches to disability.

The disability movement is a worldwide phenomenon. However, disability studies has developed furthest in the English-speaking countries, particularly in Britain and the United States. With one exception, all the chapters in this collection come from writers living and working in Britain. Moreover, there is a difference in emphasis between disability studies in Britain and America which is worth noting here. The social model, which is constitutive of the disability studies field in Britain, is far less central or accepted in American explorations of disability. Moreover I would argue that whereas British writers are mainly concerned with material factors, social relations and political power, their American counterparts have developed an approach which focuses on history, culture, literature and other aspects of discourse and meaning. Those interested to develop this comparison are referred to the recent publications of Lennard Davis and Rosemary Garland Thompson, to complement and supplement the research published in this volume.

This collection is divided into three parts. The first section provides some background, in the form of two articles from key activists in the early phase of the British disability movement, together with an account by Vic Finkelstein of the role that the Open University played in the origins of disability studies. The main section of the book attempts to cover the range of approaches within contemporary disability studies, both in terms of issues and in terms of the various disciplinary approaches, including sociology, education, geography and cultural studies. Most of the authors in the second and third parts of the collection are from the 'second generation' of disability studies researchers, moving beyond the pioneering work of Mike Oliver, Jenny Morris and others.

The final section of the book raises questions about the direction and emphasis of disability studies, in order to inform future developments. Various controversies within the field are explored, including the applicability of the social model to various groups within the disability community, the issue of impairment, the relationship between academia and the political movement, the value of theory, and the relationship to more traditional medical sociology. It is the opinion of this editor that divergences of this kind are a mark of a healthy academic discipline, and that a pluralism of approaches is essential. However, the same political commitment which is evident in the work of pioneers such as Paul Hunt and Simon Brisenden can be seen in the final chapters of the book also.

As an aid to the researcher, all the references are gathered in the bibliography at the end of the book, which has resulted in the most comprehensive list of disability studies material currently available, albeit still not exhaustive. At the end of each chapter, some indication of appropriate further reading is supplied. Researchers are also referred to the international journal *Disability and Society*, or to American publications such as the *Disability Studies Quarterly*, as well as to the international e-mail discussion list [disability-research@mailbase.ac.uk].

This collection is neither comprehensive nor exhaustive: the field is growing too rapidly for that. However, it offers an introduction to the types of intellectual and political engagements which are taking place, and some signposts as to future developments. Every year new books are published, and new academic courses initiated, and the number of disabled people working and studying in academia increases. It is my hope that disability studies will achieve the legitimacy that women's studies and lesbian and gay studies have previously attained, as a cross-disciplinary field of intellectual activity. It is vital for these explorations not to be ghettoized, or to become insular and inward-looking, because, like these other fields, this research has implications for the rest of academia. In my view this also means that disability studies must be particularly careful to retain a relationship with the disability movement, and the priorities and concerns of ordinary disabled people, rather than to emulate the increasingly irrelevant and inaccessible theoretical developments of some areas of feminist, lesbian and gay studies. It seems appropriate to end by quoting Antonio Gramsci, the disabled Italian Marxist who has inspired Mike Oliver, among others, and who wrote while imprisoned:

> The identification of theory and practice is a critical act, through which practice is demonstrated rational and necessary, and theory realistic and rational. That is why the problem of the identity of theory and practice is raised especially in the so-called transitional moments of history, that is, those moments in which the movement of transformation is at its most rapid. For it is then that the practical forces unleashed really demand justification in order to become more efficient and expansive; and that theoretical programmes multiply in number, and demand in their turn to be realistically justified, to the extent that they prove themselves assimilable into practical movements, thereby making the latter yet more practical and real. (Gramsci, 1985, p. 365)

Part One

From Activism to Academia

1

A Critical Condition

Paul Hunt (1966)

All my adult life has been spent in institutions amongst people who, like myself, have severe and often progressive physical disabilities. We are paralysed and deformed, most of us in wheelchairs, either as the result of accident or of diseases like rheumatoid arthritis, multiple sclerosis, muscular dystrophy, cerebral palsy and polio. So naturally this personal experience forms a background to the views on disability that follow.

I do not mean to exclude altogether the large number of people who today are able to lead a more or less normal life in the community; those with relatively light disabilities, or with such handicaps as defects in sight, speech or hearing, epilepsy, obesity, heart disease, and so on. I hope that much of what I say will be relevant to this latter group since they have many problems in common with us.

But apart from the obvious value of writing from my own direct knowledge, it is also true that the situation of 'the young chronic sick' (as we are officially and rather unpleasantly termed) highlights, or rather goes to the depths of, the question of disablement. Our 'tragedy' may be only the tragedy of all sickness, pain and suffering carried to extremes. But disabilities like ours, which often prohibit any attempt at normal living in society, almost force one to consider the basic issues, not only of coping with a special handicap, but of life itself.

Being cheerful and keeping going is scarcely good enough when one has an illness that will end in an early death, when one is wasting away like some Belsen victim, maybe incontinent, dependent on others for daily needs, probably denied marriage and a family and forced to live out one's time in an institution. In these circumstances the most acute questions arise and the most radical 'answers' are called for.

I am not suggesting that all of us with such devastating handicaps probe deeply into the meaning of life, nor that we automatically gain great wisdom or sanctity. We have our defences like anyone else. But it does seem that our situation tends to make us ask questions that few people ask in the ordinary world. And it also means that to some extent we are set apart from, or rather have a special position *within*, the everyday society that most people take it for granted they belong to.

I want to look at this special situation largely in terms of our relations with others, our place in society. This is essentially related to the personal aspect of coping with disablement, which I hope it will at the same time illumine, since the problem of disability lies not only in the impairment of function and its effects on us individually, but also, more importantly, in the area of our relationship with 'normal' people. If everyone were disabled as we are, there would be no special situation to consider.

This focus on the ways in which we are set apart from the ordinary does not mean that I see us as really separated from society. In fact the reverse assumption underlies everything I write. We *are* society, as much as anybody, and cannot be considered in isolation from it.

I am aware of the danger of concentrating on the ways in which disability makes us like each other and unlike the normal, and thus being trapped into the common fault of viewing people in terms of one characteristic to the exclusion of all others. Disabled people suffer enough from that kind of thing already. But whatever the differences between us, we do have certain sets of experiences in common. In dealing with this aspect of our lives I have tried not to forget two others – our uniqueness as persons and the human nature we share with the rest of mankind.

I think the distinguishing mark of disabled people's special position is that they tend to 'challenge' in their relations with ordinary society. This challenge takes five main forms: as *unfortunate, useless, different, oppressed* and *sick*. All these are only facets of one situation, but here it seems worth taking each in turn.

The first way in which we challenge others is by being *unfortunate*. Severely disabled people are generally considered to have been unlucky, to be deprived and poor, to lead cramped lives. We do not enjoy many of the 'goods' that people in our society are accustomed to. The opportunity for marriage and having children, authority at home and at work, the chance to earn money, independence and freedom of movement, a house and a car[1] – these things, and plenty more, may be denied us.

Underprivileged as we are in this sense, one point seems to be clear. If the worth of human beings depends on a high social status, on the possession of wealth, on a position as parent, husband or wife – if such things are *all-important* – then those of us who have lost or never had them are indeed unfortunate. Our lives must be tragically upset and marred for ever, we must be only half alive, only half human. And it is a fact that most of us, whatever our explicit views, tend to act as though such 'goods' are essential to a fully human existence. Their possession is seen as the key to entry into a promised land of civilized living.

But set over against this common sense attitude is another fact, a strange one. In my experience even the most severely disabled people retain an ineradicable conviction that they are still fully human in all that is ultimately necessary. Obviously each person can deny this, and act accordingly. Yet even when he is most depressed, even when he says he would be better off dead, the underlying sense of his own worth remains.

This basic feeling for the value of the person *as such* becomes fully operational, as it were, when those with severe disabilities live full and happy lives in defiance of the usual expectations. An increasing number of people do seem to overcome their misfortunes like this, and it is they who present the most effective challenge to society.

When confronted with someone who is evidently coping with tragic circumstances, able-bodied people tend to deny the reality of the adjustment. The disabled person is simply making the best of a bad job, putting a good face on it. There may be some truth in this. But when it becomes obvious that there is also a genuine happiness, another defensive attitude is taken up. The 'unfortunate' person is assumed to have wonderful and exceptional courage (although underneath this overt canonization there is usually a degree of irritation and hostility which comes to light at moments of stress). This devalues other disabled people by implication, and leaves the fit person still with his original view that disablement is really utterly tragic.

Such reactions appear to be caused by the need to safeguard a particular scale of values, where someone's sense of security depends on this being maintained. He almost *wants* the disabled person to suffer, as a confirmation that the values denied him are still worthy and important and good. If he shows no obvious sign of suffering, then he must challenge people whose own worth seems to them to be bound up with their more fortunate position in life.

So if those of us who are disabled live as fully as we can, while being completely conscious of the tragedy of our situation – this is the possibility when one has an alert mind – then somehow we can communicate to others an awareness that the value of the human person transcends his social status, attributes and possessions or his lack of them. This applies however much we recognize these 'accidents' as important, and however much we regard the 'goods' I have mentioned as the normal elements in a full life. What we oppose is only the assumption that makes them absolutely indispensable for a completely human existence.

Perhaps we can help prepare people for the almost certain day when they themselves lose, at least in old age, some of the advantages that are so highly valued. But anyway, those who implicitly believe that a man's worth depends on his good fortune must be building their lives on rather inadequate foundations, and they will perhaps find contact with us a thought-provoking experience.

A second aspect of our special position in society is that we are often *useless*, unable to contribute to the economic good of the community. As such, again we cannot help posing questions about values, about what a person is, what he is for, about whether work in the everyday sense of the word is the most important or the only contribution anyone can make to society.

There is no doubt that we do put great stress on the individual's economic contribution. Most people are wrapped up in a workaday, utilitarian world, and regard anything not visibly productive as expendable. Contemplations, philosophy, wisdom, the liberal arts, get short shrift from the average man. Those who cannot work, such as the sick, aged or unemployed, are subject to a tremendous pressure to feel useless, or at least of less value than the breadwinner.

I am not indicting some abstract Society for getting its priorities wrong; each of us shares responsibility for the prevailing attitudes. Also I am far from saying that work, in the sense of contributing to the wealth of the community, is unimportant. Of course willingness to pull one's weight is an essential part of a healthy and balanced outlook on life and other people.

But I am concerned that we should not elevate the idea of work in our minds to the point where it dominates values that ought to transcend it. It is important not to do this, if only because it causes the most acute suffering in those of us who cannot help being parasites on the economic body.

Obviously we who are disabled are deeply affected by the assumptions of our uselessness that surround us. But it is vital that we should not accept this devaluation of ourselves, yearning only to be able to earn our livings and thus prove our worth. We do not have to prove anything.

If we have a basic willingness to contribute to the community, yet cannot do an ordinary job, we may certainly contribute in less obvious ways; even, and perhaps especially, if these seem insignificant beside the 'real world of work'. Our freedom from the competitive trappings that accompany work in our society may give us the opportunity to demonstrate its essential elements. Also we can act as a symbol for the pre-eminent claims of non-utilitarian values, a visible challenge to anyone who treats his job as a final end in itself. And we do of course afford people the chance to be generous in support of the needy, thus enabling them to give practical expression to their desire to go beyond the acquisitive instinct.

At the ultimate point we may only be able to suffer, to be passive through complete physical inability. Just here we have a special insight to offer, because our position gives us an extra experience of life in the passive aspect that is one half of the human reality. Those who lead active lives are perhaps especially inclined to ignore man's need to accept passivity in relation to so many forces beyond his control. They may need reminding sometimes of our finiteness, our feminine side in the hands of fate or providence. We are well placed to do this job at least.

The next challenging characteristic of the disabled is that we are *different*, abnormal, marked out as members of a minority group. Normality is so often put forward as *the* goal for people with special handicaps, that we have come to accept its desirability as a dogma. But even if one takes a common sense meaning for the word – being like most people in our society – it is doubtful if this is what we should really fix our sights on. For one thing it is impossible of achievement, at certain levels anyway. Obviously we cannot be physically normal, are doomed to be deviants in this sense at least. Also we must be affected psychologically by our disabilities, and to some extent be moulded into a distinct class by our experiences.

But more important, what *kind* of goal is this elusive normality? If it does mean simply trying to be like the majority, then it is hardly a good enough ideal at which to aim. Whether they are physically handicapped or not, people need something more than this to work towards if they are to contribute their best to society and grow to maturity.

Of course there is a certain value in our trying to keep up with ordinary society, and relate to it; but it is essential to define the sense in which this is a good thing. Once more I am not rejecting in a sour-grapes spirit the many excellent normal goals that may be denied us – marrying, earning one's living, and so on. What I *am* rejecting is society's tendency to set up rigid standards of what is right and proper, to force the individual into a mould.

Our constant experience of this pressure towards unthinking conformity in some way relates us to other obvious deviants and outcasts like the Jew in a gentile world, a Negro in a white world, homosexuals, the mentally handicapped; and also to more voluntary rebels in every sphere – artists, philosophers, prophets, who are essentially subversive elements in society. This is another area where disabled people can play an important role.

Those we meet cannot fail to notice our disablement even if they turn away quickly and avoid thinking about us afterwards. An impaired and deformed body is a 'difference' that hits everyone hard at first. Inevitably it produces an instinctive revulsion, has a disturbing effect. Our own first reaction to this is to want to hide ourselves in the crowd, to attempt to buy acceptance on any terms, to agree uncritically with whatever is the done thing. Feeling excessively self-conscious we would like to bury ourselves in society away from the stares of the curious, and even the special consideration of the kindly, both of which serve to emphasize our difference from the majority.

But this very natural impulse has to be resisted. We must try to help people accept the fact of our unavoidable difference from them – which implies that we are attempting to integrate it within ourselves too. However, this does not mean just creating a comfortable atmosphere of acceptance around ourselves, building up a circle of able-bodied friends who treat us right, and trying to leave it at that. It is imperative that the effort should be followed through to the point where we, and those we come into contact with, understand that it is not just a case of our minds compensating for our disabilities, or something like that.

We can witness to the truth that a person's dignity does not rest even in his consciousness, and certainly that it does not rest in his beauty, age, intelligence or colour. Those of us with unimpaired minds but severely disabled bodies, have a unique opportunity to show other people not only that our big difference from them does not lessen our worth, but also that *no* difference between men, however real, unpleasant and disturbing, does away with their right to be treated as fully human.

We face more obviously than most the universal problem of coming to terms with the fact of man's individuality and loneliness. If we begin to accept our own special peculiarity, we shall be in a position to help others accept even their own difference from everyone else. These two acceptances are bound up together. People's shocked reactions to the obvious deviant often reflect their own deepest fears and difficulties, their failure to accept themselves as they really are, and the other person simply as 'other'.

The disabled person's 'strangeness' can manifest and symbolize all differences between human beings. In his relations with more nearly normal people he may become a medium for reconciling them to the fact of these differences, and demonstrate their relative unimportance compared to what we have in common.

The fourth challenging aspect of our situation follows inevitably from our being different and having minority status. Disabled people often meet prejudice, which expresses itself in discrimination and even *oppression*. Sometimes it seems to us that we just can't win. Whatever we do, whether good or bad, people put it down to our being disabled. Meeting this kind of attitude constantly can be depressing and infinitely wearing. You may produce the most logical and persuasive arguments only to have them dismissed, without even the compliment of counter-argument, as products of your disability. The frustrating thing is that there is no appeal against this. If you point out what is happening you are assured it isn't, that you are imagining a prejudice which does not exist. And immediately you know you are branded again as being unrealistic and impossibly subjective. So many people take it for granted that what you say can be explained by a crude theory of compensation, and therefore is of no account or self-evidently false. And they tell themselves that you can't really help having these ideas, poor thing.

One rather doubtful pleasure is to discover that this 'poor thing' attitude does not survive a determined rejection of the able-bodied person's assumption of inherent superiority. He admits equality as a theory, but when you *act* as though you *are* equal then the crucial test comes. Most people are good-willed liberals towards us up to this point, but not all of them survive close contact with disability without showing some less attractive traits.

Of course it is not only the 'fit' who are like this. I know I have instinctive prejudices against lots of people; against the able-bodied to start with. It is a basic human characteristic to fear and put up barriers against those who are different from ourselves. Without for a moment justifying any of its manifestations, it seems to me just as 'natural' to be prejudiced against someone with a defective body (or mind) as it is to have difficulty in accepting the members of another racial group.

Maybe it is invidious to compare our situation with that of racial minorities in any way. The injustice and brutality suffered by so many because of racial tension makes our troubles as disabled people look very small. But I think there is a connection somewhere, since all prejudice springs from the same roots. And there stirs in me a little of the same anger as the Negro writer James Baldwin reveals in *The Fire Next Time* when I remember the countless times I have seen disabled people hurt, treated as less than people, told what to do and how to behave by those whose only claim to do this came from prejudice and their power over them.

In the hospitals and Homes I have lived in one rarely sees any physical cruelty. But I have experienced enough of other kinds of subtly corrupting behaviour. There are administrators and matrons who have had people removed on slight pretexts, who try to break up ordinary friendships if they don't approve of them. There are the staff who bully those who cannot complain, who dictate what clothes people should wear, who switch the television off in the middle of a programme, and will take away 'privileges' (like getting up for the day) when they choose. Then there are the visitors who automatically assume an authority over us and interfere without regard for our wishes.

Admittedly some of these examples are trivial, and I have not mentioned all the excellent people who make any sort of life possible for us. But still I think it is true that we meet fundamentally the same attitude which discriminates against anyone different and shades off into oppression under the right – or rather wrong – conditions.

In the wider community the similarity is even clearer. Employers turn away qualified and competent workers simply because they are disabled. Restaurants and pubs give transparent excuses for refusing our custom. Landladies reject disabled lodgers. Parents and relations fight the marriage of a cripple into their family – perhaps with more reason than with a black African, but with many of the same arguments. And it's not hard to see the analogy between a racial ghetto and the institutions where disabled people are put away and given enough care to salve society's conscience.

Of course there are vast differences between our situation and that of many other 'downtrodden' people. One of these is that we are not a potential threat to lives and property. For this reason alone we can be hopeful that at least our freedom from open discrimination[2] can be achieved even though we shall never have sufficient power in the community to ensure this. It also gives us a good chance of avoiding the ever-present danger for those who are oppressed – that they will pay homage to the same god of power that is harming their oppressors.

It is true that we still have to solve the problem of means and ends; of whether, or rather in what way, we should oppose evil. But perhaps precisely because violence and power-seeking are not really practical possibilities for us, we are well placed to consider other ways of achieving freedom from injustice. However, we should be careful that our weakness here does not become an excuse for a sterile resignation.

One reason why we must resist prejudice, injustice, oppression, is that they not only tend to diminish us, but far more to diminish our oppressors. If you try to care about people you cannot be indifferent to what is happening to those who treat you badly, and you have to oppose them. If this opposition is to be by means of patience and long-suffering, then they must be directed at the abolition of evil or they are just forms of masochism.

In this section I have not only been drawing an analogy between our position in society and that of racial minorities, but also pointing the connection between all the manifestations of prejudice and discrimination. This connection means that although we cannot directly assist the American Negro, for instance, in his resistance to oppression, in one way we *can* help everyone who suffers injustice.

We do this above all by treating properly those we meet. There are always people we feel superior to or resent – the mentally ill, the aged, children, those who patronize us or hurt us. If we do not try to treat all these as fully human beings, then it is certain we would not be able to help the Negro or anyone else in a similar predicament. Here, as in so many instances, it is true that: 'What we do is a symbol of what we would do. Not only can *we* do no more than to let an act substitute for a more splendid act, *but no one can do more.* This is the reconciliation.'[3]

The last aspect of our challenge to society as disabled people is that we are *sick,* suffering, diseased, in pain. For the able-bodied, normal world we are representatives of many of the things they most fear – tragedy, loss, dark and the unknown. Involuntarily we walk – or more often sit – in the valley of the shadow of death. Contact with us throws up in people's faces the fact of sickness and death in the world. No one likes to think of such things, which in themselves are an affront to all our aspirations and hopes. A deformed and paralysed body attacks everyone's sense of well-being and invincibility. People do not want to acknowledge what disability affirms – that life is tragic and we shall all soon be dead.[4] So they are inclined to avoid those who are sick or old, shying from the disturbing reminders of unwelcome reality.

Here I would suggest that our role in society can be likened to that of the satirist in some respects. Maybe we have to remind people of a side of life they would sooner forget. We do this primarily by what we are. But we can intensify it and make it more productive if we are fully conscious of the tragedy of our situation, yet show by our lives that we believe this is not the final tragedy.

Closely involved with death and dark in the unconscious and subconscious, though really distinct, is the idea of evil. An almost automatic linkage is made not only between a sick body and a sick mind, but also undoubtedly between an evil body and an evil mind, a warped personality. There is a definite relation between the concepts of health and holiness. So many of the words used about health are moral ones – we talk of a good or bad leg, of being fit and unfit, of walking properly, of perfect physique. And disabled people find that the common assumption of good health as a natural thing often comes over to us as an 'ought', carries with it undertones of a moral failure on our part. 'If only you had enough will-power ... ' is the modern-dress version of the idea that we are possessed by an evil spirit.

Then there are traces of a desire to externalize evil, to find a scapegoat, in attitudes to the sick. Sometimes people are evidently trying to reassure themselves that they are 'saved', justified, in a state of grace. I do not mean just the feeling of gaining merit from charitable works, but rather a satisfaction got from their 'good' selves juxtaposed with the 'unclean', the untouchables, who provide them with an assurance that they are all right, on the right side.

No doubt this process works the other way too. Our experience of subjection as sick people may give us a sense of being holy and predestined in contrast to our condescending, prejudiced fellow men. But such attitudes, whether in ourselves or others, have to be constantly resisted and rooted out. They are simply products of our own fears and weaknesses, and any temporary security they give is false and dangerous.

I have dealt briefly with five interrelated aspects of disabled people's position as a challenge to some of the common values of society: as *unfortunate, useless, different, oppressed* and *sick*. A paradoxical law runs through the whole of the situation I have been describing. It is that only along the line of maximum resistance to diminishment can we arrive at the required point for a real acceptance of what is unalterable. We have first to acknowledge the value of the good things of life – of prosperity, usefulness, normality, integration with society, good health – and be fully extended in the search for fulfilment in ordinary human terms, before we can begin to achieve a fruitful resignation.

Nowadays many disabled people will have nothing to do with resignation as it used to be understood. Thriving in a climate of increasing public tolerance and kindness, and on a diet of pensions and welfare, we are becoming presumptuous. Now we reject any view of ourselves as being lucky to be allowed to live. We reject too all the myths and superstitions that have surrounded us in the past.

We are challenging society to take account of us, to listen to what we have to say, to acknowledge us as an integral part of society itself. We do not want ourselves, or anyone else, treated as second-class citizens and put away out of sight and mind. Many of us are just beginning to *refuse* to be put away, to insist that we are part of life too. We are saying that being deformed and paralysed, blind or deaf – or old or mentally sick for that matter – is not a crime or in any meaningful sense of the words a divine punishment. Illness and impairment are facts of existence, diminishment and death are there to be thought about and must be taken account of in any realistic view of the world. We are perhaps also saying that society is itself sick if it can't face our *sickness*, if it does not overcome its natural fear and dislike of unpleasantness as manifested by disability.

We are asking of people something that lies a lot deeper than almsgiving. We want an extension of the impulse that inspires this, so that it becomes a gift of self rather than the dispensing of bounty (material and other kinds) from above. To love and respect, treat as equals, people as obviously 'inferior' as we are, requires real humility and generosity. I believe that our demand to be treated like this is based on a truth about human beings which everyone needs to recognize – which is why we have a particularly important function here. But there is also no doubt that acquiring and maintaining such an attitude runs contrary to some of people's most deep seated impulses and prejudices.

The quality of the relationship the community has with its least fortunate members is a measure of its own health. The articulate person with a severe disability may to some extent represent and speak on behalf of all those who perhaps cannot interpret their predicament, or protest for themselves – the weak, sick, poor and aged throughout the world. They too are rejects from ordinary life, and are subject to the same experience of devaluation by society.

This linkage with other 'unfortunates', with the shadow side of life, is not always easy to accept. For the disabled person with a fair intelligence or other gifts, perhaps the greatest temptation is to try to use them just to escape from his disabledness, to buy himself a place in the sun, a share in the illusory normal world where all is light and pleasure and happiness. Naturally we want to get away from and forget the sickness, depression, pain, loneliness and poverty of which we see probably more than our share. But if we deny our special relation to the dark in this way, we shall have ceased to recognize our most important asset as disabled people in society – the uncomfortable, subversive position from which we act as a living reproach to any scale of values that puts attributes or possessions before the person.

Notes

1. I do not mean to imply that all these 'goods' are of the same order.
2. The elimination of prejudice is not really possible: a helpful social climate can only do so much, and each individual and generation has to renew a fight that cannot be won.
3. Doris Lorenzen in *Experiments in Survival*. New York: Kriegel.
4. I do not intend to discuss explicitly religious or philosophical questions in

this essay, but obviously the possibility of a life after death must be extremely relevant at this point.

Further reading

Hunt, P. (ed.) (1966) *Stigma*. London: Geoffrey Chapman.

2

Independent Living and the Medical Model of Disability

Simon Brisenden (1986)

Our opinions, as disabled people, on the subject of disability are not generally rewarded with the same validity as the opinions of 'experts', particularly medical experts. These reproduce the myths of disability through books, articles, lectures and other forms of sooth-saying and oracle, whilst also having the good fortune to receive a salary for their efforts. It is not, of course, in dispute that they deal with the facts – the question is rather one of whether these facts can be ade-quately interpreted from a strictly medical point of view. Is the perspective of medicine historically blinkered, such that 'the facts' are inevitably sucked into a mode of interpretation that has been pre-determined beforehand? Are these 'facts' simply processed in such a way that there is necessarily built upon them an image of the disabled person as inadequate?

Presumably it is possible, under certain conditions, to isolate a set of 'facts', in the form of a list of general physical or intellectual character-istics, that apply to each form of disability. But the use of these is limited as there cannot be a formula derived from them that will cope with the particular needs of each individual. Indeed, taken alone, the 'facts' may lead only to distortion and misunderstanding and to a view of disabled people as a category of rejects, as people flawed in some aspect of their humanity. The medical model of disability is one rooted in an undue emphasis on clinical diagnosis, the very nature of which is destined to lead to a partial and inhibiting view of the disabled individual.

In order to understand disability as an experience, as a lived thing, we need much more than the medical 'facts', however necessary these are in determining medication. The problem comes when they determine not only the form of treatment (if treatment is appropriate), but also the form of life for the person who happens to be disabled. As well as the 'facts', therefore, we need to build up a picture of what it is like to be a disabled person in a world run by non-disabled people. This involves treating the experiences and opinions of people with disabilities as valid and important; more than this, they must be nurtured and given an overriding significance, in order that they begin to outweigh the detached observations of the medical 'expert', which have invested in them the power of history. *Our* experiences must be expressed in *our* words and integrated in the consciousness of mainstream society, and this goes against the accumulated sediment of a social world that is steeped in the medical model of disability.

It is vital that we insist on the right to describe our lives, our disabilities, and that we appropriate the space and proper occasions to do so. After all, the way something is presented will condition to a great extent the way it is received, as any newspaper or television editor will tell you. If the experience of disability is always presented in the context of the medical implications it is supposed to have, it will always be seen as largely a matter of a particular set of physical or intellectual dysfunctions and little else. In this way the myth is perpetuated that disabled people require medical supervision as a permanent factor in their lives. As in society generally, the language used and the situation in which it is expressed will determine the message that goes out to those listening. There are plenty of colloquialisms that indicate the damage that can be done through inappropriate terminology. Disabled people are seen as weak, pathetic and in need of sympathy when they are referred to as 'cripples'. A person with cerebral palsy, when referred to as a 'spastic', has to suffer the indignity of being equated with a raving, dribbling, idiot – these are the facts beyond the medical 'facts'. What we have to get to, instead of this, is the real person inside the image of disability.

To begin with, we are not 'the disabled'. We are disabled people, or even people with disabilities. It is important that we do not allow ourselves to be dismissed as if we all come under this one great metaphysical category 'the disabled'. The effect of this is a depersonalization, a sweeping dismissal of our individuality, and a denial of our right to be seen as people with our own uniqueness, rather than as the anonymous constituents of a category or group. These words that lump us all together – 'the disabled', 'spina bifida', 'tetraplegic', 'muscular dystrophy' – are nothing more than terminological rubbish bins into which all the important things about us as people get thrown away. Similarly, as part of this general burial of our personality, we must note the way in which the form of presentation of a disabled person's experience can be prejudicial to whether that experience is understood. It can pre-determine the image of a disabled person's life that comes over, whilst appearing on the surface to be an objective attempt at allowing us to speak for ourselves.

Every year, at a major medical faculty in Southern England, a doctor interviews a disabled patient in a lecture theatre in front of over a hundred medical students, as part of a course on disability. The point of the exercise is to introduce the students to the problems that disabled people face in society, and to get an authentic point of view from a 'real' disabled person who can recount how a life has been affected by disability. But is an interview with a member of the medical profession – particularly in front of such a large audience – likely to be the best forum for reaching the nuances and particularities of an individual life? And does not the method of enquiry itself reinforce the established view that disabled people are 'passive' and non-disabled people 'active'? Does it not also characterize a disabled person's life as legitimately open to prying questions in front of an inquisitive public? It all seems to rest upon the fundamentally mistaken premise that you can somehow learn about a person's life by asking them questions about the nature of their disability – an idea that assumes the person to be defined by the disability. The reality of the matter is that under the guise of objective scientific enquiry a particular image of disabled people is being fostered in the minds of the audience, and it is an image full of negative implications which are in themselves disabling.

I have a fantasy that in some future world people with disabilities will be able to insist on the right to interrogate doctors, rather than be interrogated by them. In this fantasy, a doctor is placed on stage in front of a large audience of people with disabilities, in order that we may come to understand the stigma of a career in medicine, and the effect this may have on family and friends. Someone would then ask the doctor a series of searching questions, such as: 'When did your profession begin? Was it the result of an accident, or is it a deteriorating condition?' I suspect that we would learn very little about the individual beneath the white coat, but the feeling of power might prove too irresistible to be ignored.

The word 'disabled' is used as a blanket term to cover a large number of people who have nothing in common with each other, except that they do not function in exactly the same way as those people who are called 'normal'. Consequently, this large number of people are considered 'abnormal'. We are seen as 'abnormal' because we are different; we are problem people, lacking the equipment for social integration. But the truth is, like everybody else, we have a range of things we *can* and *cannot* do, a range of abilities both mental and physical that are unique to us as individuals. The only difference between us and other people is that/we are viewed through spectacles that only focus on our inabilities, and which suffer an automatic blindness – a sort of medicalized social reflex – regarding our abilities./The dustbin definition of us as 'the disabled' is a way of looking at us not as people with different abilities, and consequently different needs, but as non-people with non-abilities; not as people who can construct a life out of our different abilities, but as helpless individuals who have to be forced into a life that is constructed for them. We are the outcasts in a society that demands conformity to a mythologized physical norm, the pursuit of which leads to neurosis and is the cause of much guilt and suffering. The impossible demands made on us by this norm, against which we are measured and found to be inadequate, are at the root of our oppression.

We have been entirely defined by what are seen as our inabilities and are given the blanket label of 'the disabled'; a label which is pregnant with hidden ideological overtones. It teaches us a conditioned uselessness, which is not based upon our actual physical or intellectual capacities, but upon the desire to make us believe that we are a drain upon society's resources. It teaches us to be passive, to live up to the image of ourselves as objects of charity that we should be grateful to receive, and to ignore the possibility that we may be active people who have something to contribute to society.

This labelling process leads to us being excluded from all spheres of social life, and allows people to treat us either as morons or as creatures from another planet. Yet it is in fact the posture of society at large that constitutes the most disabling part of being disabled, not the physical effects of whatever condition one happens to have, unless it leaves the individual utterly bed-ridden or completely fatigued. On the whole, it is the organization of society, its material construction and the attitudes of individuals within it, that results in certain people being *dis*-abled. We are only people with different abilities and requirements, yet we are disabled by a society that is geared to the needs of those who can walk, have perfect sight and hearing, can speak distinctly, and are intellectually dextrous.//If society was organized on a more equitable basis, many of the problems associated with not being physically 'perfect' (as if such a concept had any logical basis), would physically disappear. The most obvious example of this has paradoxically been most clearly ignored, despite half-hearted attempts to rectify the situation. I refer to the problem of access to buildings and facilities in the community, and to the callous disregard with which our needs are ignored despite the efforts of sundry committees, working parties and other bodies on our behalf. We are disabled by buildings that are not designed to admit us, and this in turn leads to a whole range of further disablements regarding our education, our chances of gaining employment, our social lives, and so on. The disablement lies in the construction of society, not in the physical condition of the individual. However, this argument is usually rejected, precisely because to accept it involves recognizing the extent to which we are not merely unfortunate, but are directly oppressed by a hostile social environment.

The question of definition bears very directly on the outlook of the medical profession, which has exhibited an unwillingness to revise the way that it views people with disabilities. The problem, from our point of view, is that medical people tend to see all difficulties solely from the perspective of proposed treatments for a 'patient', without recognizing that the individual has to weigh up whether this treatment fits into the overall economy of their life. In the past especially, doctors have been too willing to suggest medical treatment and hospitalization, even when this would not necessarily improve the quality of life for the person concerned. Indeed, questions about the quality of life have sometimes been portrayed as something of an intrusion upon the purely medical equation. This has occurred due to a failure of imagination, the result of the medical profession's participation in the construction of a definition of disability which is partial and limited. This definition has portrayed disability as almost entirely a medical problem, and it has led to a situation where doctors and others are trapped in their responses by a definition of their own making. They cannot respond in ways that go outside the parameters of a view of disabled people which they them-selves have created. They are stuck within the medical model of disability.

The limited parameters of this model have been passed on to other professionals and to people with disabilities themselves, leading to unimaginative responses by service providers, and to low expectations on behalf of themselves by those who have a disability. This depressing situation may, to some extent, be changing, but disabled people still suffer from being viewed and defined within this medical model, with its implication that someone will – and should – always be in and out of hospital.

This way of looking at things ignores the sociological and psychological aspects of disability. It ignores the fact that frequent hospitalization and medical treatment is in itself one of the most disabling factors about being disabled. We should instead look at life as a whole, and allow people with disabilities to take decisions for themselves based on many other factors as well as medical ones. We have to look at a person's independence and ask how this can be assisted and promoted without taking the right of control away from the individual. The individual should always be allowed to determine how a specific medical suggestion fits into the overall medical economy of their life.

In order to break down this disabling definition of disability as exclusively a medical problem, with medical and para-medical solutions (which in most cases means no 'solution'), we must distinguish between a disability and a disease, for there is frequently a confusion of the two. Whereas a disease has a demonstrable physical manifestation (with the exception of the controversial area of mental illness), a disability is by no means this sort of tangible thing. It results from the things one is not able to do because of the organization of the world around you; its causes are predominantly rooted in external social factors. It is usually entirely inappropriate to see someone with a disability as a person who 'suffers' from a disease, because this will not contribute to an understanding of the life they lead. It may well constrict the possibilities of such a life by drawing the individual back within the medical model and its debilitating emphasis on physical limitations and low expectations. Many disabilities are clearly not diseases, because they result from traumatic accidents, but even in cases where a disease can be named as the cause of certain physical characteristics it is not helpful to see the individual as a 'diseased' person. It is certainly not appropriate in cases where a disease is congenital and has existed in a factor in someone's life since the day they were born. In this situation a person is simply leading a life which is in some ways different to the expected norm. To look at this person as having a disease is to ignore the fact that the disability has always been integrated within all aspects of their life, and does not represent a change from some 'norm' which was never applicable to them. The disability is simply part of being the person they are, in the context of the social world they live in. Indeed, there is literally no case in which a disabled person should be seen as 'diseased', because no disease related to disability (or anything else for that matter) extends so completely into a person's life as to define that person. To meet a disabled person and respond by asking them what 'disease' they have, is at best irrelevant, and at worst is a way of enforcing your view of us as abnormal, a different and unfortunate species of being. It is far better to respond to someone not as if the disease defines the person, but as if the person is concerned with leading a full and interesting life.

In the independent living movement we reject these definitions that limit and control us, because they do not describe our aspirations in society. In fact, the medical definition or model has to a great extent contributed to placing us outside society, in special institutions and ghettos. We describe a place *in society*, participating as equal members with something to say and a life to lead; we are demanding the right to take the same risks and seek the same rewards. Society disables us by taking away our right to take decisions on our own behalf, and therefore the equality we are demanding is rooted in the concept of control; it stems from our desire to be individuals who can choose for themselves. People with disabilities are increasingly beginning to fight against structures that deprive us of control of, and responsibility for, ourselves, and hence leave us with no real chance of participation in society. We are the victims of a vicious circle, for the control that is denied the disabled individual by the medical profession, social services, relatives, etc., conditions that individual to accept a dependent status in which their life only takes place by proxy, resulting in them being unable to visualize independent ways of living.

The control that we demand over our own lives is one that accepts that we are as irresponsible as everybody else and that we may not always do the right thing from a medical point of view. This is what I mean by the right to take risks. If we are to be treated as individuals who are due the same respect as other people, then we must be allowed to choose a way of living that confronts all the options and risks throughout life that are inherent to living in, rather than outside, society. We believe fundamentally that all individuals have the right to live independently in the community regardless of their disability. But it is important to note the sense in which we use the term 'independence', because it is crucial to everything we are saying. We do not use the term 'independent' to mean someone who can do everything for themself, but to indicate someone who has taken control of their life and is choosing how that life is led. It cannot be applied to someone living in an institutional setting, therefore, because the routine of their life will be pre-determined, to a greater or lesser extent, by the needs of the professionals in charge of the institution. However, it can be applied to the most severely disabled person who lives in the community and organizes all the help or 'care' they need as part of a freely chosen lifestyle. The most important factor is not the amount of physical tasks a person can perform, but the amount of control they have over their everyday routine. The degree of disability does not determine the amount of independence achieved.

We believe that the choice of independent living is not a privilege conferred on us by a generous society, but is the right of all individuals, regardless of disability, to live in the community. We see it as a right that has to be restored to us rather than a freely given gift. Those people with disabilities who have achieved it in our society today, usually have done so through a process of struggle that continues day in day out. Yet the benefits far outweigh the disadvantages of the struggle, and the struggle becomes less difficult as more and more people with disabilities assert their right to live independently.

Further reading

Morris, J. (1993) *Independent Lives: Community Care and Disabled People.* Basingstoke: Macmillan.
Sutherland, A. T. (1981) *Disabled We Stand.* London: Souvenir Press.

3

Emancipating Disability Studies

Vic Finkelstein

Introduction: the vulnerable

Human beings are, by nature, frail animals. We are outpaced in speed by herds of runners hunting or being hunted, at the best of times our eyesight cannot match the eagle-eye of a bird on watch, we are deaf to the sounds animals on the hoof can hear in the open plains of Africa, and compared to the fine senses of a dog sniffing for contraband drugs we could be just as well permanently without a sense of smell. However, in comprehending and dealing with this reality we have been remarkably successful. With our 'aids and equipment' we can see both further into space with telescopes and inwardly into matter with microscopes beyond the capacity of all seeing animals. Our machines enable us to move faster and further in the air than any others and our ability to manipulate the environment is creating an artificial world not only for ourselves but also for all living things, including those with superior physical prowess to ourselves.

At the centre of this achievement has been our ability to turn 'vulnerability' into a strength. Put simply, our 'natural' frailty has served as an incentive to cultivate extreme flexibility in interpreting ourselves and the world in which we live. We have acquired an accumulated body of knowledge which has enabled us to transform the 'natural' environment into a 'social' world of our own making. This singular 'adaptability' is a truly fundamental attribute of being 'human' and the point of departure between the natural and social worlds. It is arguable, however, that precisely because our capacity for 'flexible thinking' has been so successful we have lost sight of the emergent rigidity in the categories into which the social reservoir of knowledge has been assigned. Today, we are faced with a plethora of professions and academic disciplines each of which jealously defends its own territory.

Nowhere does this success in intellectual adaptability degenerate more comprehensively into dogma than in the lives of disabled people. Acquiring an impairment in the natural world, at birth or adventitiously later in life, can place any animal's survival at risk even at the best of times. In the social world, however, experience in managing human frailty has provided us with an amazing cornucopia of interventions that make possible the survival of those possessing the greatest physical and mental deficits. But the body of knowledge gained in progressing this advance has been the property of a very narrow assembly of practitioners and academics. In time this has crystallized into institutional menus of good practice expected from staff in rehabilitation centres, social services, special education, and so on. In all this activity the volume of understanding has increasingly rested on what, until recently, has been an unchallenged dogma: that the possession of an impairment leads to social vulnerability. This is despite the fact that history teaches us precisely the opposite: that the natural vulnerability of human beings has significantly shaped the development of all the machinery of modern social life.

Far from being a burden, our imperfections in relation to other animals might be regarded as one of the essential characteristics that make us human. In this respect disabled people are the most human of beings. The segregation of disabled people from our non-disabled peers, then, is not only an inhuman event, owing more to the exigencies of the natural world than to the social world, but the hiatus between specialist knowledge confined to 'disablement' and public knowledge concerned with 'normality' is no less than the emergence of a profoundly disabling pedagogical barrier in the evolution of human understanding.

The articulation of disabled people's aspirations cannot, in my view, be advanced without reviewing the demise of cerebral flexibility under the authority of rigidly constructed academic and professional disciplines. What might have been gained with the emergence of useful boundaries defining areas of knowledge now inhibits innovation. The 'assessment of needs', for example, has become an essential component in setting the agenda for informed professional interventions for disabled people. While recognizing that disabled people do have 'needs' is indeed an historical advance on the view that our impairments render us less than human, the veracity of this view was established by separating disabled people's needs from human aspirations. Our 'needs', then, are attributed to the 'problems' that we face, unlike non-disabled people whose needs are expressed by themselves for themselves in defining their own aspirations. Disabled people have others do this for them and in the process have been falsely identified as a uniquely vulnerable group in need of care.

The Berlin Wall that separates information related to disabled people from information concerned with our non-disabled peers is not inadvertent. It marks a specially constructed boundary between two distinctive frames of reference. Authority for this division was provided by the universal acceptability of dividing knowledge into scholarly disciplines and then taking care to keep on one's own side of the wall. What is perhaps not fully appreciated in the community of disabled people is that during the past two decades our agitation about the 'individual' and 'social' models of disability, etc., is not merely an *internal* discussion about the way 'disability' is understood and interventions arranged but an argument about the nature of all human beings – the essentials of being 'human'. That the discussion about models of disability has been isolated from non-disabled people is a reflection of just how disabling the boundaries of 'normal' knowledge have become. On the one side of the conceptual wall able-bodied people see themselves in terms of 'normality' with a skewed medical view of health and the impossible ambition of providing cradle-to-grave health services – they have lost sight of their own essential 'vulnerability'; and on the other side disabled people are seen as 'abnormal', 'deviant', 'people with special needs', etc., who must be provided with the equally impossible cradle-to-grave welfare (care) services.

Able-bodied people have deposited their own natural 'vulnerability', and genuine social dependency, into us as if this was unique to being disabled. Our 'vulnerability' is then seen as an attribute that separates us from the essentially normal – we are not quite human (the 'social death' model of disability: Finkelstein, 1991). This transference of vulnerability and consequent dependency into disabled people has not freed able-bodied people from their own dependency upon support systems to ameliorate their essential vulnerability but created a dangerous illusion about the meaning of 'normality'. This is no less than a disabling barrier for able-bodied people which is inhibiting the development of comprehensive knowledge about themselves. In this respect able-bodied people can be truly regarded as disabled; and the status of disabled people is merely a grand reflection of what able-bodied people have been doing to their own lifestyles over the centuries. The construction of boundaries around aggregate components of information means that both able-bodied and disabled people are handicapped by discipline.

Handicapped by discipline

As far as I am aware, prior to the 1975 presentation of the Open University course on 'disability' there were no learning materials in this field which were not located within a discipline area of an academic faculty or as a module in a professional training course. Disability was very much regarded as being *not*-able, as a deviation from the normal. Academic courses which did include the subject generally did so as a diversion from the main discussion and as an interesting consequence of human malfunction due to inherited or acquired physical and mental deficits. When I studied psychology, for example, what little mention there was of disability was raised during our study of neurophysiology when we were introduced to the concept of mental deficits in brain functioning. There were no uncertainties whether it was fitting to confine the notion of disability to the examination of abnormality – disability *was* caused by a pathology of the central nervous system. The same approach was applied to the identification of different disabilities. Blindness and deafness, for example, were mentioned in the courses I followed only in terms of problems in visual acuity and auditory loss respectively.

It is important to appreciate that in many respects the person *behind* the possession of a specific deficit was regarded as 'normal'. What rendered him or her 'abnormal' or 'disabled' was the ownership of a particular impairment. Another way of putting this is to say 'disability is a health problem of the able-bodied'. From this point of view the development of a more systematic understanding of disability was initiated through a process of creating boundaries between two separate able-bodied concerns about difficulties in living with physical or mental impairments. First, what is the nature of the problem that is possessed – the specific deficit, impairment or disability (when used as a synonym) and how life-threatening is the impairment? Second, what is the impact on personal functioning of owning an impairment – how can the activities of daily living be effectively managed for or with the impaired 'human being' (i.e. able-bodied people)? Disability, then, was interpreted as a general cause for concern and boundaries were established between the two assumed distinct problem areas: the defect and its impact on personal functioning. Within this frame of reference disabled people were regarded as really able-bodied people imprisoned in imperfect bodies. We were seen as separate to, but embedded in, our bodies; in reality separated from ourselves, and the whole 'problem' area was defined by able-bodied people in terms of what they are not, or what they do not want to be.

That disabled people were seen as imprisoned in their bodies, as able-bodied victims of an iniquity, while at the same time owning the bodies that encumber their freedom, not only embraced a contradictory interpretation of 'being disabled' but set impossible lifestyle dilemmas for us. How can we regard ourselves as able-bodied victims of 'something' that is wrong while also being disabled people because the 'something' is part of ourselves; and then at the same time hope to maintain a wholesome personal identity and a fulfilling life? Clearly in this interpretation the whole disability dilemma is internalized in the individual. We are both able-bodied (because our imperfections are regarded as secondary to the 'able' person believed to be inside the defective mind or body) and disabled (because our imperfections are regarded as the primary cause of our 'disabled' experiences). Our imperfections are both secondary and primary! Small wonder, then, that managing this dichotomous tragedy could only be viewed as a travail uniquely isolated from the everyday life experiences of able-bodied people. In my view the prevailing formal understanding of disability in academic courses and professional training was completed with this third boundary between the assumed dilemma of having to come to terms with 'disability' (to 'adjust') and assumed 'normality' of 'able-bodiedness'.

We now have three boundaries demarcating discrete fields for the separation of libraries of information about the nature of disability. In my view these are:

(a) A primary knowledge boundary dividing comprehension of the 'normal' (i.e. able-bodied lifestyles) from the *special* disability services (their needs, goals, ways of being cared for, etc. – i.e. the disabled career).

On the 'disabled' side of this fence two additional boundaries have further dismantled our integrity so that the development of knowledge can always be located in an either/or dilemma between two fields:

(b) The search for a 'cure' – the health field
(c) The provision of 'care' – the welfare field

It seems to me that, until the emergence of 'disability studies' in the late 1970s, knowledge about disabled life was incarcerated in an isolated field. Disability studies (the study of disabled people's lifestyles and aspirations) clearly could not emerge within the bounds of any discipline that had percolated out of 'normal' academic studies, simply because we had been removed from this arena and all analysis allocated to the disability experts in 'cure or care' (health and welfare) disciplines.

It was also not possible for disability studies to emerge within the bounds of the disciplines concerned with 'cure' because this field was allocated to medicine (and professions allied to medicine) where the fundamental intention is to restore 'the impaired' to the greatest approximation of 'normality'. At the very best the frustrated medical approach to curing disability spawned its own peculiar solution in the new discipline of rehabilitation. The history of this approach to intervention will be particularly informative, because for the most part the prerequisites for training medical and allied professionals excluded disabled people. Consequently we were prevented from having any real influence on the emergence and development of rehabilitation practice, ethics and philosophy. Clearly the boundaries surrounding the fields where the medical and para-medical approaches to disability had free range could never provide fertile ground for disability studies to flower.

So it was in the last field, within the community where established libraries of knowledge (the academic 'disciplines') have their weakest hold over people's behaviour and thinking, that disability studies was to get its opportunity for growth. This is where the skills and knowledge gained from the social experiences of disabled people interacted and clashed with that of non-medical professionals developing their own approach to helping disabled people.

Supporting disabled people in the community has always involved malleable ambiguities. At the one level, if 'highly skilled' professionals cannot do any more in curing an impaired body or mind, and rehabilitation has been successful (maximum 'normality' has been achieved, whatever that might mean), then it seems reasonable for social responsibility to devolve back into the hands of the family, and in any case responsibility for the majority of disabled people never completely fell under the control of qualified practitioners. Considerable power in the guidance of disabled people's lives was in the hands of non-professionals. On another level it is perfectly logical for professional workers located in medical and rehabilitation centres to be driven into the community, following their uncured patients, when 'care' is the only option left for the possessor of the impairment. The goal was to ensure that disabled people were serviced by skilled professional workers. Skilled workers were thought important because the rigid boundary between 'disability' and 'normality' made it impossible for everyday skills used in *supporting* people with abilities (e.g. selling bicycles) to be systematically and creatively applied to *caring* for people with disabilities (e.g. providing wheelchairs).

The problem was that the expertise and skills cultivated and professionalized within the boundary of 'cure' interventions, where 'impairment' is paramount, were migrating into the community where they came into contact with the expertise that had naturally emerged during lay people's support for their disabled children or peers. At this boundary an interaction is also very often a conflict. For the most part in the 1960s and 1970s this has been a 'no-contest' and the natural 'support' provided by the community was systematically eroded and then transformed into 'care' as the professionals gained the upper hand at the apogee of the 'Welfare State'.

The duel between 'care' and 'support' involved a number of players. Apart from the expanding body of professionals the main non-disabled contenders for the right to determine the direction of facilities and services in the community were parents of disabled children. Parents, however, are already in a 'care' relationship with their children and, as well-intentioned and responsible adults, want the best for them. For the vast majority this will mean that they want them to be like themselves, as 'normal' as possible. Unlike their disabled children, however, parents actively pursuing the goal of 'assimilation' into mainstream society are likely to be 'people with abilities', 'shoe-bound', aurally conversant or visually informed, etc. There was, therefore, a great deal of common ground between professional and parental interest in developing 'care' services in the 1960s, and any differences about the delivery of these services should not confuse us about their mutual affinity. Younghusband *et al.*, 1970, for example, says parents of disabled children reported that 'The need for relief from the care of a handicapped child at home was the most pressing of all personal and social needs' (p. 44). 'After personal and social needs, education came next in [their] priorities' (p. 52). Parents particularly wanted educational responsibility to move from 'the health to the education authorities'. This move from 'special education treatment' to special education administered by the education authority can be interpreted not merely as a stage on the road to 'inclusive education' but as part of the voyage disability expertise was making from the 'cure' field into the 'care' field. There was nevertheless, in my view, no significant disagreement between parents and disability experts that both care and special education were needed for disabled children.

In the 'care' field there appears to have been little prospect that non-disabled people, drawing only on their own experiences, could be any more creative in developing academic studies concerned with disability than redrafting established wisdom in the 'cure' field. What was needed to open the door to the radically new approach of 'disability studies' was the infusion of ideas directly from the experiences of disabled people.

In the late 1960s and early 1970s the voice of disabled people in the community was expressed through a growing number of organizations each focused around a particular issue. These issues were not freely chosen but arose out of the problems that specific groups of disabled people experienced as they tried to cope with the barriers in a community designed for able-bodied lifestyles. From the point of view of this chapter the most important of these organizations in the late 1960s was the Disablement Income Group (DIG). Its principal concern was that services on the 'care' side of the cure/care fence were underdeveloped and that a national disability income would help disabled people to integrate by 'compensating for disability'. Mary Greaves, Honorary Director of DIG, expressed the problem this way: 'Rehabilitation is composed of three parts – medical, rehabilitation for living and rehabilitation for work. There's a tendency to miss out rehabilitation for living' (Morris and Butler, 1972, p. 59).

Disability was seen as a problem in its own right, and thinking was dominated by the model of disability that had developed in isolation of the care sector of the Welfare State. Nevertheless, behind the focus on incomes was the broader goal of support for living in the community (integration). Referring to the Chronically Sick and Disabled Persons Act 1970 (CSDP Act), Mary Greaves is quoted as saying: 'As a disabled person, the importance of this Bill is the underlying philosophy: the integration of the disabled person into society' (Morris and Butler, 1972, p. 126). Campbell and Oliver (1996, p. 52) interpret the founding of DIG in terms of disabled people's demand for a share in the 1960s social affluence: 'The idea of a national disability income emerged and was promoted as the way to ensure that disabled people are able to share in the affluence of the time.' It was concern about 'income benefits' as well as broader problems around the issue of access to mainstream society that encouraged many disabled people to join DIG. Stephen Bradshaw, a former Director of the Spinal Injuries Association (SIA), explained: 'When I was first disabled I was very aware of the lack of state benefits. The way disabled people were treated back in 1968 when I came out of hospital was not good, and so I joined DIG straight away, because I thought that was the right way forward to gain basic and obvious things' (Campbell and Oliver, 1996, p. 34).

In a short period of time DIG grew very rapidly to become a mass organization of disabled people. Precisely because disabled people unschooled in the perspective of any established disability profession or discipline were able to meet, argue and exchange ideas in DIG made it possible to aspire to a much broader agenda than was possible from the perspective of parents caring for disabled children or professional workers either in or out of institutional settings. DIG's concentration of its resources on the single issue of incomes, however, eventually made it unable to translate any wider aspirations for integration into a deeper understanding of the nature of disability. Nevertheless, it increased awareness about the importance of 'integration' and began to challenge the dominance of the more narrow but primary rehabilitation goal of personal 'independence'.

While disabled people in organizations in the community were able to gain expertise and have an impact on professional thinking and eventually academic courses concerned with disability, there was another group of disabled people living in considerable isolation whose views and understanding of disability were almost completely unknown or ignored:

there were two parallel groups of disabled people. There were those who lived in the community. They were struggling with one set of issues and they were coping somehow in the community. Then there were those who were in the hospitals on chronic wards, geriatric wards and so on. (Judy Hunt in Campbell and Oliver, 1996, p. 29)

I will return to the influence of this group's understanding of disability on disability studies later, but I need to conclude this section with a word about the concerns and influence of those who incarcerated disabled people in residential institutions.

There has always been a variety of institutional accommodation for disabled people but it was, in my view, the development of Cheshire Homes that facilitated a very specific analysis of disability that fed into courses aimed at voluntary and professional workers with disabled people. These homes were founded on a very solid charity base by non-professional, non-disabled people, and their fundamental concern was 'care'. Disabled people were uncritically accepted as a problem, for the most part unemployable and incapable of managing much of the activities of daily living solely because we are disabled. We were essentially regarded as incapable of functioning in ordinary life and consequently invisible to, and conceptually separate from, the public: 'The problem of the incurably sick tends to be hidden from the public view and so to many people it doesn't exist' (1963 Foreword by the Duke of Edinburgh in Russell, 1980, p. 7). The 'problem', which appeared to need no clarification for the founders of Cheshire Homes, could be expressed as: 'Who will care for the disabled?' The question not asked was: 'Why is there no appropriate "support" system for disabled people in the community, similar to the elaborate public utilities that able-bodied people share between themselves?' It was, however, not only the failure to question the advantage of incarcerating us in institutions that is extraordinary in the light of the resources being committed to the Cheshire enterprise but the level of ignorance that was happily tolerated. When, in the early 1960s, questions were raised about the number of Homes that were 'needed', Russell (1980, p. 17) says: 'I realized for the first time that beneath our work was a bedrock of ignorance – ignorance of the basic facts, ignorance of the number of chronic sick in the modern world.' To this I would add 'ignorance about the nature of disability'. Ignorance characterized the whole residential institutional approach, and this was tolerated because an intellectual boundary had been placed around the world of disability preventing critical interest from non-disability academics and researchers. Ignorance also made it virtually impossible for the protest voice of disabled people to be heard at this time.

Ignorance about the nature of disability played an important role in facilitating a notorious oppressive piece of social science research targeted on institutions. In 1972 Miller and Gwynne, publicly admitting their confusion about the dynamic situation of disabled people, concluded that the function of the residential institution was to provide the 'socially dead' with transitional care until natural death occurred. There were two basic issues: how to extend this process for as long as feasible and support it humanely, and how to train staff to cope with this stressful line of work. At a time when there had been several scandals about institutional 'care' for people with mental illness and learning disability and the closure of large institutions was on the agenda, Miller and Gwynne's publication of their research was eagerly fed into education and training courses for care workers.

In the early 1970s work began on the first Open University (OU) course wholly concerned with 'disability'. It commenced in a cultural climate where academic boundaries confined the study of disability to an esoteric field peopled by a tiny minority of unchallenged experts. Out in the real world those working with disabled people were devoutly separated into cure or care concerns; practice in the latter being informed by historical assumptions without even the pretence of an underlying scholarship. The migration of the 'cure' experts and 'professional expertise' into the community, where their practice was re-labelled 'care' while their assumptions remained unchanged, had begun in earnest.

The publication reporting the outcome of the 'Lambeth studies of disablement', which were planned in 1977, captures the mood of the time: 'It is now widely accepted that the balance of health and social care for people with disability should shift from being institutional or residential to care in the community ... a complete picture of the burden of chronic illness ... demands a socio-medical definition of disablement' (Patrick and Peach, 1989, p. v). The claim to continuing medical control over the lives of disabled people in the community was unashamedly pursued.

The handicapped person in the community

The OU course began in an environment of change, with the medical model of disability about to breach the wall between institution and community, suppressing the natural evolution of social support and systematically replacing this with its administrative complement: 'care'. This was a period of instability in the informed opinion about the nature of disability. Different interpretations contested the direction of interventions and services. However, there was no dispute about the need for care and special services; disagreements amounted to no more than variations on the same theme.

The university's response to the unfolding change was also a product of its time, and we need to bear this in mind when we consider what made its first course in this field uniquely creative. The OU was not only new, having just started teaching in 1971, but there were no entry requirements apart from being over 18 years, living in the UK and being competent in English. A significant concern, and part of its Charter, was to ensure that *all* multi-media learning materials required for the completion of a course were available to all students in their own homes. Having been banned from traditional universities because poor secondary education deprived them of academic entry qualifications or because campuses were inaccessible, the Open University gave disabled people a second chance. Courses, however, were produced for the shoe-bound, aurally conversant and visually informed student with ability and it became necessary to set up a disabled students' office very early in the university's life. The approach was to make special provision for disabled students.

Since it was a new university with an untried approach to teaching and considerable scepticism from traditional institutions, an early concern was to establish the credibility of the OU courses. It was also necessary to create a system of course production which enabled an appropriate input from academics, course co-ordinators, educational technologists, editors, television and radio producers, course production planners and administrators, etc., to ensure standards and consistency. The course team became the basic unit of course production and a melting pot for the exchange of ideas. It was also accepted that the academic input from this teamwork approach could be augmented by 'consultative conferences' in order to access suggestions and opinions from non-OU experts in a proposed new course.

In the early 1970s the changing climate in 'dealing with disability' increased interest in the move towards integrated education, and the Faculty of Educational Studies began considering the preparation of a course on special education. At the time distance learning for students in the professions who wanted to improve their practice by studying upgrading courses was not an OU priority. The Education Faculty, however, always maintained an interest in the development of teachers and supported the production of post-experience courses. Phillip Williams from the Faculty was appointed Chairman of the proposed new course located in the post-experience courses programme, and a course team was brought together. This meant the new course had crossed a very significant disabling boundary. It was no longer to be constrained by a single faculty interest or bounded by an established disability discipline.

Vida Carver was a Staff Tutor in the Faculty of Social Sciences in the London Region and had played a leading role in making courses accessible to students with hearing impairments, having joined the OU from a research project with the Central Council for Education and Training in Social Work. Dr Carver not only had worked with disabled people and made courses accessible, she also knew leading disabled people personally: she was particularly friendly with Mary Greaves from DIG. Dr Carver was seconded to the course and immediately brought the wider issues discussed above into the melting pot of ideas that the course team had to consider. Dr Carver was a most persuasive advocate for change in the way disability was studied, and under her influence it was decided to broaden the course scope. The title was to be 'The Handicapped Person in the Community'. It was to be topic-based, with only one workbook concerned with special education, and the main focus on improving professional practice with disabled people living in the community.

Very early on, a consultative process took place with a large number of individuals who had been identified as interested in the field. A Consultative Conference confirmed the broader topic-based approach as an important contribution to the shifting emphasis on developing services for disabled people in the community. Leading representatives from all the main professions with a concern in 'disability' were included, as well as some of the few disabled people researching in the subject or active in disability-related organizations. It is my view that in the course team forum, outside the boundaries of established disability disciplines and traditional faculty structures, in a new and innovative pedagogic institution, in a climate of shifting emphasis from cure to care fields and in the context of general economic affluence, a new academic approach to disability started to emerge. This is clear from the course aims published in 1975 for its first presentation year: 'The aim of the course is to help you to improve your professional and social skills in order to assist handicapped people to achieve maximum autonomy.' The well-established rehabilitation goal of 'independence' has been replaced by 'autonomy' and interpreted broadly in terms of civic rights but with still some uncertainty about the meaning of a successful lifestyle for disabled people. The aims continue: 'It will call on you to examine your professional role and ideology and will encourage you to adopt an interprofessional approach to problems.' While disability is still contextualized in terms of problems, discipline boundaries are slightly breached with the promotion of an *interprofessional* approach rather than the rehabilitation concept of *multi-professional* teams. More importantly, students were encouraged to question the prevailing ideology. The aims conclude with the promotion of co-operation with 'other workers, with disabled people and with the wider community'.

This significantly broader approach to the academic study of disability is most clear in the titles of various course components. 'Difference and the Problem of Developing a Handicapped Identity' was the first unit in the course. This raised the issue of identity rather than taking for granted medical assumptions about the centrality of 'normality' in disabled people's lives and the need to 'adjust' when this was not fully attainable. 'The Medical Approach to Handicap' was only one unit in sixteen alongside traditional impairment-specific units concerned with 'Hearing Impairment', 'Visual Handicap', 'Aids for the Physically Handicapped' and 'The Social Integration of Mentally Handicapped People'.

Boundaries, however, were challenged with more global approaches to intervention. These were presented as relevant to all workers and all groups of disabled people. The 'behavioural' *Goal-setting* workbook was given a prominent place in the course, rather than professional obsession with assessment of needs. *Anticipating Needs and Matching Services* was the title of a workbook, for example, rather than 'the assessment of needs for services'. Units on personal income and costs of care raised issues that were simply absent in professional courses for therapists, teachers and medical workers with disabled people. Much of this material was entirely new and generated in production of the course. For the first time, too, disabled people contributed as colleagues, rather than as case studies, in the making of the course, including Peter Large (DIG), Fred Reid (President of the National Federation of the Blind) and others who wrote course units and were contracted as consultants to the course team.

The varied professional interests and confused meaning of disability was reflected in the course. Eric Miller was engaged to prepare a unit based upon his research with Gwynne on residential homes, focusing on the psychological problems faced by practitioners working with the tragedy of disabled people. In this case improving professional practice meant assisting workers to adjust to their emotionally disturbing jobs. This was countered by a paper on the Swedish Fokus project which aimed at enabling all disabled people to live in the community with appropriate support.

Just over 1200 students, working in all the professions with a concern in the disability field, voluntary workers and disabled people from all areas in the country studied the course in its first year. Its influence was widespread, creating waves of unease amongst those working to established disability models, giving confidence to practitioners and service users who were looking for a more comprehensive approach to disability issues, and seeding ideas for those who questioned prevailing assumptions about disability and who wanted to pursue the academic study of disability in its own right. The latter was to flower in the UK as disability studies. What was missing in the 'Handicapped Person in the Community' course was the unbounded ideas of disabled people, freed from academic and professional disciplines. This required a shift from the individual and biographical approach, which confined disabled people to a case history role in the career of disability professionals, to a social approach relocating the problem of disability to the disabling society and countering the individual model of disability concurrently relocating from the cure setting into care in the community.

The disabling society

The minimal involvement of disabled people in the production of the first OU course was not surprising. Prejudice against disabled people prevented access to employment and the prevailing fiat dictated the exclusion of disabled people from this field because of alleged inability to be objective about themselves and their situation. There were also very few disabled people at that time with the qualifications to contribute to university level courses as academics. In this light what is surprising is just how successful the OU course team was in resisting pressure and in engaging disabled people in the course production and presentation.

I became involved with 'The Handicapped Person in the Community' course in 1975 as a part-time tutor during its first presentation year, having missed the opportunity to contribute to the course production. Although I had qualified as a clinical psychologist with the original intention of working as a counsellor for disabled people in a rehabilitation centre, I had been unable to obtain a post in this specific area of psychology. The Open University, then, not only gave me the opportunity to work in the field that I wanted to but with Vida Carver's encouragement positively recruited me. At the time I was heavily engaged in a number of disability organizations, principally the Union of the Physically Impaired Against Segregation (UPIAS) where we had developed the social interpretation of disability, and we had developed a healthy scepticism towards disability-related research and courses. However, we had agreed that it was essential to find ways of engaging disabled people in disability affairs across the whole range of human endeavour, and to break down the boundaries that kept us isolated from mainstream society, maintained professional control over our lives and stunted a deeper understanding of human nature. The OU presented us with the opportunity to push a wheel in (gain a toe-hold in) the academic world where we could hope to bring our own viewpoint into the arena dominated by the medical and administrative models of disability.

'The Handicapped Person in the Community' course was presented unchanged from 1975 until 1980. During this period the voice of disabled people was growing more confident. New organizations of disabled people, such as the Spinal Injuries Association (SIA) and the National Union of the Deaf (NUD), for example, were able to support outstanding spokespeople in Stephen Bradshaw and Paddy Ladd respectively, who argued the perspective of their groups with increasing effect (see Campbell and Oliver, 1996, for a fuller discussion of this period). In Derbyshire Ken Davis and Maggie Hines had started setting up the Centre for Integrated Living (CIL) and their pioneering Grove

Road housing project (Davis, 1981); in Manchester Ken Lumb played a key role in supporting the first research project based upon the social model of disability (Finlay, 1978); and Dick Leaman, in the London Borough of Lambeth, had started working towards their CIL.

As I became employed full-time at the OU in 1976 and more settled into the job, I was able to refer to these exciting projects in the course updating material and regional 'day schools'. It was a matter of policy for me to attend a few day schools each year, and I made a point, whenever possible, of circulating copies of disabled people's writing and talking about the projects that were engaging their attention. These contacts, my involvement with my own tutorial groups, assignment monitoring and examination marking, not only provided a vast source of national feedback on what was happening at the local level but highlighted the problem of structural intransigence in the face of change.

Increased familiarity with the course and exchange of views with those who had studied or reviewed the material helped clarify both its strengths and its weaknesses. The principal problem, already mentioned, was the limited input that had originally been possible from disabled people – in particular the debate about different models of disability. I had discussed this with Paul Hunt (who had played the leading role in founding UPIAS and contributed to the development of the social model of disability) and in November 1976 he wrote to the course team suggesting changes when course materials were updated. First, he drew attention to the medical model definitions reproduced in the course and commented:

> little attempt is made to examine these definitions critically, to discuss their underlying assumptions and inconsistencies, or to put forward better definitions in their place . . . surely the crucial defect in the definitions quoted should have been pointed out: that Margot Jeffreys and Amelia Harris fail to break with the traditional view of disability as an essentially individual condition which causes certain personal and social effects.

In his conclusion he praised the course for breaking through the boundaries which separated knowledge about disability into independent fields and hoped that this would be taken further by introducing students to the social interpretation of disability:

Finally, it seems to me that part of the usefulness of the Course you have developed is that it collects together what is on the whole the more progressive thinking and practice in the field, and I hope that you will therefore be able to acquaint your students with the alternative social approach to the question of definitions.

Vida Carver replied with the view that 'the differences between us are at the level of language usage', and defended the definitions used in the course: 'The purpose of a definition is, for me, no more and no less than a statement, made in the interest of clarity, of the way in which a term will be used . . . Troubles begin when we try to incorporate attitudes or "philosophies" into definitions.' But she expressed full support for the concern behind Paul Hunt's letter: 'I have no quarrel with the sentiments that lie behind your definition of disability – indeed it was our hope that the whole course was an elaboration of those sentiments.'

This correspondence was important because it helped clarify the pace for the introduction of disability studies into the academic world. This, I knew, would begin in earnest when we were able to start remaking 'The Handicapped Person in the Community' course. I was fortunate in being able to engage Mike Oliver in this process. He had been recruited as an OU part-time tutor at an early stage in the presentation of the first course and immediately played a constructive role in disseminating ideas from the course as well as developing his own critique of the original materials. In the meantime we were collecting regular feedback from each year's presentation and quite a wide range of unsolicited correspondence from people who had seen our BBC television broadcasts, heard our radio programmes, read our textbooks or Reader, or reviewed the workbooks.

As it was the first comprehensive course in the field with a large yearly student intake there was considerable awareness about the course in what was, and still is, despite the large number of non-qualified people involved, an isolated and relatively small body of academics, researchers and professionals. The course was widely discussed in this circle, praised and criticized. For the most part this feedback was exceptionally positive. The most frequent comment was that we had omitted an element in the already overloaded course that was championed by a correspondent. The greatest controversy centred on the behavioural goal-setting approach. For some this was seen as a tool in breaking down tasks into clear logical steps to be systematically achieved by disabled people. To others it was a controversial method of controlling disabled people so that they could be moulded according to the dictates of non-disabled practitioners. Most comments from disabled people were highly critical of the workbook by Eric Miller on problems in working with disabled people, but positive comments were also received from workers who regarded the discussion helpful in addressing their own uncertainties and prejudices about disability.

In the first two years of its presentation 'The Handicapped Person in the Community' course was available only in the post-experience courses programme, but after that it was also open to undergraduate students. In the early years a large number of students had come from the teaching professions. Later on professional and voluntary workers in the community had become the dominant student groups. There were always a small number of disabled students, mostly following the course out of interest, but with a few who were trying to find a path into employment in this area. In the undergraduate programme we also attracted a small number of students with no obvious interest in the field.

The medical profession, however, was always underrepresented, given their role in the lives of disabled people, and for the most part paid little attention to the course. There had been some input from medical consultants when the original course was planned and a unit on the medical approach to disability was included. Subsequently, one medical consultant raised concerns about the 'sociological bias' of the course, and argued for a more 'medical and practical' approach.

In taking into consideration all the above feedback, opinions from respected leading disabled people and professionals and caution in over-reaching the interest of practitioners who had to work within structures suffused with enduring assumptions and models of disability, it was decided that the course would be remade over three years, replacing a few units at a time while retaining the basic structure and reworking the topics already within the course. The medical unit was to be retained, although remade along with the rest of the course.

Conclusion: mainstreaming the vulnerable

A new course team began rewriting the materials for the first units to be replaced in the 1980 presentation. All the components were replaced by 1982, and although the course retained its old title it was in fact entirely new and, in my opinion, could now be properly identified as a course in disability studies. When the team was assembled we engaged in a number of brainstorming sessions, trying to ensure that the new ideas emerging from the community of disabled people were considered alongside the more progressive views coming from the established professions and voluntary bodies.

Amongst the several external consultants involved in the new course was Mike Oliver. I was to rely heavily on his input because the boundary isolating disabled from non-disabled people made it difficult for even the most sympathetic academics familiar with the field to get a full grasp of the new ideas in the short space of time leading up to actually preparing course components. The transformation of the original 'Handicapped Person in the Community' course for entry into disability studies was a remarkable learning experience for us all.

The first workbook to be replaced was, of course, concerned with the work Miller and Gwynne had carried out on residential care. The associated television programmes and set book were also replaced and in a very real way the removal of these materials marked a turning point in the development of disability studies. The driving force behind course content now came into the hands of disabled people, and the concerns of service providers were not ignored but interpreted in this context. We also made an effort to challenge traditional ways of dividing disability up into discussion areas. Rather than considering blindness and deafness, for example, we merged this discussion and looked at barriers to communication. The significance of physical impairment was studied in relation to disabling barriers and the means to overcome these. Learning disability was located in a consideration of personal relationships and the support society is prepared to make available. Considerable space was given to reworking personal, professional and public assumptions about disability. In keeping with the focus of all the health and social welfare courses at the OU the emphasis was on improving services, working with disabled people and thinking through appropriate services rather than revitalizing existing approaches and professionalism.

The new course received a mixed reception. Many workers found the materials invigorating and rich in ideas, but difficult to translate into practical approaches in service settings totally directed by the individual, medical and administrative models of disability. Over a period of time, however, there is no doubt that the course ideas began to penetrate the wider scene. A substantial reason for this is because the disability movement began to have a much more substantial impact on challenging the comfortable assumptions that had for so long fed the direction of servicing disabled people. There was a powerful concord between the OU course and the groundswell of opinion emanating from the national and international disability movement.

In 1989 work began on the final version of this disability course. It was to be produced in modular form with the completed course called 'The Disabling Society'. There was much greater input from leading disabled people who had played a role in reshaping our understanding of disability. The concern about developing appropriate services was maintained together with an enhanced role for disabled people, as the new Centres for Integrated Living (CILs) were set up by disabled people and began providing some services. The separation between purchasing and providing services had perhaps opened up new possibilities for service development and at the same time direct payments to disabled people and civil rights legislation finally completed the long haul from institutional approaches to community-based approaches.

While the introduction of 'community care' can be regarded as an important development, it has, as I have argued above, been the main vehicle for transporting into the community traditional cultures of intervening in the lives of disabled people. While there are many reasons for the decline in the number of students following the introduction of 'The Disabling Society' course, it is my view that 'community care' has been the greatest contributor. I believe this has been a pernicious influence in maintaining the boundary between disability and normality and allowed the relocation of disability into this new field which is now struggling to become an academic discipline. Professional workers have taken to this approach with enthusiasm, often claiming that it fits in with the social model of disability. In my view this is nothing more, nor less, than the old separation of disability from mainstream life under a new name. It is a formula for trying to revitalize moribund professionalism at a time when, more than ever, we should be discussing the dismantling of a fragmenting health and welfare service and replacing this with a National Medical Service and a service concerned with supporting people in achieving their lifestyles. We should be debating the unpacking of current professions in order to identify those skills which may be reassembled in more appropriate professional configurations for the twenty-first century.

If there was a compelling lesson from over twenty years developing disability studies at the Open University and introducing over 8000 students to a different way of understanding human behaviour, it is that we should be looking at ways of breaching boundaries. Dismantling the faculty system and making topic-based courses across the disciplines, for a start, might bring back some of the innovative teaching that first characterized the OU. Disability studies, in my view, can play an important role in drawing attention to these issues. Failure to do so is likely to result in the new discipline becoming just one amongst many where an academic elite avoids the opportunity of our time.

Note

A longer version of this paper, including footnotes, is available from Vic Finkelstein, c/o The School of Health and Social Welfare, The Open University, Walton Hall, Milton Keynes MK7 6AA.

Further reading

Brechin, A., Liddiard, P. and Swain, J. (eds) (1981) *Handicap in a Social World*. Sevenoaks: Hodder & Stoughton and Open University Press.

Campbell, J. and Oliver, M. (1996) *Disability Politics: Understanding Our Past, Changing Our Future*. London: Routledge.

Linton, S., Mello, S. and O'Neill, J. (1995) Disability studies: expanding the parameters of diversity, *Radical Teacher*, vol. 47, pp. 4–10.

Swain, J., Finkelstein, V., French, S. and Oliver, M. (eds) (1993) *Disabling Barriers – Enabling Environments*. London: Sage with the Open University.

Part Two

The Developing Discipline

4

Sociology, Disability Studies and Education: Some Observations

Len Barton

In writing this chapter I have approached the task from the perspective of being a non-disabled sociologist working in the field of education. The brevity of the chapter has involved me in a set of judgements and selections from a vast range of possible concerns and issues. This is dissatisfying but inevitable. Nevertheless, I hope I have been able to provide the reader with an indication of some of the exciting and challenging issues we need to engage with. It is part of a fundamental process of re-learning.

A sociological approach

Sociology is a contentious subject and has been the object of a range of criticisms emanating from both academic and popular sources. These include the contention that sociology is a pseudo-science, that it rarely produces any useful knowledge and that it encourages a form of discourse that is inaccessible and alienating.

In such a brief chapter as this I cannot engage with distinguishing between the ignorant, misinformed and mischievous nature of some of the criticisms, nor identify those that deserve a more serious response. However, I do think it is necessary to briefly highlight some of the key characteristics of a sociological approach and why I feel it is important when applied to the question of disability.

Sociologists are interested in social relations. This includes relations of individuals and groups in and across different social contexts and periods. Sociologists are obsessed with trying to understand how social relationships are established, maintained and changed. Thus, they are constantly asking questions about the social conditions under which people act (Halsey, 1995).

Sociology is not a homogeneous discipline (and within this brief account it is not possible to discuss the more recent sociological developments in the form of postmodernism and post-structuralism). It is characterized by internal disputes over conceptualizations, methods and interpretations. Thus, for example, whilst there is a strong historical interest within sociology over the questions of inequality and power, there are different explanations offered with regard to their meaning, sources and consequences (Lukes, 1979).

In seeking to understand the relationship between the individual and society as well as establishing the value of a sociological approach to this issue, C. W. Mills (1970) maintains, we need to make a distinction between 'personal troubles' concerned with the immediate and personal concerns of individuals and 'public issues' which arise from the larger structures of social and historical life. The sociological imagination, Mills argues, is characterized by its 'capacity to range from the most impersonal and remote transformations to the most intimate features of the human self – and to see the relations between the two' (1970, p. 14). Part of the difficulty of this task is due to sociology being 'inherently and inescapably part of the subject matter it seeks to comprehend' (Giddens, 1986, p. 156). A further aspect of the challenge facing sociological analysis concerns the uniqueness of the human subject. People are able to generate a range of conceptions of what the 'good life' might be like and express such hopes through the complex medium of language (Halsey, 1995). Finally, whilst human beings are actively involved in the creation of meanings, they also produce outcomes which they neither intended nor anticipated (Giddens, 1986).

In engaging with this urgent and difficult task sociologists, Giddens (1986) argues, need to develop a 'historical sensibility' so that by understanding the past we can, it is hoped, be helped to change the future. It is also a means by which ethnocentrism can be critiqued. Finally, such an approach will teach sociologists 'sobriety' (p. 13) and help them to recognize that knowledge of history and of ourselves is always tentative and incomplete.

A sociological approach to the study of disability provides an alternative perspective in which individualized, homogenized and disabilist conceptions of policy and practice are subject to critical analysis. Sociologists are interested, for example, in how in different historical periods disability is defined, by whom, in what contexts and with what consequences. Furthermore, they are interested in how the particular vested interests of professionals serve to encourage a culture of expertise in which disabled people experience relationships of dependency. Finally, there is a growing interest in the development of social movements and how members generate alternative sets of values, priorities and practices that encourage various forms of opposition to the dominant conceptions. The voices of disabled people and the importance of the disability movement are more recent interests attracting various sociological analyses (Oliver, 1996; Barnes and Oliver, 1995; Barton, 1996).

As a non-disabled person I have experienced an extensive learning curve with regard to the question of disability. In coming to terms with ideas supporting a social model of disability, my own disabilist assumptions and expectations have had to be critically engaged with. Making connections between personal attitudes and institutional discriminations has been a central aspect of this development. This has been a particularly disturbing experience because in relation to education I was also committed to the belief in the importance and appropriateness of special segregated forms of school provision, including residential ones.

Given that many readers of this book will be, like me, non-disabled and also have little experience of interacting with disabled people, it is important to outline some of the key features of a social model approach. The intention is to provide a critique of those powerful social perceptions of disability that view it as a personal tragedy or individual deficit and to affirm some alternative, positive images of disability.

A social model

A particularly important issue relates to the question of how a society defines and excludes specific individuals or groups. Historically the conditions and factors which have influenced the status and experience of disabled people have changed over time. Deeply held fears and prejudices have at particular historical periods led to strong custodial measures being viewed as the most appropriate response for those individuals who were defined as a *menace* needing total institutional provision, or a *burden* needing sterilizing and even exterminating, and as *vulnerable* thus in need of protection (Wolfensberger, 1993; Scull, 1982; Ryan and Thomas, 1980).

Official definitions powerfully influenced by medical and psychological concerns and interests, often enshrined in legislation and taken up in a populist discourse increasingly influenced by mass media images, have been used to define disabled people negatively. They include: 'deformed', 'cripple', 'spastic', 'mentally handicapped' and 'subnormal'. This has resulted in not only a hierarchy of impairments, but a growing appreciation on the part of historical and social analysts that disabled people have been 'divided, categorised, and controlled on the basis of individual impairments' (Campbell and Oliver, 1996, p. 132).

The approach adopted in this chapter finds its definitional support in the statement on Fundamental Principles of Disability which resulted from a discussion between the Union of the Physically Impaired Against Segregation and the Disability Alliance. The UPIAS (1976) position is quite clear:

> In our view, it is society which disables physically impaired people. Disability is something *imposed* on top of our impairment by the way we are unnecessarily isolated and excluded from full participation in society. Disabled people are therefore an oppressed group in society. (my emphasis)
>
> Thus we define *impairment* as lacking part or all of a limb, organ or mechanism of the body; and *disability* as the disadvantage or restriction of activity caused by a contemporary social organization which takes no or little account of people who have physical impairments and thus excludes them from participation in the mainstream of social activities. Physical impairment is therefore a particular form of social oppression. (p. 14) (my emphasis)

This statement has provided the basis for the development of a social model of disability. This approach is critical of official perspectives, including medical ones, which focus on and legitimate conceptions of the individual in terms of their loss and inabilities, and of unacceptable features of their person. Problems from this perspective are individualized, and disabled people are viewed as 'other' or negatively different.

To be a disabled person means to be discriminated against. It involves social isolation and restriction. This is because of an essentially inaccessible socio-economic and physical world (Finkelstein, 1994).

Disability is thus a significant means of social differentiation: the level of esteem and social standing of disabled people are derived from their position in relation to the wider social conditions and relations of a given society. Particular institutions have a crucial influence on social status including the level and nature of employment, education and economic well-being (Equality Studies Centre, 1994).

Status is influenced by the cultural images which, for example, the media portray about particular groups, the legal rights and protection afforded them and the quality and duration of their educational experiences (Equality Studies Centre, 1994). Disabled people experience the tyranny of normality, as Morris (1991) so powerfully contends:

> Our difference is measured against normality and found wanting. Our physical and intellectual characteristics are not 'right' nor 'admirable' and we do not 'belong'. It is particularly important to state this because – having given such a negative meaning to abnormality – the non-disabled world assumes that we wish to be normal, or to be treated as if we were. (Morris, 1991, p. 16)

Pam Evans, a wheelchair-user, has identified a number of assumptions which, she maintains, are the ideas that make up the essence of the prejudice disabled people experience on a *day-to-day basis*. Here are a few of the assumptions:

> That we feel ugly, inadequate and ashamed of our disability.
> That our lives are a burden to us, barely worth living.
> That we crave to be 'normal' and 'whole'.
> That we are asexual or at best sexually inadequate.
> That any able-bodied partner we have is doing us a favour and that we bring nothing to the relationship.
> That if we are particularly gifted, successful or attractive before the onset of disability our fate is infinitely more 'tragic' than if we were none of these things.
> That our need and right to privacy isn't as important as theirs and that our lives need to be monitored in a way that deprives us of privacy and choice. (quoted in Morris, 1991, pp. 19, 20, 21)

People with learning difficulties have experienced some of the most major impositions of professional judgements over their lives, so much so, Ryan and Thomas (1980) argue, that their identity has always been imposed by significant others who claim that such actions are in the interests of these 'vulnerable' people.

Advocating the social nature of oppression involves, as Abberley (1987) suggests, 'that these disadvantages are dialectically related to an ideology or group of ideologies which justify and perpetuate this situation. Beyond that it is to make the claim that such disadvantages and their supporting ideologies are neither natural nor inevitable' (p. 7). An extensive range of research findings have clearly demonstrated the extent of the institutional discrimination which disabled people experience in our society. This involves access and opportunities in relation to work, housing, education, transport and support services. Thus the issues go far beyond the notion that the problem is merely one of individual disabilist attitudes. These are not free floating but are both set within and structured by particular material conditions and social relations. Good will, charity and *ad hoc* responses are insufficient to address the profundity and stubbornness of the factors involved (Glendinning, 1991; Barnes, 1991b; Oliver, 1993b; Morris, 1993b; Oliver, 1996).

The issue of how we define disability is therefore crucial because it will influence both our interactions and our expectations. Individualized tragedy perspectives need to be critically engaged with and removed. These are part of the barriers to participation and empowerment. Given the degree of institutional discrimination which disabled people experience daily, their anger, as Morris (1991) maintains, 'is not about having "a chip on your shoulder", our grief is not a "failure to come to terms" with disability. Our dissatisfaction with our lives is not a personality defect but a sane response to the oppression which we experience' (p. 9). Disabled people's history needs to be viewed as part of an increasing struggle to establish and maintain positive self-identities (Shakespeare, 1994c). It is about developing self-respect, self-confidence and solidarity. This is part of their struggle for rights, choices and participation in society. Essential to this form of action is the demand for anti-discrimination legislation (Barnes and Oliver, 1995; Barnes, 1996d).

Extending the disabling labels

Within the educational context the category 'disabled children' needs to be understood in terms of including a *range* of official definitions in which the individuals have no necessarily observable physical impairment. This includes those pupils defined as having emotional and behavioural difficulties (EBD) and the rapidly increasing numbers of children diagnosed as suffering from Attention Deficit Disorder (ADD).

What is common to all these classifications is that the 'problem' is located *within* the individual, necessitating the intervention of various professional agencies. One of the outcomes of this process is the establishment of a culture of dependency between disabled children and professionals. Another outcome is that of social restriction and thus exclusion from particular interactions, contexts and opportunities. Thus, as Oliver (1990) so perceptively notes:

> All disabled people experience disability as social restriction, whether those restrictions occur as a consequence of inaccessible built environments, questionable notions of intelligence and social competence, the inability of the general population to use sign language, the lack of reading material in Braille or hostile public attitudes to people with non-visible disabilities. (Introduction, p. xiv)

Compounding or cushioning these experiences are such influential factors as race, gender, age and class. This also provides the context in which we are to understand an individual experiencing *multiple* oppressions (Vernon, 1997a).

A key factor is that of social relations and the degree to which such encounters are found to be enabling. This raises the complex and fundamental issue of *power* and the extent to which disabled people are able to exercise control over decisions and actions that have a real impact in their lives. This has motivated disabled researchers to advocate for a 'close involvement of disabled people both individually and collectively in the planning, establishment, delivery and evaluation of services' (Finkelstein and Stuart, 1996).

School context

Schools are characterized by intense social interactions within confined geographical spaces. They are significant socializing institutions attempting to instil in young people appropriate ways of thinking and behaving. This includes the inculcation of particular social and moral values and responsibilities through, for example, processes of routine, ritual and repetition. In this context pupils' self-identities and esteem are developed in positive and negative ways. The quality of teachers' expectations is thus a crucial factor shaping pupils' experience and outcomes (Vlachou, 1997).

Historically, schools have been viewed as sorting and sifting institutions in which competition and selection have significantly influenced the increasing introduction of assessment-led curriculum planning and course developments. In the current climate the public image of an institution has become of central importance and the populist discourse of parental choice and school accountability have supported critiques of schools, teachers and previous forms of policy and practice. This is all part of a serious and systematic attempt to restructure the educational system in terms of its governance, financing, content and outcomes of provision (Ball, 1994; Hargreaves, 1994; Ranson, 1994).

Schools face several contradictory tensions. For example, to what extent do they contribute towards maintaining existing social conditions and relations, in contrast to how far they work towards identifying, challenging and removing disabling barriers in the pursuit of a more equitable system of provision? The latter is part of what has become known as inclusive education. This is an approach to educational change increasingly supported by organizations of disabled people who advocate, for example, that special segregated schooling should be abolished (Campbell and Oliver, 1996; Barnes, 1991b).

Inclusive education is about the education of *all* children which *necessitates* serious changes, both in terms of society and its economic, social conditions and relations and in the schools of which they are a part. Thus, an interest in removing disabling barriers is part of a politics of disablement and, as Barnes (1996) contends, this is 'about far more than disabled people; it is about challenging the oppression in *all* its forms . . . It is impossible, therefore to confront one type of oppression without confronting them *all* and, of course, the cultural values that created and sustain them' (Foreword, p. xii, my emphasis). In relation to the position of education this raises some key questions, such as: What are schools for? How far are schools committed to the principle of diversity? Do/can schools make a difference in the lives of pupils?

Whose interests do particular educational policies and practices serve? What definition of 'difference' do schools legitimate in a market-driven system of provision? Is a market-driven system of provision and practice contributing to an increase in segregated special education and other forms of exclusionary practices?

Identifying institutional barriers to participation in education – in terms, for example, of the organization and nature of the system of provision, the curriculum, pedagogy and assessment practice – is thus an urgent and crucial task demanding serious and systematic attention. It is an essential part of the process of engagement that the struggle for inclusive policy and practice involves.

The social construction of disability

Part of a disability studies approach involves a serious interest in how we define disability and challenging the disabilist assumptions that legitimate forms of professional and common sense thinking and practice (Darke, 1994; Corbett, 1994). Within the field of education this is a fundamentally important issue because it is part of the process of the social construction of disability. Through the use of disabilist language, barriers to participation and dignity get legitimated in the daily interactions of life within educational institutions (Vlachou, 1997).

One particular example is the use of the terms 'special' or 'special needs'. Educational literature of both an academic and an official nature contains many examples of deficit thinking. This form of thinking is applied to children from a variety of black and poor white working-class backgrounds who have failed the system or whose behaviour is deemed unacceptable, and thus in need of 'special provision'. Writing about the impact of deficit thinking on schools in the United States in particular, Pearl (1997) maintains that there is a resurgence of racial stereotypes through such popular publications as *The Bell Curve* by Herrnstein and Murray (1994) in which racial or ethnic differences in intelligence are claimed to be genetically based. In relation to African American and Mexican American pupils, Pearl (1997) argues that 'Deficit thinking is deeply embedded in every aspect of American life. It is so much part of the landscape that it is difficult to recognize, let alone address' (p. 211). In England and Wales the term 'special' or 'special need' is an example of a 'disabling culture' generating and maintaining a distance between disabled and their non-disabled peers

(Finkelstein and Stuart, 1996). In a convincing analysis of the power of naming, Corbett (1996) maintains that the label 'special needs' implies relative powerlessness on the part of those to whom it is applied. In relation to disabled pupils it 'is the language of sentimentality and prejudice' (p. 5). According to Ballard (1995) the continual use of the term 'special needs' inhibits the development of critical analysis and 'the culture of separate special education will continue for as long as the term "special" is part of the vocabulary of education' (p. 3).

Emancipatory research

Disability studies has also been very influential in raising fundamental critiques about the nature of research and the relations of production that such practices involve. This is part of a more general interest in establishing an 'emancipatory' approach to researching disability (Oliver, 1992b; Oliver, 1997). Questions concerning the relationship between the researcher and researched, the notion of expertise and the issue of who controls the process of research production are raised alongside critiques that emphasize technical and objective criteria. Researchers are presented with a major issue in the questions Oliver (1992b) poses: 'do researchers wish to join with disabled people and use their expertise and skills in their struggle against oppression or do they wish to continue to use these skills and expertise in ways which disabled people find oppressive?' (p. 102). This particular issue is not unrelated to the previous concern with the question of definition. Seriously engaging with developing an emancipatory approach to research will necessitate critical self-awareness, including how we contribute to the creation of disabling research practices through the language that we use and the expectations it supports.

A great deal of research within the field of *education* does not reflect such concerns and exemplifies the sorts of perspectives and practices that increasing numbers of researchers within disability studies are critical of. We have a long and disturbing journey ahead although there are some encouraging indications that such developments are taking place (Fulcher, 1989; Slee, 1995; Corbett, 1996).

Clough and Barton (1995) have attempted to place such issues on the agenda for those researchers working in the field of education. The central aim of the book is to provide specific insights into the ways in which 'special educational need' is variously constructed through research. The contributors to the book were asked to engage critically with the following questions:

- What assumptions about SEN/disability do I have which are inevitably present in the way I conceive of the study?

- What specific questions – in the light of these – am I asking in this particular study, and which events and circumstances prompted them and gave them a particular urgency?

- Why and how did these assumptions, questions and circumstances suggest or require the particular methods which I chose? What assumptions about 'how the world operates' – and how we can know it – are given with these methods? Why, then, are they particularly suitable for investigating the phenomena in question?

- How did the process of my research change or qualify my assumptions? In what ways am I changed by the research?

- And in what ways is the community's understanding changed by what I have achieved? If, as we are trying to suggest, research actually defines the field, what redefinition (however small) is suggested in my work? What might – or what would I have – another researcher learn from my experience? (p. 3)

A key aim of this approach is to explore the hidden and taken-for-granted aspects of research relations and production. This entails, for example, confronting issues of power, representation and purposes, and the ownership of research.

Conclusion

In producing this chapter I have been selective in what, how and why I have considered particular issues. Thus, as in all research, the end product is partial and incomplete. Nor does this perspective undermine the seriousness with which issues have been approached, nor I hope, the importance attached to specific aspects of the analysis offered.

I have attempted to identify some of my sociological predispositions to my work and to outline briefly some of the essential features of a social model of disability. Drawing on the contribution of disability studies to the issue of how we define 'disability' and what constitutes

'emancipatory research', the limitations and possibilities of work emanating from the field of education has been briefly examined.

It is essential that we should understand the *context* in which the
engagement with barriers to inclusion within education have to be
undertaken. These include the structural, political and ideological
conditions and relationships. In a book of papers which seeks to affirm
the Comprehensive ideal and challenge some of the myths and stereotypes that critics have developed as part of a sustained undermining of
the system of state-maintained provision, Pring and Walford (1997)
contend that the restructuring of the educational system has been based
on the values of selection and competition. This has resulted in the
establishment of 'unequally funded schools which will provide very
different educational experiences for children of different abilities,
social classes and ethnic groups. It will fail to raise educational standards for all' (p. 6). The drive for change within education informed by
market-led visions, definitions and values is making the challenge to
deficit thinking more difficult and the development of an emancipatory
approach to research much more demanding. This reinforces the
seriousness with which the removal of disabling cultures needs to be
engaged with. The stakes are too high for anything less than this.

Further reading

Barton, L. (ed.) (1996) *Disability and Society: Emerging Issues and Insights*.
    Harlow: Longman.
Fulcher, G. (1989) *Disabling Policies? A Comparative Approach to Education
    Policy and Disability*. Lewes: Falmer Press.

5

The Social Model of Disability: A Sociological Phenomenon Ignored by Sociologists?

Colin Barnes

Background

The idea that disability is a medical problem affecting a small proportion of the population is no longer sustainable. In the 1980s government figures suggested that there were 6.5 million disabled people in Britain (Martin, Meltzer and Elliot, 1988). A more recent study concludes that four out of every ten adult women and men have a 'long term illness or disability' (CSO, 1996). Internationally there are around 50 million disabled people in Europe (Daunt, 1991), and approximately 500 million worldwide (Disabled Persons International, 1993). Although there are significantly more disabled people in the under-resourced, 'developing' nations of the world, the prevalence of disability is greatest in wealthier, 'developed' societies (Helander, 1993). Moreover, the combination of an ageing population and new medical interventions which prolong life will ensure that the number of disabled people will increase substantially over the next few years. The economic, political, and social implications will be far-ranging (Hills, 1993).

Over recent years there has also been an unprecedented expansion of self-help groups and organizations controlled and run by disabled people on a worldwide basis (Davis, 1993; Driedger, 1989). In the UK the mobilization of disabled people led to the setting up in 1981 of the British Council of Organisations of Disabled People (BCODP) which now represents 113 national and local organizations and has a membership of over four hundred thousand disabled individuals (British Council of Organisations of Disabled People, 1996b). There has been a parallel emphasis on political campaigns and demonstrations leading to the introduction of a variety of policies to combat the systematic exclusion of disabled people from the mainstream of economic and social life by governments in rich and poor countries alike (Doyle, 1995; Gooding, 1994; Northern Officers Group, 1996).

The 'big idea' underpinning the recent politicization of disabled people, certainly in Britain, is the 'social model of disability' (Hasler, 1993). Although the roots of this phenomenon are now over thirty years old, it is one which is generally ignored by the majority of mainstream sociologists. In this chapter I will present a broad overview of the development of this perspective, and suggest that sociology is the poorer for this omission.

Medical sociology and the politicization of disability

It is important at the outset to distinguish between the traditional individualistic medical approach to disability and the socio-political approaches discussed below. Within the context of sociology the former, recently termed the 'socio/medical model of disability' by Mike Bury (1996), is rooted in the work of the American sociologist Talcott Parsons and his discussion of sickness and sickness-related behaviour. Writing in the late 1940s, Parsons argued that the 'normal' state of being in Western developed societies is 'good health', consequently sickness, and by implication impairments, are deviations from 'normality'. Subsequently sociologists, particularly medical sociologists, have focused almost exclusively on the experience of 'illness', whether chronic or acute, and the social consequences which flow from it, notably stigma management (Goffman, 1968b), rather than the environmental and social barriers faced by disabled people, and the politicization of disability by disabled people and organizations controlled and run by them (Barnes and Mercer, 1996).

At the centre of this approach is the World Health Organization's International Classification of Impairments, Disabilities and Handicaps (ICIDH). Here impairment denotes 'any loss or abnormality of psychological, physiological, or anatomical structure or function', disability 'is any restriction or lack (resulting from an impairment) of ability to perform an activity in the manner or within the range considered normal for a human being' and handicap 'is a disadvantage for a given individual, resulting from an impairment or a disability, that limits or prevents the fulfilment of a role that is normal (depending on age, sex, social and cultural factors) for that individual' (Wood, 1980, pp. 27–9).

Produced with the help of medical sociologists in the late 1970s, this typology was rejected from the outset by organizations controlled and run by disabled people including the BCODP and Disabled Peoples' International (DPI), also formed in 1981. DPI is the international equivalent of the BCODP, with over ninety member organizations (Driedger, 1989). The WHO scheme is criticized for a variety of reasons but largely because it identifies impairment as the determining factor in explaining disability and the multiple deprivations associated with it (Oliver, 1996). At their inception both the BCODP and the DPI adopted a definition of disability similar to that developed by the Union of the Physically Impaired Against Segregation (UPIAS) in 1975 – four years before the ICIDH entered the public domain (see below).

Although in Britain the politicization of disability by disabled people and their organizations can be traced back to the nineteenth century with the setting up of organizations such as the British Deaf Association (BDA) and the National League of the Blind (NLB) (Pagel, 1988), the momentum increased significantly in the 1960s (Finkelstein, 1993b; Miller and Gwynne, 1972; Oliver, 1990). For example, the link between poverty and impairment was first placed on the political agenda by two disabled women, Megan du Bosson and Berit Moore, when they formed the Disablement Income Group (DIG) in 1965. Their campaign for a comprehensive disability income was quickly joined by a host of other organizations – both of and for disabled people. The latter are traditional paternalistic organizations controlled and run by non-disabled people. These came together in 1972 under the umbrella of the Disability Alliance (DA).

But the mobilization of disabled people exacerbated existing tensions between disabled activists and non-disabled social scientists. These tensions had their roots in disabled residents' struggle for control of residential homes during the 1960s. In 1961 researchers from the Tavistock Institute were invited by residents to conduct research on power relations within long-term institutions for people with physical impairments in order to evaluate their demands for greater autonomy and control. After an extensive review the researchers, Eric Miller and Geraldine Gwynne, concluded that such demands were unrealistic. Their solution was a rehash of traditional wisdom known as the 'enlightened guardian model of care' (Miller and Gwynne, 1972); this represented nothing less than a betrayal of trust by the disabled residents (for a review of this research from the residents' perspective see Hunt, 1981). These conflicts surfaced in UPIAS's (1976) critique of the DA and its dominance by non-disabled academics such as Peter Townsend – a founder member of the DA and an aspirant associate member of the Union in 1975 (UPIAS, 1976, p. 3).

The Alliance was regarded as a forum where others speak on behalf of disabled people; UPIAS was adamant that disabled people must speak for themselves:

> We reject the whole idea of 'experts' and professionals holding forth on how we should accept our disabilities, or giving learned lectures about the psychology of impairment. We already know what it feels like to be poor, isolated, segregated, done good to, stared at, and talked down to – far better than any able bodied expert. We as a Union are not interested in descriptions of how awful it is to be disabled. What we are interested in is the ways of changing our conditions of life, and thus overcoming the disabilities which are imposed on top of our physical impairments by the way this society is organized to exclude us . . . We look forward to the day when the army of 'experts' on our social and psychological problems can find more productive work to do. (UPIAS, 1976, pp. 4–5)

Moreover, contrary to the views of medical sociologists (Bury, 1996; Williams, 1996), these developments had a significant and lasting effect on some established academics. Townsend is a good example; besides containing detailed evidence of the relationship between poverty and impairment his *Poverty in the United Kingdom*, published in 1979, four years after the first UPIAS Policy Statement, also casts doubt on the usefulness of conventional individualistic definitions of disability:

> Although society may have been sufficiently influenced in the past to seek to adopt scientific measures of disability, so as to admit people to institutions, or regard them as eligible for social security or occupational or social services, these measures may not be applied at all, or may even be replaced by more subjective criteria by hard pressed administrators, doctors and others. At the very least, there may be important variations between 'social' and objective assessments of severity. (Townsend, 1979, p. 688)

Furthermore, alternatives to traditional individualistic analyses of the disability experience had begun to emerge.

In broad terms, these socio-political theories of disability can be divided into three distinct but linked traditions. The first draws heavily on American functionalism and deviance theory, and explains the 'social construction' of disability as an inevitable outcome of the evolution of contemporary society. The second is rooted in the historical materialism of Karl Marx (1973) and the work of the Italian Marxist Antonio Gramsci (1971), and maintains that disability and dependency are the 'social creation' of industrial capitalism (Oliver, 1990). Both approaches have been criticized for their neglect of the role of culture by the third group, a 'second generation' of British writers concerned primarily with the experience, rather than the production, of both impairment and disability. I shall look at these three traditions in turn.

American socio-political approaches to disability

In the late 1960s and early 1970s the impact of functionalism, labelling theory, the rising cost of state welfare, and the radicalization of young disabled Americans in the Independent Living Movement (ILM) precipitated several American social theorists to re-evaluate the traditional medical approach to disability. The American ILM emerged in the early 1970s partly from within the university campus culture and partly in consequence of some 'enlightened' professionals' efforts to influence US disability legislation (Anspach, 1979; De Jong, 1979; Hahn, 1986).

One of the ILM's early advocates, Gerben De Jong, challenged the validity of the 'medical model', arguing that disability was in large part a social construct, and that environmental factors are at least as important as biophysical ones in the assessment of a disabled person's capacity to live independently. Although De Jong gave tacit approval to Safilios-Rothschild's notion of the 'rehabilitation role', he claimed to be establishing a new paradigm in the celebrated tradition of Thomas Kuhn (1961) by which the current body of knowledge on disability would be rendered obsolete (De Jong, 1979).

This approach and the activities of the early ILM are firmly entrenched in the philosophical and political traditions which De Jong refers to as 'radical consumerism' (De Jong, 1979, p. 242). This, he contends, was the driving force behind the other political movements which swept the USA during the 1960s. For De Jong the ILM is wedded to the core assumptions that form the ideological cornerstones of capitalist America: ideological and political freedom, consumer sovereignty and self-reliance. But such a position tends to disregard history and the stark inequalities of a 'free' market economy. These omissions have precipitated the assertion that the philosophy of the American ILM favours only a specific section of the disabled community; in particular young, intellectually able, middle-class, white Americans (Blaxter, 1984; Williams, 1984; 1991).

In the early 1980s, however, the problem of history was partially addressed by an American political scientist, Deborah A. Stone. In work reminiscent of the theories of Max Weber (1949), a fact she fails to acknowledge, Stone (1985) argues that capitalist development is accompanied by a process of intensifying rationalization and bureaucratization. Through a detailed historical account of social policy developments in America, Britain and Germany she asserts that all societies function through a complex system of commodity production and distribution, the principal means of allocation being work. But because not everyone is able or willing to work, a 'distributive dilemma' arises concerning how to allocate resources on the very different principles of work and need.

The problem is resolved through the development of the concept 'disability': a boundary category through which people are allocated either to the work-based or to the needs-based system of commodity distribution. For Stone the increasing specialization of both categorization and provision is the outcome of the increased rationalization and bureaucratization of the Western world. Thus, the 'social construction of disability' is the result of the state's need to control access to the state-sponsored welfare system and the inevitable accumulation of power by those charged with the responsibility for allocation: the medical, rehabilitation and legal professions. The escalating cost of this seemingly ever expanding and increasingly rigid needs-based system will bring about an eventual system breakdown. This, Stone suggests, can be resolved only by a retreat from state-sponsored welfarism and a re-emphasis on individual responsibility and prevention (Stone, 1985).

This line of argument is extended further by a Canadian theorist, Wolf Wolfensberger (1989). In a short but incisive analysis of the recent experience of Western societies Wolfensberger argues that the social construction of disability and dependence is a latent function of the unprecedented growth of 'human service industries' – examples include the medical, rehabilitation, and legal professions – in the post-1945 period.

Although these agencies have manifest or stated purposes or functions, it is the latent or unacknowledged functions which are the most powerful. These are the covert functions of human services that are achieved in subtle and indirect ways. Wolfensberger maintains that in a 'post primary production economy', where manufacturing is no longer the main economic activity, human service industries have become more important. Their unspecified function is to create and sustain large numbers of seemingly dependent and, therefore, devalued people in order to secure employment for others. This is in marked contrast to their stated function which is to rehabilitate such people back into the community (Wolfensberger, 1989).

A more comprehensive analysis is provided by an American sociologist, Gary L. Albrecht. In *The Disability Business* (1992) Albrecht argues that, in contrast to perceptions of disability as a medical condition, a form of social deviance, and/or a political or minority group issue, 'disability' is produced by 'the disability business'. Drawing on the limited anthropological and historical material available, Albrecht shows how the kind of society in which people live produces certain types of disease, impairment and disability.

Utilizing what he terms an 'ecological model', he traces the ways in which the physical, biophysical, and cultural environments interact to produce particular biophysical conditions and social responses to impairment. Hence, in the modern USA, the combination of industrialization, the subsequent growth of the human service sector and the more recent politicization of 'disability rights' by the American disabled people's movement have transformed 'disability' and 'rehabilitation' into a multi-million-dollar enterprise. This poses particular economic and social problems for the future. His solution is the further development of a 'pluralist political economy of rehabilitation', based on the present American system, in which 'persons with disabilities [*sic*] must either accept the socially constructed definitions laid on them or fight for a *personal* redefinition' (Albrecht, 1992, p. 375) (emphasis added).

Undoubtedly each of the above represents, to varying degrees, an alternative to conventional individualistic interpretations of disability, yet they each fail to address some of the key structural factors precipitating their application. Indeed, in common with much of the literature on disability, they draw on the work of established academics rather than that produced by disabled people and their organizations; particularly in the UK. As a consequence they each opt for the traditional terminology of the medical profession (see Barnes, 1992a). Consequently, disabled people are treated as an abstraction somehow distinct from the rest of the human race, and the crucial question of causality is fudged rather than clarified. For example, Albrecht states that 'disability is constituted both by impairments and the disabling environment. The concept of disabling environments, however, forces us to acknowledge that disabilities are physically based but socially constructed. Societies, then, produce disabilities differently from impairments' (1992, p. 35).

Equally important is the fact that the central value system, or 'ideological cornerstones', upon which Western society rests goes unchallenged. Certainly in a later paper Wolfensberger (1994) addresses what he terms 'modernistic values' but these are the direct outcome of the 'collapse of western society' in the latter half of the twentieth century. Albrecht's notion of the 'cultural environment' encompasses abstract concepts like the 'human populations', 'economy', 'means of production', 'social organization' and 'ideologies' – his discussion of the latter is limited to half a page. He concedes that issues like poverty, race, ethnicity, gender and age are significant factors in the construction and production of disability, but the theoretical and cultural implications of these insights are never fully explored. As noted above, in policy terms the outcome for disabled people is rather depressing.

The social model of disability: a materialist account

A more penetrating assessment clustered around what has become known as the 'social model' of disability can be found in the work of British authors, many of whom are disabled people themselves. Building on personal experience rather than academic insights, the social model was initiated by a small but influential group of disabled activists in the late 1960s and early 1970s (UPIAS, 1975; 1976). The seeds of this radical new approach are contained in a book first published in

1966 entitled *Stigma: The Experience of Disability*. This collection of essays by six disabled men and six disabled women was one of the first to call for a focus on the social rather than biological factors in understanding disability. Probably the clearest example of this shift in emphasis can be found in Paul Hunt's essay arguing that disabled people pose a direct challenge to commonly held cultural values (reprinted as Chapter 1, above).

Such insights, coupled with the gradual but significant politicization of disability over the following decades, generated a more sophisticated theoretical grounding for the social model of disability. A major influence was the formation of the Union of the Physically Impaired Against Segregation (UPIAS) in 1972 and the formulation of the redefinition of disability which makes a clear distinction between the concepts of impairment and disability. Thus impairment concerns the biological 'lacking part of or all of a limb, or having a defective limb, or mechanism of the body' – and disability is about the social: 'the disadvantage or restriction of activity caused by a contemporary social organization which takes no or little account of people who have physical impairments and thus excludes them from participation in the mainstream of social activities' (UPIAS, 1976, p. 14). As noted above, this definition was later broadened to accommodate all impairments – physical, sensory, and intellectual – and adopted by other organizations including the BCODP and DPI.

Building on the lessons learnt in the struggles for the control of residential homes in the 1960s, UPIAS's reformulation of disability as social oppression was a holistic approach which rejects the traditional paternalistic and patronizing approach to social policy (UPIAS, 1975; 1976; Campbell and Oliver, 1996). Moreover, a theoretical grounding for the social model of disability was provided by another founder member of UPIAS, Vic Finkelstein, a disabled South African exile and psychologist living in Britain.

In *Attitudes and Disabled People* (1980) Finkelstein argued that disability is the direct result of the development of Western industrial society. Using a conventional materialist framework, Finkelstein divides history into three distinct sequential phases. The first, Phase One, broadly corresponds to the feudal period before European industrialization. Here economic activity consisted primarily of agrarian or cottage-based industries; a 'mode of production', he maintains, which does not preclude people with perceived impairments from participation.

But in Phase Two, round about the nineteenth century, when industrialization took hold, people with impairments were excluded from employment on the grounds that they were unable to keep pace with the new factory-based work system. Hence they were segregated from the mainstream of economic and social activity into a variety of residential institutions. Finkelstein's Phase Three, which he maintains is only just beginning, will see the eventual liberation of disabled people from such oppression through the development and use of technology, and their working together with helpers and allies towards commonly held goals.

For Finkelstein, therefore, disability is a paradox emerging out of the development of Western capitalist society. On the one hand, disability implies 'a personal tragedy, passivity and dependence' (Finkelstein, 1980, p. 1). On the other, it can be seen as societal restriction and discrimination. In Phase One people with impairments were dispersed throughout the community; but in Phase Two, owing to the emergence of large-scale industry with production lines geared to 'able bodied norms' and 'hospital based medicine' (p. 10), they were separated from their social origins into a clearly defined devalued group. Phase Three will witness the end of the paradox as disability will be recognized as social restriction only.

Although intended as an aid to understanding rather than an accurate historical statement, Finkelstein's analysis has been criticized for being over-simplistic and over-optimistic. It is over-simplistic in that it assumes a simple relationship between the mode of production and perceptions and experiences of disability. It is too optimistic in its assumption that technological development and professional involvement will integrate disabled people back into society. Technology for disabled people can be disempowering as well as empowering, and, hitherto, professional vested interests have proved one of the biggest barriers to disabled people's empowerment (Barnes, 1990; Oliver, 1986; 1990; 1996).

Nonetheless, in the following decade the notion of disability as social oppression was used extensively by disabled writers and activists to explore their own experiences of prejudice and discrimination. Notable examples include Alan Sutherland's (1981) *Disabled We Stand* and the various contributions to disability journals such as *In from the Cold* (the journal of the Liberation Network of People with Disabilities published between 1981 and 1987) (Barnes, Mason and Mercer, 1997) and *Coalition* (the journal of the Greater Manchester Coalition of Disabled People, started in 1986 and still going strong).

In 1987 a disabled sociologist, Paul Abberley, called for a more comprehensive theoretical approach. Besides marshalling empirical evidence sustaining the claim that disabled people are in a worse position than non-disabled peers because they are perceived as disabled people, he argued that a theory of disability as social oppression must also

> argue that these disadvantages are dialectically related to an ideology or group of ideologies which justify and perpetuate this situation. Beyond this it is to make the claim that such disadvantages and their supporting ideologies are neither natural nor inevitable. Finally it involves some beneficiary of this state of affairs. (Abberley, 1987, p. 7)

Such an analysis is provided in Mike Oliver's *The Politics of Disablement* (1990). This book provides a comprehensive materialist account of the creation of disability, placing 'ideology' at the centre of the argument. Here ideology refers to a set of values and beliefs distinct from theology or metaphysics but rooted in notions of post-Enlightenment rationality which underpins social policies and practices including those in the workplace, medical intervention, welfare services and the leisure and culture industries. Hence the material and social disadvantages associated with impairment are related to the core ideology of individualism, and the peripheral ideologies of medicalization and rehabilitation – all of which emerged within the context of capitalist development. Anthropological evidence is also provided to show that these disadvantages are not apparent in all societies, demonstrating that this group of ideologies is neither natural nor inevitable. Moreover, it is the system as a whole which benefits since, economically, disabled people form part of a 'reserve army of labour' and, ideologically, they 'serve as a warning to those unable or unwilling to work' (p. 70).

In short, economic development, the changing nature of ideas and the need to maintain order during industrialization influenced social responses to and, therefore, the experience of impairment. The rise of the institution as a means of both social provision and control coupled with the individualization and medicalization of 'social problems' in the eighteenth and nineteenth centuries precipitated the emergence of the individualistic medical approach to impairment. Moreover, this 'personal tragedy theory of disability' has, in turn, achieved ideological dominance or 'hegemony' (Gramsci, 1971) in that it has become translated into common-sense and everyday assumptions and beliefs.

Elsewhere I have argued that the social oppression of disabled people can be traced back to the very foundations of Western society. At its core lies the pursuit of physical and intellectual perfection, or the 'myth of the able bodied' ideal associated with Graeco-Roman culture, and that this oppression has been exacerbated by industrialization and its accompanying ideologies (Barnes, 1996c).

Unlike the work of their American counterparts, these accounts suggest that the basis of disabled people's oppression is linked to the material and ideological changes associated with capitalist development. This has far-reaching implications in social policy terms both for disabled people and for society as a whole. Policy recommendations include comprehensive and enforceable anti-discrimination legislation, a Freedom of Information Act, user-led services, direct payment schemes, inclusive education policies and the development of a disability culture (see for example Barnes, 1991b; Campbell and Oliver, 1996; Morris, 1993d; Oliver, 1990).

The social model, diversity and impairment

However, in the early 1990s the focus on the structures of oppression was criticized by a second generation of British writers working from within a feminist or postmodernist framework. Emphasizing the link between culture and prejudice, they have argued that the social model of disability has neglected the everyday experiences of disabled people – with particular reference to gender (Morris, 1991; 1996), minority ethnic status (Stuart, 1992; Begum et al., 1994; Vernon, 1996a), sexuality (Hearn, 1991; Killin, 1993; Shakespeare et al., 1996) and impairment (Crow, 1992; 1996; French, 1993a; 1994; Morris, 1991).

But it is important to remember when evaluating these criticisms that, although the emergence of the social model of disability has a history spanning well over three decades, its rise to prominence was gradual and, for many, is located in the late 1980s. Hence much of the early material produced by disabled writers and disabled people's organizations was not widely available, either in public libraries or in academic institutions. Consequently many people, some of whom are mentioned above, are apparently unaware that it emerged out of the direct experience of disabled people themselves. Moreover, because of this unfortunate situation much of the earlier work on the experiences of disabled people has been overlooked. There is, for instance, a quite extensive literature dealing solely with the experiences of disabled women. One notable example is Jo Campling's (1981) *Images of Ourselves*, a collection of 24 essays by disabled women of varying ages, backgrounds and impairments from all over Britain talking about their everyday lives.

The net effect is that academics and researchers are impelled to go over the same ground rather than build on what has gone before. This is important because although much has already been achieved there is still much that needs to be done – particularly with reference to the way in which disability interacts with other oppressions and, as a consequence, how it is experienced differently by different sections of the disabled population such as disabled members of minority ethnic groups.

Furthermore, the lack of information may also help to explain why some disabled writers have called for the integration of the experience of impairment, notably, with reference to the experience of physical pain, fatigue and depression, into the social model of disability. But, as noted above, there is a vast and, indeed, ever expanding literature produced by medical sociologists and others dealing explicitly with these issues which effectively blurs the crucial distinction between the experience of impairment and the experience of disability. Most of this writing represents either 'sentimental autobiography or else preoccupied with the medical and practical details of a particular condition' (Hunt, 1966, p. ix). Hitherto it has served only to endorse negative cultural stereotypes of disabled people and, in so doing, detract attention away from the material and cultural forces which compound disabled people's disadvantage (Barnes, 1996a). Furthermore, the experience of pain, fatigue and depression is not unique to people with accredited impairments. Many 'non-disabled' people encounter them on a regular basis during the course of their everyday lives; as a result of a particular type of employment, for instance. Equally, large numbers of disabled people may never encounter these experiences; deaf people are but one important example.

It is appropriate, therefore, to conclude by reiterating that the social model of disability is, first and foremost, a focus on the environmental and social barriers which exclude people with perceived impairments from mainstream society. It makes a clear distinction between impairment and disability: the former refers to biological characteristics of the body and the mind, and the latter to society's failure to address the needs of disabled people. This is not a denial of the importance of impairment, appropriate medical intervention or, indeed, discussions of these experiences. It is, however, a concerted attempt to provide a clear and unambiguous framework within which policies can be developed which focus on those aspects of disabled people's lives which can and should be changed (Barnes, 1996a) – something which hitherto sociology has failed to provide.

Conclusion

This chapter has suggested that theorizing about the experiences of both impairment and disability within the context of sociology has spanned the latter half of the twentieth century. However, it is clear that the bulk of this work, particularly that produced by medical sociologists, has tended to adhere, at least implicitly if not explicitly, to traditional wisdom and policy solutions. In spite of this, a more radical approach, commonly known as the social model of disability, has emerged from within the disabled people's movement. In theoretical and policy terms this has far-reaching implications both for disabled people and for society as a whole. Yet hitherto the phenomenon of the social model of disability has escaped the attention of most sociologists. For me this raises a number of important and uncomfortable questions about the nature and role of the discipline which have yet to be answered.

Further reading

Albrecht, G. L. (1992) *The Disability Business*. London: Sage.
Oliver, M. (1990) *The Politics of Disablement*. Basingstoke: Macmillan.
Oliver, M. (1996) *Understanding Disability: From Theory to Practice*. Basingstoke: Macmillan.

6

The Spectre at the Feast: Disabled People and Social Theory

Paul Abberley

The first thing you need to do when writing about disability today is to clarify your terms, and this immediately gets you into the realm of theory, since the most fundamental issue in the sociology of disability is a conceptual one. The traditional approach, often referred to as the medical model, locates the source of disability in the individual's supposed deficiency and her or his personal incapacities when compared to 'normal' people. In contrast to this, social models see disability as resulting from society's failure to adapt to the needs of impaired people.

The World Health Organization, for example, operates in terms of a four-part medically based classification, developed by Wood (1980), known as the International Classification of Impairment, Disability and Handicap (ICIDH). This functions to link together the experiences of an individual in a logic which attributes disadvantage to nature. A *complaint*, like a spinal injury, causes an *impairment*, like an inability to control one's legs, which *disables* by leading to an inability to walk, and *handicaps* by giving the individual problems in travelling, getting and retaining a job, etc. Thus the *complaint* is ultimately responsible for the *handicap*. A social model of disability, on the other hand, focuses on the fact that so-called 'normal' human activities are structured by the general social and economic environment, which is constructed by and in the interests of non-impaired people. 'Disability' is then defined as a form of oppression: 'The term "disability" represents a complex system of social restrictions imposed on people with impairments by a highly discriminatory society. To be a disabled person in modern Britain means to be discriminated against' (Barnes, 1991b, p. 1).

Such a model is advanced by the Disabled Peoples' International, of which the British Council of Organisations of Disabled People is a member, and is increasingly utilized in the field of disability studies. For a social model, both the notion of normality in performance and the disadvantage experienced by the 'deficient' performer are oppressive social products. Thus the meaning attached to 'disability' here spans the area covered by the two WHO terms 'disability' and 'handicap'. It is such a definition, with its bipartite distinction between impairment and disability, that I employ and discuss in this paper.

The political impetus for the development of new sociological approaches to disablement in Britain has doubtless been the increase in the self-organization of disabled people. Amongst disabled and non-disabled sociologists who see their work as supporting this process, this development has involved a re-examination of and reorientation towards the general social theory in terms of which they have hitherto seen the world. Insofar as the process has involved dragging the study of disablement from a quiet backwater of medical sociology or deviancy theory into the mainstream of social enquiry, it equally entails the interrogation of mainstream theories as to their adequacy for the task of providing the groundwork for a liberative analysis of disablement. The most common response of modern social theory to the disabled per-son's enquiry 'What about me?' is silence. This very silence is itself telling, but we may go further than this. For while a theory may make no explicit reference to disabled people, we may derive implications from its general approach and analysis of social existence. If we find these implications unacceptable, we are obliged to criticize the aspects of them from which they derive as ideological or culturally constructed rather than as natural or a reflection of reality (Alcoff, 1988). The alternative is to regard the disadvantage of disabled people as inevit-able, to regret it emotionally but accept it intellectually. This is a recipe not for social change but for Quixotic posturing. The disability move-ment needs to develop views of what it would mean for impaired people not to be disabled at all, if it is to move beyond the first stages of the struggle to abolish disablement. And this requires social theory, devel-oped by the activist, the academic or a symbiotic relationship between the two.

Functionalism and disability

The founding father of functionalist sociology, Emile Durkheim (1964), posits a fundamental distinction between non- or preindustrial societies and industrial ones. In the former social integration is characterized as based on the similarity of roles in the social division of labour, 'mechanical' solidarity. After industrialization, with a growing separateness and distinction of the individual from the group as the division of labour is increasingly specialized and individuated, a good society is one with strong bonds of 'organic' solidarity. These bonds are constituted through the recognition of the role of others in the complex division of labour that makes up that society. The venue where this solidarity is to be forged is the occupational associations. Thus to be deprived of such a role is to be deprived of the possibility of full societal membership. Whilst some of his polemical writing like the essay 'Individualism and the Intellectuals' (Durkheim, 1971), written as an intervention in the Dreyfus Affair, places great stress upon the necessity for the good society to recognize diversity, there is no suggestion that this extends to the incorporation into society of those unable to work.

It is then as a consequence of theoretical consistency that Topliss, operating from a functionalist perspective ultimately traceable back to the work of Durkheim, comes to advance the following argument for the inevitability of discrimination against disabled people:

> While the particular type or degree of impairment which disables a person for full participation in society may change, it is inevitable that there will always be a line, somewhat indefinite but none the less real, between the ablebodied majority and a disabled minority whose interests are given less salience in the activities of society as a whole.
>
> Similarly the values which underpin society must be those which support the interests and activities of the majority, hence the emphasis on vigorous independence and competitive achievement, particularly in the occupational sphere, with the unfortunate spin-off that it encourages a stigmatising and negative view of the disabilities which handicap individuals in these valued aspects of life. Because of the centrality of such values in the formation of citizens of the type needed to sustain the social arrangements desired by the ablebodied majority, they will continue to be fostered by family upbringing, education and public esteem. By contrast, disablement which handicaps an individual in these areas will continue to be negatively valued, thus tending towards the imputation of general inferiority to the disabled individual, or stigmatization. (Topliss, 1982, pp. 111–12)

For Topliss the inevitable disadvantage of disabled people, in any possible society, stems from our general inability to meet standards of performance in work. This can be contrasted to other perspectives, like interactionism, where some writers (Haber and Smith, 1971) suggest that the core 'deficiency' of disabled people is an aesthetic one. However, aesthetic judgements may themselves be related, albeit in a complex manner, to the requirements of production, so it seems unlikely that the aesthetic explanation, however attractive it may be in certain cases, possesses the irreducibility ascribed it by its proponents.

Marxism and disability

Given the political unacceptablity of the implications of such perspectives as functionalism and interactionism to sociologists committed to the liberation of disabled people, one major source which we have drawn upon is Marxism. This has occurred in part because of the theoretical and political backgrounds of the sociologists involved. But equally, I think, because Sartre's 1960 judgement that all thinking has to operate in relation to the dominant philosophy of the age, Marxism, still holds correct (Sartre, 1963). However, this utilization has occurred at a fair distance from the fundamental economic and philosophical basics of the theory. Such notions as oppression (Abberley, 1987; 1992a) and hegemony (Oliver, 1990; 1996), the former owing its initial credentials to Lenin's analysis of imperialism and the latter to Gramsci's work on ideology, have been found useful by some researchers and members of the disability movement. But as far as the nuts and bolts of the critique of political economy are concerned, we have largely been silent. For my part this has been not accidental, but because I have come to see profound problems in utilizing a Marxian model of human beings for the liberation of disabled people.

The clearest and most explicit reference to disabled people to be found in the Marx/Engels corpus occurs in *The Condition of the Working Class in England*, written in 1844–45. Engels argues that the Industrial Revolution creates the proletariat in a gigantic process of concentration, polarization and urbanization, and with it, despite expansion of the whole economy and an increased demand for labour, a 'surplus population' which Marxists were later to refer to as the 'reserve army of labour'. He was concerned to explore the conditions of life and the collective and individual behaviour that this process produced, and the greater part of the book is devoted to the description and analysis of these material conditions. His account is based on first-hand observations, informants and printed evidence, such as Commission reports and contemporary journals and periodicals. 'Cripples' are cited as evidence of injurious working practices: 'The Commissioners mention a crowd of cripples who appeared before them, who clearly owed their distortion to the long-working hours' (Engels, 1969, p. 180).

He cites the evidence of a number of doctors who relate particular kinds of malformation and deformity to working practices, as an 'aspect of the physiological results of the factory system' (p. 181). He continues: 'I have seldom traversed Manchester without meeting three or four of them, suffering from precisely the same distortions of the spinal columns and legs as that described . . . It is evident, at a glance, whence the distortions of these cripples come; they all look exactly alike' (p. 182). He continues for some pages to relate particular forms of impairment to factory working conditions and to condemn 'a state of things which permits so many deformities and mutilations for the benefit of a single class, and plunges so many industrious working-people into want and starvation by reason of injuries undergone in the service and through the fault of the bourgeoisie' (p. 194). He concludes his description of 'the English manufacturing proletariat' thus: 'In all directions, whithersoever we may turn, we find want and disease permanent or temporary . . . slow but sure undermining, and final destruction of the human being physically as well as mentally' (p. 238).

Engels here establishes the main form of Marxism's concern with disabled people. We are exemplary of the predations of capitalism and, as such, have propaganda value as one of the things socialism will abolish: the significance of disabled people is as historically contingent victims. The analysis is not then one of disablement but of impairment, and rates of impairment.

A hundred years later Hannington uses a similar analysis and sources of evidence, this time to condemn not factory work but the lack of it: 'These youths . . . meet problems which render them increasingly conscious of the way in which their lives have been stunted and their young hopes frustrated and of the results of the physical impairment which they have suffered through the unemployment and poverty of their parents' (Hannington, 1937, p. 78). Doyal (1979) refines this general thesis, and documents a relationship between 'capitalism' and impairment on a wide variety of fronts, adding consumption, industrial pollution, stress and imperialism to the labour-centred concerns of Engels and Hannington.

Now I in no way wish to dispute the general accuracy and pertinence of these studies. My point is rather that such an analysis, linking impairment to capitalism as a very apparent symptom of its inhumanity and irrationality, is of little use in the struggle against disablement. All it implies is that, with the state, impaired people would wither away in a society progressively abolishing the injurious consequences of production for profit. But there are two crucial objections to the notion of the problem of disability ending up in the dustbin of history. First, whilst socially produced impairments of the kind outlined by Doyal *et al.* may decrease in number, it is inconceivable that the rate of impairment should ever be reduced to zero. Second, and of significance for disabled people today, it is an issue whether such a situation, could it occur, would be desirable. As long as there is a general eugenicist consensus between left and right that impaired modes of being are undesirable, disabled people must challenge such views as, in essence, genocidal.

Why, when in practice the propagation and implementation of right-wing theories of disability are a real and ever-present problem for disabled people, should I criticize Marxism? Is this a matter of getting on a popular bandwagon and exhibiting the spurious maturity espoused by so many ageing radicals? I think not. The social models of disability propagated as liberative of disabled people by the disability movement are necessarily perspectives 'of the left' since they involve the radical overhaul of the status quo. Thus, in developing our understanding of disablement and working towards its abolition, it is with perspectives which claim a critical and oppositional standpoint that we must come to grips. In particular, we need to understand the failure of Marxism to provide concepts which we may employ to develop further a liberative social theory of disability.

I have argued above that Marxist analyses, since they address impairment rather than disability, are exclusively concerned with prevention and cure. However, this emphasis is no accidental consequence of the marginality of disabled people to Marxism's primary concern with production relations under capitalism, rather it is deeply grounded in Marxist notions of humanity. It will thus apply across modes of production and historical eras. To see why this is the case, it is necessary to consider the Marxist model of human beings, and in particular the role labour takes in the constitution of humanness. For Marxism, whilst all human societies must produce their own material conditions of exist-ence, the commodity is the form products take when this production is organized through exchange. The commodity has two aspects. First, it can satisfy some human want – it has use value; second, it can be exchanged for other commodities, a property Marx calls simply 'value'. Since a commodity has both a use value and a value, the labour producing it has a dual character. Any act of labour, 'productive activity of a definite kind, carried on with a definite aim' (Marx, 1974a, p. 49), is useful labour productive of use value. This can be contrasted to pseudo-labour (familiar to many who have undergone occupational therapy): 'Nothing can have value, without being an object of utility. If the thing is useless, so is the labour contained in it; the labour does not count as labour, and therefore creates no value' (p. 48). This 'is a condition of human existence which is independent of all forms of society; it is an eternal natural necessity which mediates the meta-bolism between man and nature, and therefore human life itself' (ibid., ch. 1).

In analysing capitalism, however, he goes on to explore that aspect of labour which endows its product with value, and this is linked to the idea of the average worker:

> Any average magnitude ... is merely the average of a number of separate magnitudes all of one kind, but differing as to quantity. In every industry, each individual labourer, be he Peter or Paul, differs from the average labourer. These individual differences or 'errors' as they are called in mathematics, compensate one another and vanish, whenever a certain minimum number of workmen are employed together. (Marx, 1974a, ch. 1)

This abstract labour, productive of value, is equivalent to socially necessary labour time:

> the labour-time required to produce any use-value under the condi-tions of production normal for a given society and with the average degree of skill and intensity of labour prevalent in that society ... which exclusively determines the magnitude of the value of any

article is therefore the amount of labour socially necessary, or the labour-time socially necessary for its production.

Approximation to this norm serves to define the normal worker. Thus the whole project of capital resting on the notion of abstraction from real data on wages, prices, profit, etc. involves the construction of a norm of 'human being as worker'. Marx's and Engels's description of capitalism captures the way in which capitalism creates both disabled people and a concept of disability as the negative of the normal worker. But this is not an aspect of capitalism Marx seems to present as transcendable. So, whilst Marxism provides powerful theoretical tools for understanding the origin and nature of the oppression of disabled people, it seems of less use in conceptualizing a future for those impaired people unable to work. Thus if we remain within the problematic which has served us well in analysing the oppression of disabled people in the present era, we seem to be obliged to propagate what appears in terms of that theory to be a myth, namely that a society is possible in which all impaired people could have a meaningful role in production.

This becomes clearer if we consider the way in which Marx and Marxists present human freedom, the condition supposed to develop through the transcendence of capitalism and its vestiges. Marx occasionally seems to reduce the problem of human freedom to free time, in for example the 1847 'Wage-Labour and Capital' (Marx, 1969). On such a view there should be no problem for those unable to labour: free time would occupy the whole of life. But this position is more generally ridiculed and in the 1857–58 *Grundrisse* it is asserted that 'Really free working is at the same time precisely the most damned seriousness, the most intense exertion' (Marx, 1973, p. 611).

In the 1875 'Critique of the Gotha Programme' Marx makes the well-known statement that 'in a more advanced phase of communist society . . . when labour is no longer just a means of keeping alive but has itself become a vital need . . . [we may then have] from each according to his abilities, to each according to his needs' (Marx, 1974b, p. 347). But this implies that impaired people are still deprived, by biology if not by society. Impairment, since it places a limit upon creative sensuous practice, is necessarily alienatory, for those who accept that this term should be seen as an element of a Marxist terminological canon. This is not perhaps a problem in relation to free time, since even in Utopia people would not be expected to take part in all possible recreational and cultural activities. It does however constitute a restriction in relation to work, which is an interaction between agent and nature which results in production of social value.

Whilst the distinctions between productive, reproductive and unproductive labour are crucial to the analysis of capitalism, rather than the exploration of a Marxist Utopia, the ability to labour in some socially recognized sense still seems a requirement of full membership of a future good society based upon Marxist theory. Whilst children as potential workers, and elderly people as former ones, may be seen as able to assume a status in a paradise of labour, it is hard to see how despite all efforts by a benign social structure an albeit small group of impaired people could achieve full social integration. Following Marxist theory thus understood, some impaired lives cannot then, in any possible society, be truly social, since the individual is deprived of the possibility of those satisfactions and that social membership to which her humanity entitles her, and which only work can provide. For impaired people to be adequately provided for in the system of distribution, but excluded from the system of production – that is, on a superior form of welfare – would be unsatisfactory, since we would still be in the essentially peripheral relationship to society we occupy today. There is then for Marxism an identity of who you are with the work you do which transcends capitalism and socialism into the concrete utopia of the future to constitute a key element of humanity, and a key need of human beings in all eras. Whilst other needs can be met for impaired people, and this can perhaps be done in a non-oppressive manner, the one need that cannot be met for those unable to labour is the need to work. This appears to be true for a whole range of Marxist thinkers.

William Morris, whose *News from Nowhere* envisages a profound erosion of barriers between necessary labour and the rest of human life, therefore attributes to work a crucial role in human happiness and identity: 'I believe that the ideal of the future does not point to the lessening of men's energy by the reduction of labour to a minimum, but rather to the reduction of pain in labour to a minimum ... the true incentive to useful and happy labour is and must be pleasure in the work itself' (cited by Levitas, 1990, p. 108). Marcuse, whilst believing that work can be more pleasant than it is today, points to a deep coincidence of analysis between Marx and Freud: 'Behind the Reality Principle lies the fundamental fact of scarcity ... whatever satisfaction is possible necessitates work, more or less painful arrangements and undertakings for the procurement of the means for satisfying needs' (Marcuse, 1955, p. 35).

Andre Gorz, at the opposite pole from Morris in his advocacy of the minimization of socially necessary labour and the maximization of free time, still sees purposive activity and competence as a condition of social inclusion: 'the abolition of work does not mean abolition of the need for effort, the desire for activity, the pleasure of creation, the need to cooperate with others and be of some use to the community'. He continues: 'the demand to "work less" does not mean or imply the right to "rest more"' (Gorz, 1982, pp. 2–3). But this is precisely the kind of right that impaired people do demand, today and for the future.

This suggests that Gouldner was correct in his judgement that

> Marxism never really doubted the importance of being useful . . . Its fundamental objection to capitalist society was to the dominating significance of exchange-value, not to use-value. It objected to the transformation of men's labour into a commodity, but it continued to emphasise the value and importance of work. (Gouldner, 1971, p. 406)

It seems that Marxism, on these interpretations, along with allopathic medicine which has been so tied in to the disablement of impaired people in the modern era, can never be other than a project of the Enlightenment. It shares with other such enterprises a rationalist adherence to aspirations of 'perfection', and can identify non-workers only with the historically redundant bourgeoisie, one aspect of whose alienation is their failure to participate in social production.

Work and disability theory

How does this feed back into analyses of disability in society today and the needs of the disability movement? With less than one-third of those in the relevant age-group in employment in Britain today (Martin, Meltzer and Elliot, 1988), for many disabled people the demand for access to work is seen as a crucial component of the struggle for equality. This is reflected in the focus of the government's feeble proposals to 'tackle' disabled people's oppression which focus on the workplace. Equally BCODP, in fighting the government's cutbacks on the Access to Work scheme, asserts 'The right to a job is a fundamental Human Right' (BCODP, 1996, p. 3). Recent work (Lunt and Thornton, 1994) has surveyed some of the issues involved in implementing employment policies in terms of a social model of disablement – but the aim itself is left unexamined.

At the level of more general theory, Finkelstein has pointed out repeatedly (1980; 1993a) 'that the predominant factor contributing to the disablement of different groups is the way in which people can participate in the creation of social wealth' (1993a, p. 12). He goes on to argue that since

> assumed levels of employability separate people into different levels of dependency ... By trying to distance themselves [groups of people with particular impairments or degrees of impairment] from groups that they perceive as more disabled than themselves they can hope to maintain their claim to economic independence and an acceptable status in the community. (1993a, p. 14)

He cautions against doing this for what are essentially political reasons, that it will divide the movement, and points out that those who did this would be surrendering to the logic of the medical model, which they claim to reject. Now this appeal to unity and theoretical consistency, whilst appropriate to its context, seems to me to pass over an essential issue for disabled people – that, even in a society which *did* make profound and genuine attempts to integrate impaired people into the world of work, some would be excluded, by their impairment. Whatever efforts are made to integrate impaired people into the world of work some will not be capable of producing goods or services of social value, that is 'participating in the creation of social wealth'. This is so because, in any society, certain, though varying, products are of value and others are not, regardless of the effort that goes into their production. I therefore wish to contend that, just because a main mechanism of our oppression is our exclusion from social production, we should be wary of drawing the conclusion that overcoming this oppression should involve our wholesale inclusion in it. As Finkelstein recognizes, a society may be willing and in certain circumstances become eager to absorb a portion of its impaired population into the workforce, yet this can have the effect of maintaining and perhaps intensifying its exclusion of the remainder. We need to develop a theory of oppression which avoids this bifurcation, through a notion of social integration which is not dependent upon impaired people's inclusion in productive activity.

Feminist analyses

One area where the analysis of oppression has become rich enough to deal with this issue is feminist theory. Feminism has pointed out that Marxism is deeply marked by the maleness of its originators – and never more so than in the key role assumed by work in the constitution of human social identity. It is argued that the apparent gender-neutrality of Marxist theoretical categories is in reality a gender-bias which legitimizes Marxism's excessive focus on the 'masculine sphere' of commodity production. Whilst some approaches in feminist sociology have reproduced, though from a broader perspective, the concern with work as definitional of social inclusion (Abberley, 1996), others have more profoundly disputed labour-dependent conceptions of humanity.

One aspect of this involved feminist conceptions of the human body, far less abstract than classical Marxist formulations. In exploring the politics of human reproductive biology, feminism opens up other aspects of our biological lives, and thus impairment, to critical reflection. Another is that it has pointed out that the traditional technological solutions have not resulted in a better society for women. 'One fact that is little understood . . . is that women in poverty are almost invariably productive workers, participating fully in both the paid and the unpaid work force . . . Society cannot continue persisting with the male model of a job automatically lifting a family out of poverty' (McKee, 1982, p. 36). In *Black Feminist Thought* Patricia Hill Collins quotes May Madison, a participant in a study of inner-city African Americans who has pointed out that

> One very important difference between white people and black people is that white people think you ARE your work . . . Now, a black person has more sense than that because he knows that what I am doing doesn't have anything to do with what I want to do or what I do when I am doing for myself. Now, black people think that my work is just what I have to do to get what I want. (quoted by Collins, 1990, pp. 47–8)

Whilst white male non-disabled sociologists may interpret this as evidence for the thesis of the alienated or instrumental worker, we should perhaps see it as documenting the social basis of an alternative theory of social membership and identity. This negative evaluation of the significance of 'work' and 'technology' in the present is not construed as explicable in terms of 'deformations under capitalism', but is carried forward into a critique of the viability for women of a society organized around 'work' and the 'technofix'. Such issues are, I think, of significance to the development of theories of disablement. Schweickart, amongst many, represents another strand in arguing that 'The domination of women and the domination of nature serve as models for each other. Thus, science and technology have a place in a feminist utopia only if they can be redefined apart from the logic of domination' (1983, p. 210).

This debate seems an important one for disability theory, both in terms of such detail as the desirability of care activities being performed by machines and in terms of wider issues of how far it would be correct to transform impaired people to give us access to the world. Thus amongst the 'deep' issues of the relationship between human beings and nature raised within feminism are many which echo in disability theory.

Conclusion

The theoretical perspectives I have considered above seem to me to imply an important distinction between disablement and other forms of oppression. Whilst the latter involve a utopia in which freedom can possibly be seen as coming through full integration into the world of work, for impaired people the overcoming of disablement, whilst immensely liberative, would still leave an uneradicated residue of disadvantage in relation to power over the material world. This in turn restricts our ability to be fully integrated into the world of work in any possible society. One implication that can be drawn from this, which finds most support in classical sociological perspectives, with their emphasis on the role of work in social membership, is that it would be undesirable to be an impaired person in such a society, and thus that the abolition of disablement also involves as far as possible the abolition of impairment.

The work-based model of social membership and identity is integrally linked to the prevention/cure-orientated perspective of allopathic medicine and to the specific instrumental logic of genetic engineering, abortion and euthanasia. Ultimately it involves a value judgement upon the undesirability of impaired modes of being. However, this logic allows for the integration of perhaps a substantial proportion of any existing impaired population into the work process, but only insofar as the interface between an individual's impairment, technology and socially valued activity produced a positive outcome. Thus the abolition of an individual's disablement is ultimately dependent upon and subordinate to the logic of productivity. Recent events in China, where a genocidal eugenics law and state-sponsored infanticide have been accompanied by significant equality legislation for some disabled people, exemplify this logic, which I suggest is perfectly consistent with that state's ideology.

An alternative kind of theory can be seen as offering another future insofar as it reflects work as crucially definitional of social membership and is dubious about some of the progressive imperatives implicit in modern science. But such perspectives are not mere piecemeal modifications to existing ideas of the good society. They also involve a distancing from the values of 'modern' society in so far as they involve the identification of persons with what they can produce in such a system. A liberative theory of disability requires the posing of values counter to the classical sociological and revolutionary consensus, the assertion of the rights of the human 'being' against the universalization of the human 'doing'.

This is by no means to deny that the origins of our oppression, even for those with jobs, lie in our historical exclusion as a group, from access to work, nor is it to oppose campaigns for increasing access to employment. It is, however, to point out that a consistently liberative analysis of disablement today must recognize that full integration of impaired people in social production can never constitute the future to which we as a movement aspire. If we must look elsewhere than to a paradise of labour for the concrete utopia that informs the development of theories of our oppression, it is not on the basis of classical analyses of social labour that our thinking will be further developed. Rather it involves a break with such analyses, and an explicit recognition that the aspirations and demands of the disability movement involve the development and proselytization of values and ideas which run profoundly counter to the dominant cultural problematic of both left and right. This is a matter not of choice but of the future survival of alternative, impaired, modes of being. I am thus arguing that we need to develop theoretical perspectives which express the standpoint of disabled people, whose interests are not necessarily served by the standpoints of other social groups, dominant or themselves oppressed, of which disabled people are also members.

Such sociology involves the empowerment of disabled people because knowledge is itself an aspect of power. Disabled people have inhabited a cultural, political and intellectual world from whose making they have been excluded and in which they have been relevant only as problems. Scientific knowledge, including sociology, has been used to reinforce and justify this exclusion. New sociology of disablement needs to challenge this 'objectivity' and 'truth' and replace it with knowledge which arises from the position of the oppressed and seeks to understand that oppression. It requires an intimate involvement with the real historical movement of disabled people if it is to be of use. Equally, such developments have significance for the mainstream of social theory, in that they provide a testing ground for the adequacy of theoretical perspectives which claim to account for the experiences of all a society's members.

Further reading

Abberley, P. (1996) Work, utopia and impairment, in L. Barton (ed.) *Disability and Society: Emerging Issues and Insights*. Harlow: Longman.

Engels, F. (1969) *The Condition of the Working Class in England*. St Albans: Granada Publishing.

Gleeson, B. J. (1997) Disability studies: a historical materialist view, *Disability and Society*, vol. 12, no. 2, pp. 179–202.

7

The Best Burgers? The Person with Learning Difficulties as Worker[1]

Stephen Baron, Sheila Riddell and Heather Wilkinson

The purpose of this chapter is to consider the construction of the person with learning difficulties as worker in the context of UK vocational education and training policy, where changes reflect shifting understandings of employment in post-industrial society. Before providing a brief commentary on the implications of 'reflexive accumulation' (Lash and Urry, 1993) for people with learning difficulties, we consider why work is such an important issue for this group in terms of the attainment of adult status, and some of the ways in which, historically, the economic productivity of disabled people has been regarded. Data from interviews with training managers in Local Enterprise Companies are drawn upon to illustrate competing constructions of the person with learning difficulties as marginal or paradigm workers.

The significance of employment for adults with learning difficulties

At one level, both childhood and adulthood are relative concepts, interpreted differently at particular historical periods and in different cultures (Ariès, 1973). None the less, within the UK in the late twentieth century, childhood generally denotes a state of relative dependence and adulthood relative independence (Jones, 1997). Over recent years, coinciding with the seemingly inexorable rise of structural unemployment in Western industrialized countries, there have been recurring moral panics over the possible dangers to the social fabric of young people failing to make a successful transition to adulthood. Excluded from mainstream society and deprived of a range of rights and responsibilities, the fear is frequently expressed that, in the absence of employment, such young people may join the shadowy world of the underclass, characterized by poverty, drug dependence and general degeneracy. Social commentators such as Willis (1984) confirmed these fears, maintaining that unemployment inevitably generated a form of 'profane culture'. He argued:

> Properly to understand unemployment, we need to understand what is missing – the wage. The wage is not simply an amount of money ... It is the only connection with other social possibilities, processes and desirable things. As such it operates as the crucial pivot for several other processes, social and cultural transmissions quite unlike itself. (p. 34)

Other commentators, such as Coffield *et al.* (1986), Hutson and Jenkins (1989) and Jones (1997), took a less pessimistic stance, suggesting that in the absence of paid employment a range of other factors might come into play, encouraging and sometimes coercing young people from childhood into adulthood. Some markers of adult status kicked into play automatically; for instance, legal rights and obligations generally depended on the attainment of a certain age rather than any other qualification. These included the right to withhold or give medical and sexual consent; to marry with or without parents' agreement; to claim benefit from the state; the obligation to pay tax and make national insurance contributions. Leaving the parental home, even if this might involve a period of homelessness, was another way in which young people might seek to attain adult status, and, particularly for young women, becoming a parent might represent the attainment of adulthood.

Despite these alternative routes to adulthood, coupled with what has been described as the dynamic of transition (Riddell, forthcoming), a powerful force pushing and pulling young people away from childhood, questions continued to be raised as to whether young people possessed both the skills and the attitudes not only to act as responsible parents but also to ensure the future international competitiveness of the UK economy. An earlier generation of social researchers considered that neither education nor vocational training made much difference to young people's life chances (e.g. Coleman *et al.*, 1966) and the economic health of the nation (e.g. Stronach, 1988). The distribution of wealth within a society and the state of the global economy were, it was maintained, far more salient. School effectiveness researchers (see Riddell and Brown, 1991, for commentary) transformed this perception, maintaining that both schools and education systems played a crucial part in determining individual and national economic success. Furthermore, international league tables were able to demonstrate that some of the top performers such as Singapore and the Czech Republic were working with far more meagre resources and with larger classes than the UK, thus (supposedly) demonstrating that greater efficiency and effectiveness were quite compatible with reduced public expenditure. Within this economistic formulation, the entire purpose of education and training is seen in terms of enabling people to compete effectively with others to secure scarce jobs and for nations to compete successfully against rival states. In a later section there is exploration of the implications of human capital theory for people with learning difficulties in the labour market.

The question remained, however, as to whether people with learning difficulties were to be included in the education/training market or should be regarded as intrinsically unworthy of national investment in the light of their (assumed) relatively poor potential as competitors in the labour market. Historically, the view resurfaces that disabled people, including those with learning difficulties, should be pressed into gainful employment to prevent them from becoming a burden on the state. Unlike the 'sturdy beggars' featured in Elizabethan Poor Law, who were to be whipped and sent back to their parish of origin to obtain gainful employment, it was felt that slightly less harsh, though nonetheless controlling, treatment was appropriate for disabled people. Thus the Egerton Commission of 1889 argued: 'It is better for the state to expend its funds on the elementary technical education of the blind, than to have to support them through a life in idleness.' In Edinburgh basic education in manual skills was first extended to deaf and blind people in such institutions as the Asylum for the Industrious Blind, founded in 1773, and Donaldson's Hospital (now School) for the Deaf, founded in 1850. Under the terms of the Education (Scotland) Act 1906, School Boards were permitted to provide 'special educational treatment' for 'epileptic, crippled and mentally handicapped children' who were deemed unable to benefit from mainstream schools but were not sufficiently impaired as to require institutional care. Special schools were often linked to occupational centres where disabled people were likely to spend their working lives, having been in a limited and stereotyped range of occupations (e.g. basket-weaving, packing items for distribution). The fundamental problem remained, however, as to whether the purpose of this work was intended to be a form of personal therapy or whether it was intended to make a real economic contribution. The answer to this dilemma seemed to depend, at least to some extent, on the state of the economy.

In the 1940s, for example, 80 per cent of school leavers from Glasgow special schools moved into employment, working in jobs such as unskilled labouring on building sites. As the world economy moved into recession in the 1970s in the wake of the oil crisis, previously unthinkable levels of unemployment became accepted as inevitable. It is salutary to remember that the Labour Party lost the 1979 general election in part because of its failure to tackle unemployment; with 1.5 million on the dole, the Tories reminded the nation that 'Labour isn't working'. Throughout the 1980s, the method of calculating unemployment changed many times and by the end of the decade it was approaching 3 million. During this period, despite the rhetoric of training young people for work, the reality was that for many there was only a remote likelihood that employment would follow their youth training scheme. For young people with learning difficulties, the notion of 'significant living without work' referred to in the Warnock Report (1978) was often used to justify this situation, with the implication that this group was essentially unemployable despite its previous involvement in the open labour market.

More recently, the salience of employment in the lives of disabled people, including those with learning difficulties, has been reaffirmed. Disabled people themselves maintained that employment and a wage were essential to avoid dependence on inadequate state handouts (Brisenden, 1989). It was suggested that other markers of adult status might be particularly difficult for people with learning difficulties to attain, and therefore employment for this group was perhaps even more important than for other young people (Riddell, Ward and Thomson, 1993). Organizations of and for disabled people developed supported employment schemes, based on the idea that employment in the open labour market should be regarded as the goal for most people, with appropriate help available as required. These 'real jobs' programmes were justified in terms of both the needs of the economy and the interests of disabled people (Kilsby and Beyer, 1997). Although the

state was reluctant to commit funds to supported employment programmes, none the less there was concern about the proportion of
GNP being spent on unemployment benefit. The Labour government
elected in May 1997 committed itself to a welfare to work programme
and pledged to reduce the number of those classified as disabled and
therefore unable to work. The following sections of the chapter discuss
in more detail the restructuring of capitalist production and its implications for the person with learning difficulties as worker.

The restructuring of capitalist production

As indicated above, the shifting fortunes of people with learning difficulties were intimately linked with the changing nature of global
capitalism analysed, *inter alia*, as 'disorganised capitalism' (Lash and
Urry, 1987), 'flexible accumulation' (Harvey, 1989) or 'economies of
signs and space' and 'reflexive accumulation' (Lash and Urry, 1993).
While there are substantial differences between these interpretations
and others not reviewed here, there is unanimity that the capitalist
mode of production is undergoing a qualitative change to a different
form of capitalism, an epochal change. The waning form of capitalism,
Fordism or organized capitalism, is based on the concentration and
centralization of capital into large monopolistic manufacturing or
extractive firms within relatively few regions globally. The scale of plant
is large, seeking vertical integration and economies of scale, and it is
characterized by a detailed division of labour (Lash and Urry, 1987,
pp. 3–4). In this version of the capitalist mode of production the labour
process is broken up into single, specialized tasks requiring a minimum
of training and a maximum of externally imposed labour discipline
(Harvey, 1989, pp. 177–8). From the early text of organized capitalism,
F. W. Taylor's 1911 *Principles of Scientific Management* (Taylor, 1947),
through to the Marxist critics of its high stage (Beynon, 1973; Braverman, 1974) the labourer is presented as an extension of the tool: to
Taylor an ox to be given the right-sized shovel according to what is
being shifted; to Beynon the production line worker paid to endure the
boredom of the rapid repeat cycle of the production line.

The emerging form of capitalism, flexible accumulation to Harvey,
fragments the (intended) long-term industrial, social and political
structures of organized capitalism, substituting a strategy of short-term,
profit-maximizing forays. In his darker moment of the crisis of the

'third cut', Harvey sees these as leading to the necessary devastation of regions by war as capital seeks locations to (re)colonize profitably (Harvey, 1982). Emphasis shifts to smaller-scale units producing small batches to specific orders. In this type of production labour power is applied to multiple tasks, with discipline being enforced by quality assurance systems and more horizontal management structures. Learning off and, crucially, on the job becomes of central importance. For 'core' workers co-responsibility and commitment to, and by, the firm are *leitmotifs*; for the increasing number of 'non-core' workers unemployment or casualization and poor pay are the relevant themes (Harvey, 1989).

Lash and Urry (1993, p. 60) criticize the concept of 'flexible accumulation' on the grounds that it underestimates the role of services in the developing mode of production; it underestimates the role of knowledge and information in contemporary economic growth; it focuses on production and thus ignores consumption; it fails to grasp the extent to which both production and consumption are permeated by the symbolic processes of cultures external to the economy. Lash and Urry offer the concept of 'reflexive accumulation' as an alternative way of conceptualizing current restructuring to 'flexible accumulation'. In 'reflexive accumulation' Lash and Urry posit a 'double hermeneutic' in the economy: a hermeneutic concerned with the 'question of increasing information intensity as a way of coping with a complex and uncertain economic environment' and a hermeneutic 'in which the very norms, rules and resources of the production process are constantly put into question' (1993, p. 61).

What are the consequences of these changes in the nature of global capitalism for those with learning difficulties?

One immediate reaction to such a question is to refuse it. First, many concerned with learning difficulties reject the categorization, arguing that every individual is special. This argument is addressed, with special reference to children, by Dumbleton (1994), who suggests that the positing of a seamless spectrum of abilities in which differences disappear 'is a comforting one and is similar to the idea that we are living in a classless society. However neither is true.' The search for such (false) comfort he traces to 'the unease that disability engenders in various ways' and the hope that it 'may help to isolate us from the pain felt by those who have greatest difficulties'. Sally French makes similar points autobiographically in 'Can you see the rainbow – the roots of denial' (French, 1993b). Dumbleton challenges us to imagine if 'anyone would choose to move further along the spectrum of eyesight towards the blind end or [along] the spectrum of learning difficulty towards the severe difficulty end' (p. 3).

Second, for some adherents of the social model of disability such a question (. . . those *with* learning *difficulties*) presents structural issues of discrimination and exclusion as if issues of personal deficits. As Chappell notes (Chapter 14, below) there is unease in the disability literature about the status of the concept, and experience, of 'impairment' with a reluctance to grant a realist status to impairment for fear of re-enabling an individualist, medical model of impairment/disability. Ironically, we suggest, this returns some 'materialist' readings of disability to an idealism. That 'social and environmental manipulation' (French, 1993a, p. 22) may remove barriers for those with, for example, a mobility impairment is both true and politically important to argue. While we personally work with the faith of the educator that, properly taught, anyone can learn anything, it is important to recognize that this is a myth, a constructive myth: no amount of 'social and environmental manipulation' is going to enable our friends with learning difficulties or, in all modesty, us to resolve Fermat's Last Theorem. Accepting the reality of cognitive impairment, as Christie challenges us to do (Christie, 1992), demands that we try to think of differences *both* as a quality of the individual *and* as an actively reproduced social relation rather than *either* as an individual trait (as in the medical model) *or* as a social construction (as in versions of the social model). It is from this perspective that we are exploring the nature of a 'learning society', as refracted through the structural position of adults with learning difficulties, in the ESRC programme of that name; and it is from our initial interviews with various policy makers and professionals that we draw our data in order to explore the question posed above.

One, perhaps the, common feature of 'learning difficulties' is difference in the symbolic ordering and manipulation of the world: for some (for example those, in medical terms, severely damaged by vaccines) symbolic exchange may be limited to the few (carers) who have learnt the different code; for those classified as autistic there may be a lower level of reciprocity in symbolic exchange or there may be an elaborate and eloquent alternative symbolic order (sponsored as art in instances such as Wiltshire, 1991); for the catch-(almost) all category of 'moderate learning difficulties' there may be a comparative slowness in assimilating symbols or a comparatively limited repertoire of symbols or the overly formulaic use of symbols. Each of these symbolic differences may be seen as differences in degrees of reflexivity (either an under- or an over-reflexivity).

Such individual impairments are made particularly significant by, and we suggest offer particular analytic purchase on, the epochal changes in the capitalist mode of production noted above. Chappell argues (properly) for the inclusion of issues of learning difficulties in the social model of disability (Chapter 14, below). We may go beyond this critique to suggest that, while issues of non-standard bodies enabled the social model to develop a general critique of exclusion in Fordist capitalism, the issues of reflexive difference which learning difficulties present are a privileged 'moment' which will enable the social model to develop a general critique of exclusion in the reflexive accumulation epoch of capitalism.

First, as major parts of the economy move towards 'economies of signs', those for whom manipulating symbols is difficult are disqualified from these sectors of employment. While, for example, the significance of skills in information technology can be vastly overplayed, there are increasing demands which many people with learning difficulties cannot meet. Similarly in the food services sector, a traditional niche for people with learning difficulties, the McDonaldization of services (Ritzer, 1995) has placed increased emphasis on the cultural correlates of food, especially the symbols of speed, snappiness and self, the manipulation of which is difficult for many people with learning difficulties (but see the interesting counter case below).

Second, in production, 'learning difficulties' signify either a slower pace of 'learning' than 'normal' or a limit to what might be learnt that is lower than 'normal' (or both). In the classic text of organized capitalism Taylor's 'ox' who provided the muscle behind the different-sized shovels was treated, in theory and reality, as a mechanical being for whom speed or quantum of 'learning' was of little relevance (Taylor, 1947). Similarly the classic study of 'Fordism' (Beynon, 1973) shows the assembly-line workers as adjuncts to machines with repetitive tasks requiring endurance of monotony rather than 'learning'. As we have suggested above, people with learning difficulties could find niches in this organization of production: with a shift towards the double hermeneutic of reflexive accumulation the word 'learning' is increasingly being added to the nouns of production, and such niches are harder to find or create.

Why is 'learning' suddenly so important? It would be optimistic to see the shift towards reflexive accumulation as bringing with it a more fulfilling labour process; the trend to casualization and de-skilling for many is clear. What reflexive accumulation does promise is perpetual instability, a bourgeois permanent revolution, where tasks change rapidly and start-up costs are to be minimized in the increasing frantic search for profitable investment. People with learning difficulties tend to learn slowly; slow learners are expensive. People with learning difficulties tend to produce slowly; slow producers are less profitable.

If, following Willis (1977), we take those seeking to make the transition from school to work as our test category then the position in the emerging organization of production of those with learning difficulties is highlighted. Of leavers from special schools in Edinburgh in 1996 only some 9 per cent went into work while 28 per cent undertook Skillseekers training as a preparation for work. The remaining 63 per cent became 'clients' of social-work-type services from which employment is only a remote possibility or remained 'at home'. In our interviews with the Local Enterprise Companies (LECs, the Scottish equivalent of English TECs) the reasons offered for the lack of success of people with learning difficulties in the competition for jobs 'out there', a recurrent phrase redolent of the jungle and the survival of the fittest, became clear.

Skillseekers, the guaranteed programme for those seeking to make the transition from school to work, was seen by its providers as a low-status service: 'It's all down to Guidance and Guidance Teachers who see Skillseekers as a last resort.' Within Skillseekers people with learning difficulties were subsumed into the category of 'Special Training Needs' (STN), some 15 per cent of the Skillseekers defined by their inability to gain a Level 2 Vocational Qualification without special support (if at all): young people 'with no aspirations' or 'invariably it'll be a behavioural or social problem . . . it just tends to be immaturity and behavioural stuff'. Within this STN group people with learning difficulties were a small minority.

The STN group as a whole was seen as that which was most unlikely to get a job, with employment rates of 4–6 per cent being estimated.

Those with learning difficulties, presumably among the most 'employable' of that category, were seen as particularly difficult to provide training and employment for, with single cases being adduced as evidence of success. Under Scottish Enterprise's 'output'-related funding system, providing training for people with learning difficulties was thought 'not economic' or 'a big risk' with attributions to training providers of feelings of 'We've got to take the winners' or 'Well the client group. They are not going to make a lot of money with the client group . . . Well, a private training organization is there for one purpose and that is to make money.' The recent policy attention to STN by Scottish Enterprise was seen as unusual: 'It's not a Conference Centre, it's not a Festival Theatre, it's not a photo-opportunity.'

Many people with learning difficulties were thus expected never to take up employment, leading to a tension in LECs between the 'soft social ethic' and the 'hard business ethic': 'I, hand on heart, went to X's [specialist provider for people with special needs] training place today and looked round. You could probably say that half of these people will never work. Perhaps I should be harder but I'm achieving the Outcomes [overall] which I need to keep my masters happy' or, on the other hand, 'I've had, very nicely, to write back [to organizations seeking funding for training people with learning difficulties] and say "We're about economic development. Yes. We will help but only if people are, have the potential to be, economically active." It may be cruel but that's part of life' or, more forthrightly, 'work as a means of integration is being seen as beyond these individuals'.

'Progress', as required for Scottish Enterprise's outcome-based funding formula, was gradually being re-defined by LECs as a succession of training courses: 'a merry-go-round of [Course A] to [Course B] to [Course A] to [Course C]. Where else do people go?' or 'The way we measure outcomes at the moment [is a problem]. I think there should be different types of outcome. I still think that if you say it doesn't matter what happens to the youngster . . . you're going to have training workshops where you go through until you're 65 and get a pension and a lollipop . . . there needs to be some sort of progression. There also need to be places for people who, let's face it, won't be able to work, produce very little. That does not mean to say they should be kicked into touch. Everyone wants the best [workers] – it's the Health & Safety culture.' Such merry-go-rounds were rejected by some LECs, who saw the priority as being 'to meet the needs of individuals and not to lead them up the garden path in any way and give them training which should lead them to being economically active. This might mean telling people the hard thing: "How many people with your disability have done that?" '

The implications of our interviews with LEC officials are clear: those people with learning difficulties who try to gain employment through the training system of LECs become a small minority at the tail end of a wider category of persons for whom, overall, employment is unlikely. The discourse of skills–employability–profitability constructs these people with learning difficulties as expensive to train and slow to produce and thus low in 'employability'. Their inclusion in the LEC discourse is contested, being explicitly attributed to the gaps in community care, and their presence maintained largely through the budgetary dexterity of committed LEC officials: 'we bend Government policy as far as we can although we don't break it'.

There is, however, a minority, alternative discourse in the LECs which constructs people with learning difficulties differently, as capable of employment if the conditions were appropriate. For one LEC this meant ensuring that the appropriate support structures were present, and it sought to establish a progression from training to sheltered workshop to part-time work to full-time work to sustained full-time work by way of supported employment. For other LECs the key to employment lay not in such structures but in the personal encounter with an employer – the chance 'to get a foot in the door' or to be 'kept on'.

More strikingly there was an inversion of the lack of 'employability' discourse in some LECs, with people with learning difficulties being constructed as model employees, the value of which most employers were missing: 'Just because someone has learning difficulties does not mean that they are not going to be very capable employees. I think probably the opposite, maybe a more capable employee and would certainly give the employer a loyal work member' or 'People are seeing how if you give people with learning difficulties a job they do it to the letter and they've been so reliable. We had one lad working in McDonald's and he was incredible – the best burgers that they had ever seen, the burger in the middle of the bun, the relish in the middle of the burger. He accepts nothing else, nothing slap happy about. One woman who is a cleaner and she is meticulous, keeps the place much cleaner than any of the other cleaners they've got there.'

This logic of this inversion suggests that employers, prejudiced, are acting against their own interests. People with learning difficulties are here constructed as loyal, hard-working and punctual. The contrast was explicitly made with other groups of workers, particularly new entrants such as school leavers and other Skillseekers, who are seen as lacking precisely these virtues of obedience and conformity: people with learning difficulties would seem to be especially docile bodies (Foucault, 1977).

The apparently contradictory constructions of people with learning difficulties both as marginal workers and as paradigm workers are united in being part of a utilitarian discourse: the person with learning difficulties is constructed in the narrow terms of how they might contribute to profitable production, such contributions being seen as deriving from the personal capacities of the would-be workers. Constructing a person, and production, in terms of such individual characteristics, and their aggregation, warrants the label 'human capital', the economistic approach to education and training which has dominated much academic and policy thinking for thirty years (classically, Becker, 1964). In recent years there has been increasing interest in the idea of 'social capital' as a complement or, for some, an alternative to constructions of 'human capital'. What might be the implications of a 'social capital' construction of people with learning difficulties?

Learning difficulties, reflexive accumulation and the circulation of social capital

'Social capital' is a concept which is in danger of ranking with 'community' as one which exudes such warm overtones that it is excused critical scrutiny. As we have noted elsewhere (Riddell *et al.*, 1997), societies characterized by high social capital, such as Nazi Germany, might be deeply unpleasant places in which to live, especially if you have learning difficulties.

The current popularity of the concept can be traced to James Coleman's 1990 attempt to offer a post-Parsonian, synthetic theory of social action (Coleman, 1990), although he traces the concept to earlier papers by Loury. Coleman is attracted to the concept as a way of repairing the deficiencies of the necessarily individualist basis of his social action theory, and as a way of articulating his theory with

neoclassical economics: 'social capital inheres in the structure of relations between persons and among persons. It is lodged neither in
individuals nor in the physical implements of production' (1990, p.
302). Social capital is defined by its function – it takes its place
alongside physical capital and human capital: 'like all forms of capital it
is productive' (1990, p. 302), 'like human and physical capital social
capital depreciates if it is not renewed' (1990, p. 321). Coleman's
ultimate aim for the concept is for it to take its place in the pantheon of
quantitative concepts of financial, physical and human capital. For
Coleman one form of social capital is obligation:

> a credit slip held by A to be redeemed by some performance by B.
> If A holds a large number of these credit slips from a number of
> persons with whom he has relations, then the analogy to financial
> capital is direct: The credit slips constitute a large body of credit on
> which A can draw if necessary. (1990, p. 306)

Similarly social capital may take the form of information potential (e.g.
(implausibly) a social scientist keeping up to date through conversa-
tions with colleagues); of norms and sanctions (e.g. community
rewards for high achievement in school); of authority relations (e.g.
(interestingly abstract) 'if Actor A has transferred rights of control to
another Actor, B, then B has available social capital in the form of those
rights of control' (1990, p. 311)); of appropriable, or of intentional,
social organization providing collective resources for the realization of
individual purposes.

'Trust', one component of Coleman's theory of social capital, is
taken up and developed by Francis Fukuyama (1995), who takes the
'end of history' not only as having arrived ('convergence . . . around the
model of democratic capitalism' (1995, p. 4)) but as having found its
Hegel, Fukuyama (1992). Social engineering of 'the great society' is
assumed no longer to be a realistic (or desirable) goal and 'virtually all
serious observers understand that liberal political and economic institutions depend on a healthy and dynamic civil society for their vitality'
(1995, p. 4).

Fukuyama claims that 'a nation's well being, as well as its ability to
compete, is conditioned by a single, pervasive, cultural characteristic:
the level of trust inherent in the society' and this depends on 'the
crucible of trust', social capital (1995, pp. 7, 33). Fukuyama goes on to

distinguish between societies characterized by high trust or low trust and between forms of solidaristic organization which are 'older, economically harmful or inefficient' and those which are 'wealth creating' (1995, p. 159). The test criterion in each case is economic progress, 'in Schumpeter's phrase ... a process of creative destruction'. Japan is hailed as the contemporary nation with the most appropriate form of 'spontaneous sociability' (1995, p. 159). The lean manufacturing of Mr Ono, where 'each worker has a cord at his workstation by which he can bring the entire assembly line to a halt if he sees a problem', is presented as the model of a 'high trust workplace' where the role of the worker is 'not to manipulate a simple operation on a complex machine, as in Adam Smith's pin factory, but to contribute their judgement to help run the production line as a whole' (1995, pp. 258–9). Increasingly, apparently, workers in addition to docile bodies need selectively active minds.

What are the implications of these visions of social capital, and lean manufacturing, for the (would-be) worker with learning difficulties? The work of Coleman and Fukuyama envisages an untrammelled capitalism seeking 'friction free economies' (Fukuyama, 1995, p. 149) in which the primacy of profit is not questioned by a trusted and trusting workforce, dedicated to the enterprise. The search for 'efficiency' is seen as necessarily destructive of social relations which inhibit (or, perhaps even, which do not directly contribute to) it. This version of social capital thus turns the utilitarian screw tighter and we would expect the majority discourse we found in the LECs, the adult with learning difficulties as a marginal worker unlikely to contribute to profitability, to strengthen. The inversion of this discourse, the adult with learning difficulties as paradigm worker, is also threatened by the neoclassical vision of social capital: the lean manufacturing systems envisaged, with their emphasis on a certain autonomy and judgement of the worker, are the antithesis of Taylorist formal and real subsumption which were the basis of celebrating the adult with learning difficulty as docile worker. Rather than just placing the burger in the centre of the bun, the relish in the centre of the burger, the worker in a lean fast-food operation (if that is not an oxymoron) would be expected to contribute to the design of the bun, burger and relish, and may even get to rescript the customer greeting.

Such visions of social capital are fetishistic in the Marxist sense: they attribute an autonomous existence and causal power to putative objects which are, at heart, social relations (Marx, 1974a).[2] Rather than seeing social capital as a quantum, greater or smaller, ranked alongside physical, financial and human capital as forces of production, we suggest social capital is a process in which social relations in production are formed and re-formed with material consequences. Viewed from this perspective the introduction of a person with learning difficulties to a workplace, for example through a Supported Employment Project, offers a privileged moment for both the analysis and the expansion of social capital. For Lash and Urry the second hermeneutic of reflexive accumulation is the hermeneutic 'in which the very norms, rules and resources of the production process are constantly put into question' (1994, p. 61). In the Coleman/Fukuyama version of this hermeneutic this questioning is blinkered to and by profitability: production teams 'are given time to discuss the operation of the line and are continually encouraged to make suggestions as to how the production process could proceed more efficiently' (Fukuyama, 1995, p. 259).

As our LEC interviews suggested above, the person with learning difficulties is, perhaps by definition, something of an 'outsider' to reflexive production organized for maximum profitability: Schutz's spontaneous Stranger for whom the seen but not noticed may have to be explained (Schutz, 1974). The introduction of a person with learning difficulties (plus job coach) into a workplace may thus be seen from this perspective not as an isolated moment of human capital formation (teaching the skills) but as a moment when the usually hidden nature of the social relations of production is made apparent and different ways of organizing production explored. The second hermeneutic of Lash and Urry, faced with an 'unprofitable' and symbolically different worker, could question 'the very norms, rules and resources of the production process' by *challenging* the primacy of profit/efficiency and exploring alternative practical ethics such as self-realization, dignity, reciprocity and social integration. Why must lives be dedicated to ensuring that the burger is in the middle of the bun, the relish in the middle of the burger?

Notes

1. The research reported here is part of the ESRC's Learning Society Programme, Grant L123 25 1042, 'The Meaning of the Learning Society for Adults with Learning Difficulties'. This chapter is a development of

some ideas presented as 'The Learning Society: The Highest Stage of Human Capitalism' at a Learning Society Programme Conference on Skills Formation held in Bristol in May 1997. That paper will appear in a collection on skills formation edited by Frank Coffield (Policy Press, 1998).

2. To present, as Coleman aspires to, 'social capital' as *dinglich* (thing-like) in Marx's terms would represent perhaps the ultimate achievement of political economy.

Further reading

Lash, S. and Urry, J. (1993) *Economies of Signs and Space*. London: Sage.

Philpot, T. and Ward, L. (eds) (1995) *Values and Visions: Changing Ideas in Services for People with Learning Difficulties*. London: Butterworth–Heinemann.

Riddell, S., Baron, S., Stalker, K. and Wilkinson, H. (1997) The concept of the learning society for adults with learning difficulties: human and social capital perspectives, *Journal of Education Policy*.

8

Researching a Disabling Society: The Case of Employment and New Technology

Alan Roulstone

This chapter will focus on the research issues surrounding the enabling potential of new technology for some disabled people in the field of employment. It will be argued that new technology, if used appropriately, can enable a number of disabled people to gain access to or keep employment. However, the chapter will also explore the need to redefine in a critical way the discourse that surrounds these perceived benefits. It will be argued that this discourse has to date been firmly premised on a medical model of disability, one which obscures the wider potential of new technology, and which has placed a cultural boundary around the discussion of these benefits.

It will be argued that employment rehabilitation itself has perpetuated a disabling discourse around the question of gaining employment generally and the benefits of new technology specifically. This dominant medical model of technology benefits will be challenged by the adoption of a social barriers model of these benefits. It will be observed that the two models arrive at very different understandings of the functions of new technology in the enabling process and provide very different research techniques with which to study these issues. As Hughes notes: 'every research tool or procedure is inextricably embedded in commitments to a particular view of the social world' (Hughes, 1990).

In order to illustrate the usefulness of a social barriers model in this context, an exploration of the application of this model to the author's own research will be made. This research and its findings offer insights into the theoretical relevance of a social barriers model of disablement, its research applicability and the implications for the way research is conducted. It will be argued that the long-established hegemony of rehabilitation writers in the field of employment policy and research can be severely challenged by such a reframing of the research question within a social barriers model.

Disabled workers and new technology

At the level of contractual employment, the wider configuration of barriers disabled people have faced has been seen to stem from the impact of industrial capitalism, the physical nature of the factory and its demands for an average worker (Finkelstein, 1980; Gleeson, 1991; Oliver, 1990; Ryan and Thomas, 1980). This process of designing out of the bodies and potentialities of disabled people can be seen to have resulted in continued environmental and attitude barriers to the employment of disabled people (Graham *et al.*, 1990; Kuh *et al.*, 1988; Lonsdale, 1986; Martin *et al.*, 1989; Morrell, 1990; Oliver in Brown and Scase, 1991; Prescott-Clarke, 1990). Whilst such evidence suggests that the industrial capitalism of the late nineteenth century casts a long shadow in employment terms, the last eighty years has seen the growth of white-collar, office-based employment environments.

More recently, the technological shift has been from manual work systems to the computerized collation, storage, manipulation and transporting of information (see Gallie, 1988; Hamnett *et al.*, 1989; Littler, 1984). The growth of white-collar work also encompasses the advent of jobs which do not easily fall into the traditional blue/white collar dichotomy: laboratory workers, medical scientific officers and telephone engineers. What is clear from even a cursory glance at the changing world of work is a shift away from the image of wide-scale factory work.

The advent of the microchip, its potential for interactive functions and its rapid diffusion offer new working environments for some disabled people (Francis, 1986; Forester, 1989; Lyon, 1988). Many environments that formerly relied on physical processes and an ability to negotiate disabling physical structures have been redesigned to allow new computer-based working, one where many previous manual tasks of filing, data handling, storage and communication are handled electronically. This is not to argue that these new ways of working are non-alienating (see Boddy and Buchanan, 1986; McLoughlin and Clarke, 1988; Thompson, 1983) nor that new technology is inherently progressive and socially neutral (Braverman, 1974; Cockburn, 1985; Finnegan and Salaman, 1987; Gill, 1985; McKenzie and Wajcman, 1985). However, there is evident a serendipitous benefit of new technology for some disabled people, one that is not a result of altered economic imperatives but one which simply reflects new environmental practices which cannot be read off from economics.

This positive but unplanned development for some disabled people is the reverse of the negative development of mechanized factory technology, which, whilst not designed to exclude disabled people, in assuming 'average' body shape, function and ergonomics, had this effect. Therefore the unplanned benefits of new technology stem from the microcosmic character of some new-technology-based work, where formerly very physical workspace and tasks are replaced by small-scale, desk top working environments. We can acknowledge the parallel, if limited, development of specialized new technologies which are designed to allow alternative means of access to the written or spoken word (see Chamot, 1989; Schofield, 1981; Church and Glennen, 1992).

The promise of new technology can be read at two levels. First, the promise of new technology to allow access to new working environments by opening up formerly disabling employment environments. Second, the scope for the expression of abilities that new technology allows may in some instances allow for a redefinition of disability itself. Here the role of specialized technologies specifically might allow disabled people not simply to perform employment functions but to illustrate abilities formerly excluded by disabling environments.

The recognition of the promise of new technology is not new; there is much available work detailing this promise. However, to date, the discussion of benefits of new technology have been firmly grounded in a medical individual model of disability (Ashok, Hall and Huws, 1985; Busby, 1990; Carew and West, 1989; Cornes, 1984; 1987; 1989; 1990; Floyd and North, 1985; Gibler, 1989; Hazan, 1981; MacFarlane, 1990; Moses, 1988; Murray and Kenny, 1990; Perlman and Hansen, 1989; Rajan, 1985; Stevenson and Sutton, 1983). Such a framing of 'the promise' of new technology comes from writers and professionals working in technology procurement and rehabilitation. Within the rehabilitation approach the role of new technology is viewed in a social vacuum, one which fails to address the power politics of employment and in some instances issues of access to new technology. Generally it is assumed that mainstream new technology will simply make itself available in education and employment settings in an inevitable, almost evolutionary way. This can be conceptualized as a form of techno-logical determinism, one where technological diffusion will unfold by its own logic and in turn will shape economic and political decisions. The work of post-industrial theorists helped popularize this form of technological determinism (Bell, 1974; Toffler, 1980; for a critique see Elliot and Elliot, 1976; Kumar, 1978; Lyon, 1988).

It is the contention of this chapter that at a most general level medical model theories of the benefits of new technology are inadequate at the level of explaining such benefits. The result is an apolitical and anodyne image of the 'technical fix' provided by new technology. Of great significance, the fix that new technology allows is explicable in medical model terms as the positive effect new technologies have in attenuating or compensating for the physical or sensory problems a disabled person has. Alternatively, the benefit is expressed in terms of augmentation of the incomplete or impaired body. Together this emphasis on augmen-tation, attenuating and compensation – words which feature liberally in the rehabilitation literature – can be summed up as a 'deficit' model of technology benefits. In understanding the deficit model we need to root its theoretical premises in labour market economics.

Employment rehabilitation staff, it can be argued, see the main function of new technology, in its correction of deficits, to be the enhanced supply of employment-ready disabled people. Here the affin-ity between the deficit model and the supply-side emphasis of a rehabilitation approach can be observed. Within a deficit model, the refusal of employers to employ disabled people, and to employ them fully, is explained by the deficits the disabled individual has. The logic suggests either that disabled people are unable to perform a range of tasks, or that they are simply undereducated or undertrained. The role of rehabilitation is to rehabilitate the disabled person into the demands of the contemporary employment domain. Where disabled people are concerned, the reliance on a deficit rehabilitation model suggests a clear course of action to try to correct their bodily, educational and training deficits. Here, not only have rehabilitation workers arguably obscured the mechanisms by which new technology enables people with impairments, but they have in their writings created a cultural boundary around the way these benefits are analysed. By adopting terminology such as 'augmentive' or 'compensatory' technology they have established the rules of this particular 'language game' while constructing the individual body as the focus of and solution to the employment problem.

Models of new technology benefits

The key differences between a deficit model and a social barriers model can now be applied to the question of the benefits of new technology. Within a deficit model of disability, new technology is seen as significant in the following circumstances:

- when it begins to attenuate or compensate or augment a bodily deficiency. No scope exists for there to be a benefit without concomitant physical change.
- when new technology is seen as beneficial because of having reduced bodily deficits, and employment is more likely to result from this correction.
- where, because employment is still not obtainable, it is likely that the individual is too severely disabled (physically impaired) and is therefore unemployable. Here, technology simply cannot attain the level of correction demanded of an able-bodied world. The only hope here is that rehabilitation and the exhortation of employers (begging?) may make the difference between employability and unemployability.

We can contrast a deficit model of technological aid to employment with a social barriers model. Within this model the benefits of new technology accrue for the following reasons:

- Technology becomes significant at the point at which employment barriers begin to break down. Here the 'enabling' potential of new technology is clearly connected with enabling environments (Swain *et al.*, 1993). Note that no bodily change needs to have occurred as suggested in the deficit model. Here new technology, its potential, moves from being seen as a technical fix for broken bodies to being viewed as a useful tool in overcoming the barriers of an oppressive working environment (Abberley, 1987; Barnes, 1990).
- A barriers model, unlike a deficit model, does not assume that work is the likely sequel to having technological support and experience. The model acknowledges that technology is only one facet of the

enabling process. There is nothing inherent in new technology which qualifies it to reduce barriers. Access to and use of new technology, as with access to work and society generally, may be shaped by pre-existing disabling forces.

• A failure to obtain or keep work, then, is due to the continued attitude and physical barriers faced by disabled people. This clearly equates with a demand-side model of disability and employment, that disabled people are unemployed or underemployed because of inadequate demand for and recognition of their skills. Such awareness of skills clearly needs to extend to technological skills, but also to the enabling potential of new technology; and such technology should be viewed alongside ramps and doors as access aids and issues. Here the cultural boundary equating technology with a fixing of broken bodies is shattered, hopefully never to be revisited.

The dominance of a deficit model of new technology benefits is obvious even from a cursory glance at the literature. The work of Paul Cornes has been central to the discussion of these benefits. Here Cornes discusses new technology in therapeutic terms: 'The role of new technology in this context therefore is to be considered from the perspective of its contributions to therapeutic procedures to restore sensory, physical or mental functioning or technical aids to augment, compensate or substitute for reduced or lost functions' (Cornes, cited by Oliver, 1991, p. 103). Here we see evidence of an individualizing of the disability problem being at the heart of a deficit model. This is evidenced again in Cornes's work where he discusses the specific benefits of technology in 'enabling persons with paraplegia to walk' and 'enabling persons without speech to speak'. The language of rescue and revelation at the heart of these assertions also seems to reflect a tragedy model of disability. Technology does not simply assist the body, but elevates people with impairments to a point closer to accepted normality. For some disabled people, their bodies are too impaired for such a membership of the honorary able-bodied. Here technology can however release the energies of disabled people in a way that makes them more acceptable. MacFarlane is discussing the impact of new technology on the cosmologist Stephen Hawking:

This is where Information Technology comes to the fore. Through its use many a brilliant mind can be released from a crippled and inhibiting carapace. Just look at Professor Stephen Hawking ... however, one does not have to be the proverbial 'egghead' [...] ordinary mortals can benefit just as much. (MacFarlane, 1990, pp. 179–91)

This general potential is also reflected in the work of Sandhu when he notes: 'Developments in information technology are helping more and more people overcome disabilities [impairment]' (Sandhu, 1987, p. 600).

Together, the generalized promise of allowing more people to overcome their bodily problems and the more impairment-specific scope for 'overcoming' blindness, immobility and so on captures the flavour of deficit models of new technology as an employment-assistive force. Although some writers in this tradition do acknowledge social factors in their analyses (Ashok *et al.*, 1985; Carew and West, 1989; Cornes, 1989, p. 33; 1993, p. 109; Rajan, 1985), these factors are seen as possible compounding factors in the working lives of disabled people, not the source of the disability problem. The result of such a primary focus on the individual body combined with a supply-side rehabilitation ethos is that research directly reflects these deficit model ideas.

The adoption of deficit premises in rehabilitation-based and labour-market studies can be observed in the research that has been undertaken. Studies are conducted by credentialed 'experts': they rarely involve disabled people in the framing, piloting or doing of the research. The voices of disabled people are usually absent in what are predominantly macro-level feasibility studies (Sandhu, 1987; Stevenson and Sutton, 1983); studies of labour markets and technological impacts on labour markets (Ashok *et al.*, 1985; Rajan, 1985); internal organizational reviews of provision for disabled people (Carew and West, 1989); and most commonly 'best practice' research (Cornes, 1987; 1989; Murray and Kenny, 1990).

Best-practice research embodies the central ethos of a rehabilitation-deficit approach. By seeking out only a snapshot of 'positive' experiences of new technology and access to work, the research filters out experiences that do not accord with best practice. This way the studies ignore the wider forces facilitating and limiting use of enabling technology. This snapshot approach and use of best-practice case studies can be seen as the result of a rehabilitation function which is to market disabled people to previously unwilling employers. The message seems to be that with the appropriate technology even disabled people can be employed.

Cornes captures this in his 1989 study in which he admits to a search for 'a general state-of-the-art impression of the kinds of employment opportunities available for young people with severe disabilities, [the research] had a restricted focus on young people who were already in employment, as opposed to those who had tried and failed' (Cornes, 1989, p. 4). Cornes's work can be compared to any other form of marketing, where a commodity is presented in an uncomplicated and unambiguous way, one where only successful disabled people are portrayed, for to include images of barriers and failed employment attempts would be to risk diluting the clarity of the marketing message. The historical emphasis on employment 'winners', although in some ways useful in conveying some positive messages of disabled people, ultimately distorts the relationships between work, new technology and disablement. Cavalier (in Gartner and Joe, 1987, pp. 129–41) sums up the medical-model character of rehabilitation-based work in his analysis of the 'technocratic' nature of this work. For Cavalier this approach focuses on, first, the technology provided rather than the enabling process, second, the needs of the provider rather than the requirements of the applicant, and third, the focus is on dis-abilities rather than abilities.

Research findings

During the period 1990–92 the present author undertook research into the enabling potential and role of new technology in disabled people's employment and search for employment. The following reflects the author's own attempts to redress the balance back towards a social barriers model: one which connects this theoretical model with an alternative research strategy, one which throws up quite different research findings.

The work was a direct response to the disabling deficit premises of most previous research. The research was also strongly informed by the growing literature on emancipatory, participatory and non-alienating research (Oliver, 1992b; Roberts, 1981; Stanley, 1990; Zarb, 1992). At the heart of its theoretical project was the aim of letting disabled people 'drive' the research, its focus, parameters and priorities. Here the voices of disabled people were educed via focus group meetings and piloted research. It was only from such a discussion that I could begin to ground the theoretical concerns in an appropriate set of research methodologies. It was from such meetings and indeed correspondence with a range of people with varied impairments and experiences that the research progressed.

The initial research question set asked: 'Has new technology been significant for you as a disabled worker?' This question allowed for responses which perceived the role of new technology in positive, negative or in some instances ambivalent ways. The question did not exclude critical responses: indeed a small number of responses were from disabled people who felt that their impairment was produced by or exacerbated by new technology, more specifically its intensive use.

The piloting process raised a number of issues as to the research questions that needed to be asked: first, what methods should be adopted given the diversity of experiences picked up in the piloting process. Here a research method had also to explore in depth the qualitative issues surrounding the role and benefits of new technology. It was felt that a social barriers model, one which had to explore the exact significance and meaning of new technology, environments, 'ability' and 'disability', had to be primarily qualitative in form. It was felt, however, that although fitting squarely into a 'verstehen' tradition (Weber, 1949), a more quantitative picture of the range and spread of experiences had also to take place. (On combining quantitative and qualitative methodologies see Bryman, 1988; Fielding and Fielding, 1986; Weber, 1949.)

It was decided that a two-stage research methodology would be adopted, one where the first stage represented a detailed quantitative measure of the kinds of experiences disabled workers or jobseekers were having. From this a second qualitative sub-set (30) would be drawn which reflected the diversity and spread of the first group (96). The process of selection was an imperfect one, but is meaningful at the level of an illustrative rather than definitive sub-group of the quantitative research. (On the question of compatibility of quantitative methodology and enabling research see Barnes, 1992b.) In-depth interviews took place at the disabled participant's preferred venue, exploring biographical questions, the route taken to working with new technology, the perception of new technology, the perceived benefits of new technology in relation to the body and the working environment.

The attempt at non-alienating research extended to the production of questionnaire and interview methods that took account of impairment. This translated into enlarged print questionnaires, tape-recorded questions for stage-one participants with visual impairments, and a personal helper and interpreter for two interviewees.

The piloting process provided support for a social-barriers model. Although some participants discussed the significance of new technology in terms of its individual corrective role, when questions were framed in a way that allowed a free discussion of the role of new technology it was clear that the effect of new technology on the previously disabling employment environment was clear. This then directly shaped the nature of the questions adopted for the research.

For purposes of brevity the research findings and their illustration of the value of the barriers model will be applied to three selected areas of the research: first the immediate benefits of new technology, second the wider realization of abilities that often resulted from the use of new technology at work, and finally a glimpse at the barriers that continue to limit the disabled workers and jobseekers researched.

The microcosmic nature of much office technology, its concentration of functions in one work station, provided many benefits for disabled employees:

> The main benefit for me is that I am able to do a multiplicity of things in one place . . . this is made even easier with 'Windows' as it has a clock and a calculator. (Paul, systems engineer, spinal injury)

Another comment refers to the value of computers in reducing the physical demands of the workplace:

> The personal computer is less tiring than the electronic typewriter, because with that you are reaching for the paper tray, going for files and having to put them back. (Gill, purchasing officer, rheumatoid arthritis)

A similar point again refers to the contrast with the previous, more physical working environment:

> With the old manual system the work was more tedious, your work had to be spread out, with a lot of paper to use. With the PC, it's all

on one screen. For a disabled person you haven't got to lump walloping great files around. (Dennis, self-employed accountant, polio)

One key way in which new technology was seen as enabling was in its role of equalizing the working environment. By framing the research questions in terms of altered working practices, the responses pointed to reduced physical hurdles but also to the enhanced similarities of the way work is performed:

> There's no doubt about it in my mind that technology of the sort that I'm using [standard PC] does enable me to work very much on an equal footing as an able-bodied person. What I find is you survive the physical demands of the workplace much more. (Barry, computer consultant, polio)

The next comment refers explicitly to the similarity of working with new technology, that is, the ergonomics of PC working:

> When I'm behind the PC I feel like anybody else, there is no restriction. Other people have to sit down to be proficient. So we become equal. Also, in my chair [gesture pointing to the wheel-chair] I am at the same height as every other PC user, it was different before with people moving about above my level all of the time. (Ahmed, computer officer, spinal injury)

The enabling potential of new technology was commonly seen to stem from the flexible manipulation of information, words and data, the stuff of much post-industrial work routine. In a number of instances the shift away from disabling communication was more significant than the shift away from large-scale physical barriers — for example, small typed or written words and poor-quality definition on Gestetner printed material. Here, for workers with a visual impairment, the enlargement and contrast manipulation some PC software and hardware allows provides access to this 'core text' of contemporary employment:

> I wouldn't be able to programme if it wasn't for the large screen and the speed of being able to do the job, and error reduction. I used to have clerical help when I was having to read the small print. But now I sling a lot into the wordprocessor and mainframe. I can access quite quickly with the [enlarged] screen, it's enhanced my

independence. Written communication is the biggest, most fundamental boost I've had, I can express myself, do better work.
(Trevor, programmer, visual impairment)

Often a mixture of specialized and standard PC developments has in
some instances serendipitously enabled some workers to gain more
control over the communication environment:

> E-mail has had special benefits for me as a blind person. With it I
> can get access (via speech output) to memos and details of what's
> going on in my section. I can communicate without having to walk
> about as well. So I don't have as much trudging to do. I can let my
> fingers do the walking. (Graham, programmer, blind)

The apotheosis of enabling technology was observable where disabled workers detailed the benefits of working with new technology for
their understanding of the ability/disability interface. Here Clive, self-
employed, reflects:

> I am aware that it [new technology] may allow me to say something
> about my ability to those who don't realize what I'm capable of.
> There have been a number of examples of local firms asking me to
> work [for them] once they are aware of my abilities. Some were
> obviously surprised at what I could do. (Clive, self-employed
> computer consultant, cerebral palsy)

This revelation of abilities was symbolic for Clive, as he had been told
that he was unemployable at the age of 20 and although substantial
contracts have eluded him and barriers remain, he is personally aware
of the falsity of the medical model in this context. Here Clive's cerebral
palsy has not changed, but the immediacy with which he can express his
abilities has changed with IT work. Clive notes how able-bodied
expectations are shattered by his computer-based work, but also notes
how the effect is relatively short-lived.

The ability to communicate ability was also mentioned by another
participant; this time communication had the dual meaning of literal
communication and symbolic communication of abilities:

> Computers do allow me to communicate, and express my abilities
> through the text [screen] rather than through the spoken word. I

feel as if my work will be judged for what it is rather than for who produced it. (Stewart, programmer, hearing impairment)

Whilst this provides evidence for only limited benefits of new technology, it does suggest that computer-based working can, at an immediate level, allow more equalized relations and working environment. For some workers, being able to write in the same medium as other workers was itself significant in allowing access to what can be called the 'core text' of employment. Here Mary reflects on the role of new technology in her work:

I use computers to enable me to do paperwork, and to do database work; I couldn't do without it. Basically being able to write in a way that is legible, it puts me on an equal footing. (Mary, part-time access officer and sports development worker, athetoid cerebral palsy)

So we can view new-technology work, if it is used in a non-disabling context, as allowing benefits at the immediate level of enhanced access and at the more fundamental level of allowing a redefinition of the ability/disability equation. However, it was evident from the research findings that the benefits of new-technology work were tempered by the broader working environment and the attendant work processes. What, then, were the factors continuing to limit disabled workers?

The paradox of enabling technology is that its promise lies in its potential to redefine the attitude and structural barriers disabled workers and jobseekers face; however, its use is itself constrained by these factors. This does not discount the enabling potential, as is clear from the above evidence, but in many instances barriers continue to constrain the extent of these benefits. Here environmental, 'technical' and attitudinal barriers were all cited as remaining in the working lives of disabled people or jobseekers.

Despite the enabling potential embodied in new technology, continuing evidence of wider disabling barriers was noted. Commonly this would take the form of a manual duplication of work, where computerized work was backed up with manual records 'just in case'. In some instances this negated many of the benefits of technology:

As time passes, we will be using the PC for more and more functions, although we keep manual records for everything. You see my supervisor has been there [work] for thirty years and she says as long as she's there a manual back-up will stay. (Jane, clerical officer, polio)

Similarly:

At work we have a suspended filing system and I cannot use it because my arms are not strong enough to get files out. I have to rely on others. I cannot understand why we don't just use computers, that's what we got them for. (Susan, purchasing officer, rheumatoid arthritis)

Other examples of wider disabling barriers diluting the enabling potential of new technology were of workers having to use goods lifts, inaccessible toilets, heavy doors and knobs, even in an otherwise 'high-tech' environment. One disabled worker, who detailed the myriad of ways in which his PC enabled him to work more fully, then related how he had been put at a desk too small to accommodate his computer and had to shuffle across a six-foot gap each time he wanted to do PC work:

I haven't got room on my desk for a PC so I have it on the table behind me. It is about six to eight feet away. I have to go from place to place, it can be very frustrating having to do this. (Richard, principal planning officer, multiple sclerosis)

One factor cited by participants as limiting the enabling potential of new technology was the intensive nature of the wider working environment. Here the speed, rhythm and pressure of work was felt to negate the benefits of new technology. In a few instances the initial benefits of new technology were soon outweighed by the working regime.

It was noted that these reports came exclusively from women, women doing routine non-manual work. The general literature on new technology at work suggests that women, because of their structured position in the employment hierarchy, are more susceptible to intensive, 'top-down' and uncontrolled use of IT applications (see Cockburn, 1983; 1985; Crompton and Sanderson, 1990, pp. 123–4; Harvey in Lee and Loveridge, 1987). Here a participant relives her experience of new technology in her banking job:

> When I began using the word processor I seemed to be getting more and more work to do. I would start at eight in the morning, it was a long day, this was purely to get all of the work done. I was using the computer all of the time. My boss seemed to have used new technology to get more from us. It led to a 'flare up' in the end. I transferred to another job and went part-time to relieve the strain. (Joan, part-time secretary, multiple sclerosis)

Joan eventually left banking, as part-time work was similarly intensified. She now works part-time in a land agency, where she can work more flexibly with new technology and her work load is more manageable.

A similar experience was noted by another female participant, but in this instance the work led to a serious deterioration in her arthritis:

> When the VDUs [PCs] were introduced they decided to go all audio. Well I don't like audio typing, it is easy and effective as a technique, but I found that it was as though nothing else existed except his [the manager's] voice and my fingers really. Before then I was using electric [typewriter] and doing shorthand, the little breaks mean all the difference. (Margaret, unemployed secretary, psoriatic arthropathy)

Here not only did repetitive use lead to a physical deterioration, but the work itself was alienating compared to earlier working conditions. The advent of faster, more manipulable technology encouraged a shift to audio-based transcription. Here there was nothing inevitable about the intensification of work, but this clearly was an impetus behind the introduction of the new technology. These two experiences were fortunately a tiny minority of experiences, representing about 3 per cent of the disabled people researched. However, these experiences are a sobering thought and need to be built into our understanding of the role of new technology.

A more common scenario in the research was that of workers who felt that, whilst enabling benefits clearly accrued, the negative attitudes of colleagues were a major and continued problem. Here negative attitudes included

• jealousy over the provision of specialized technologies to disabled employees and any extra training and workplace adjustments;

- resentment or disbelief at some disabled workers' employment success;
- active discrimination against workers with impairments.

Attitudes represent the most significant and most commonly cited barriers in the research. In general terms these attitudes reflect Oliver's formulation of negative perceptions of difference (Oliver, 1990). Here pity, existential discomfort and aesthetic shock all seemed evident. On pity:

> The boss I have at the moment is very young, she is 24, a high flier, when she sees me helping Janet [another disabled employee], and as I use my teeth to help her put her coat on ... She once said: 'When I look at you and Janet it makes me feel so lucky.' (Denise, purchasing officer, hemiplegia)

On existential discomfort:

> I have got one now [line manager] who just cannot come to terms with having a blind secretary, she doesn't like me doing the doing. She just cannot seem to accept that I'm happy being a blind secretary. (Mandy, secretary to a senior hospital social worker, blind)

On aesthetic shock:

> If I went for a job with six able-bodied girls I am unlikely to get the job. People go by appearance, they want someone presentable to meet people, the hospitality bit. (Val, senior personal assistant, polyarthritis)

Here Val was discussing the way in which this aesthetic valuation impacted on her wider career trajectory, noting later that her boss was accepting of a disabled PA, but that many others in the same organization were not, given the front-line nature of PA work.

The above examples capture the generalities of attitudes, but it is the more specific attitudes that seem to convey the resilience of these barriers. Here a disabled senior planning officer relates the attitudes and dismay of his superiors when he asked for a parking space closer to his office. As it was, the office was about 400 yards away across a busy road:

> When I raised the fact that I was having difficulty walking across the car park and 'could I have a space nearer the door?' there was a lot of opposition saying that it would mean one less space for senior management. The implication was that it was outrageous that I should want to even dare ask. (Richard, senior planning officer, multiple sclerosis)

The most shocking attitudes were those that evidenced actual employment discrimination. Here Ahmed discusses his experience of gross exploitation:

> When I started I was contracted to do a four-day week and was paid on that basis, later they [employers] realized they would need me five days per week. So they did, but they did not change my salary. I was paid for four days; this is what comes of being disabled, because I knew if I said no to them . . . I was relatively powerless. (Ahmed, computer officer, spinal injury)

Ahmed represents a clear instance of someone who benefited from new technology in his present job, it giving him access to the wider environment; however, he had experienced wider barriers in the form of low employment expectations and discriminatory attitudes. For example, Ahmed had been a computer-based seismic geologist before his spinal injury: rehabilitation and training had prepared him for lower-grade work, with the assumption that he would not return to this work. Ahmed took a job as computer officer, a job with more modest pay and prospects, and once there faced discriminatory practices. Ahmed also had difficulties attending courses in word processing and spreadsheets as his local college delivered its computing courses on the first floor and there were no lifts. The first few years of work as a computer officer were described as a struggle and as something of a 'come-down' for Ahmed.

The final quotation points up the dilemma of enabling potential in an unpropitious working environment. Edward is a middle-years administrative officer in the civil service; he finds new technology has held promise for him as a hearing-impaired worker. Unfortunately Edward's ambition to move from administrative work to programming has always eluded him. He has been told at a series of unsuccessful promotion interviews that he cannot enter programming unless he reaches executive officer status. He is in a Catch-22; he has no chance of attaining EO status at his age and he would prosper only were he working in programming where he states that problems of communication would be lessened.

> Personally, technology is not the problem. It is people. I can take advantage of new technology, it is getting the opportunity to use it. But it is probably going to be denied to me. You talk about technology allowing me to communicate my abilities. In order to communicate something like that I need a recipient. There is no recipient. Technology has not been allowed to give me that chance. (Edward, administrative officer, hearing impairment)

Conclusion

The foregoing provides a mixed picture of the experiences of new technology in disabled people's employment. It has been shown that by adopting a social model of disability a wider picture of the dynamics of the enabling process, and factors inhibiting this process, can be identified. By framing research questions in terms of barriers we have been able to see how new technology is beneficial in its potential to reduce environmental and to a lesser extent attitude barriers. Here the notion that research methodology shapes the kind of responses is clearly supported. In contrast with the best-practice research promulgated by the medical model, one which ignores the role of barriers and focuses on the successful 'correction' of impairment, the social model provides a holistic image of the role of new technology over time and the framing of the research questions by disabled people. From this perspective the factors continuing to limit the potential of new technology are as important as its benefits.

Here macro-level prognostications are exchanged for immediate experiences, best-practice research exchanged for holistic measures of benefits and continued barriers, questions which are premised on the assumption that new technology corrects the body changed to questions which ask how environments are reconstructed by technology. For example key questions in this research asked: 'Please detail any physical barriers in your work that new technology has enabled you to overcome' and 'What barriers in your work would you see as presenting the greatest level of difficulty?'

It was clear from the qualitative stage of this research that new technology enhanced the employment experiences of many disabled people whilst the status of the participant's body remained exactly the same, i.e. 'uncorrected'. No disabled participant discussed the benefits of new technology in terms of it augmenting or compensating for their bodies. The way forward is clearly to build on this use of a social-barriers model of disablement in other research contexts. Indeed disability researchers are duty-bound to establish at the outset the research issues disabled people themselves raise and the model of disability being adopted. The research participants were not schooled in the social model of disability: only two of those interviewed belonged to a disability organization of any kind. In this way the research cannot be criticized for using an unrepresentative study group. The findings of this research augur well for future research applying a social model of disability.

Further reading

Swain, J., Finkelstein, V., French, S. and Oliver, M. (eds) (1993) *Disabling Barriers – Enabling Environments*. London: Sage and Open University Press.

Zarb, G. (ed.) (1995) *Removing Disabling Barriers*. London: Policy Studies Institute.

9

Oppression, Disability and Access in the Built Environment

Rob Imrie

> As materials for culture, the stones of the modern city seem badly laid by planners and architects, in that the shopping mall, the parking lot, the apartment house elevator do not suggest in their form the complexities of how people might live. What were once the experiences of places appear now as floating mental operations. (Sennett, 1990, p. xi)

In the last decade access for disabled people to public buildings and facilities in cities has become an important part of the political agenda, and many public authorities internationally are promoting strategies for accessible built environments. In particular there is more awareness that disabled people, in their everyday lives, are having to confront hostile built environments, ones where access to buildings, streets and places is often impossible. Western cities are characterized by a design apartheid where building form and design are inscribed with the values of an 'able-bodied' society. Thus, from steps into shops to the absence of induction loops in public and civic buildings, disabled people have to confront built environments which were never designed to cater for a range of bodily differences. This has led some commentators to regard the built environment as disablist, that is, projecting 'able-bodied' values which legitimize oppressive and discriminatory practices against disabled people purely on the basis that they have physical and/or mental impairments.

For instance, day-to-day artefacts which the able-bodied take for granted are usually (literally) out of reach, or unavailable, for the wheelchair-bound person. Thus, most cash-dispensing machines are placed too high for wheelchair users to reach, while clothes retailers have few changing facilities for people in wheelchairs. Moreover, Barnes (1991) indicates that society's ignorance of sign languages generally excludes the deaf and hard-of-hearing from a range of public places, while concluding that disabled people's ability 'to perform even the most routine of daily tasks is thus severely diminished because of a predominantly inaccessible environment' (p. 180). Indeed the urban environment is generally inaccessible for a range of people with disabilities, characterized as it is by, for example, the interwar expansion of the suburbs, which, aligned to the postwar spatial divisions of city functions, generated cities which increasingly placed a premium on individual mobility. As Hahn (1986) notes, in his discussion of Los Angeles, for people with disabilities the city is a vast desert containing few oases.

Critical to the production of such disablist and disabling environments are the roles of architects and/or design professionals. Indeed architects, and other design professionals, are implicated in the production of the built environment, in developing aesthetic values and propagating specific conceptions of design. In this sense architectural ideas and practices are of importance to explore in order to gain some understanding of how disablist spaces in the built environment are developed and perpetuated. In discussing such themes I divide the chapter into three. First I consider the interrelationships between architects, power and the built environment, and develop the argument that the perpetuation of disablist spaces is critically linked to the socio-institutional practices of architects and the wider design professions. Second, I relate such ideas to the importance of modernism in the construction of the disablist city. While modernism, as a set of ideas and related socio-political practices, is not exclusively responsible for the construction of disablist cities, it can be argued that it has been the dominant force in their postwar reconstruction. In a concluding section I consider the possibilities for the development of emancipatory architecture and accessible environments.

Architects, power and the built environment

Over the last twenty years a powerful critique of the role of the architect, in the perpetuation of gendered, racial, and other divisions in the city, has emerged (Dicken, 1980; Knox, 1987). It is premised on the idea that the interplay between the ideologies and institutional practices of the design professions, within the wider context of particular socio-economic strictures, has served to exclude minority interests while reinforcing an alienating and oppressive built environment. The documentary material ranges widely from accounts which show how the built form is inattentive to the needs of women to those which suggest that spaces are segregated on a racialized and disablist basis. Indeed, as Matrix (1984) notes, there is an assumption by architects of 'sameness', of normality, amongst the population, 'that all sections of the community want the environment to do the same things for them' (p. 3). Such ideas have been sustained through three interconnected dimensions of the design process, that is, the (ideological) assertion of the aesthetic or privileging the idea of building form over use; the professionalization of architectural and other design practices, thus creating a new technical, 'expert' elite; and the rise of the corporate economy as the dominant clientele.

In considering the relationship between aesthetic values and the production of the built environment, Ghirardo (1991) has noted how many architects still see their practices as about the designer providing buildings with critical capacities, so that the architect can engage 'with contemporary problems through formal manipulation' (Ghirardo, 1991, p. 12). In such views it is assumed that architecture is a form of artistic expression and endeavour, and, in Ghirardo's (1991) terms, 'that art has a high moral purpose in the formation and transmission of culture . . . of the design of aesthetically pleasing forms of poetic spaces' (p. 9). This, then, projects the architect as a purveyor of beauty and truth, an elevated being somehow with the abilities and skills to construct for (in distinction to with) the population as a whole. Indeed such conceptions have performed a powerful ideological role in architecture, especially, as Sennett (1990) has argued, one of self-legitimation through the perpetuation of discourses which seek to elevate the practices of architects to a form of objective neutrality, the idea of the rational technicist operating for a willing and compliant clientele.

In particular, as McGlynn and Murrain (1994) note, it has never been a feature of the culture, social ethics and/or practices of design professionals to see themselves as part of wider political processes. As they comment, architects seem to have limited understanding of the relationships between values, design objectives and the design intentions derived from them, with design theory tending to concentrate on the technocratic and technological, reducing questions of access and form to the functional aspects of the subject, yet ignoring what Davies and Lifchez (1987) have termed the social psychology of design or trying to understand what it is that people really want (see also Dicken, 1980, p. 353). In this sense, as Davies and Lifchez (1987) have argued, the popularization of architecture as 'high art', or pure design, is underpinned by a capacity to perpetuate an impersonal, often alienating, practice, given that the focus is about the aesthetic, or the building form, not the user and/or the pragmatics of the functioning of the building. Buildings, then, in this interpretation, are treated as an abstraction, something over and beyond, somehow able to transcend, the socio-political contexts within which they are produced.

Such conceptions, as the next section of the chapter will show, reached their apogee under the postwar modern movement where the emphasis on minimalist form sought to reduce the complexity of human movement and building use to a singular set of rules and/or laws, or the idea that all human action is knowable and controllable. As Sennett (1990) and others have commented, the idea of control, coupled with the perpetuation of the ideology of architect as artist, was simultaneously disarming and disabling in a number of interrelated ways. Foremost, it perpetuated a representation of the architect as 'expert', so providing a legitimation to practise unfettered by wider public and/or corporate controls. In this sense the architect was more or less untouchable. In addition the 'expert' characterization, reinforced by architects aligning themselves to the idea that their practices were somehow underpinned by a scientific rationalism, was crucial in signalling to a wider public that they were there to be 'acted on', that architectural knowledge was something to be handed down, or a form of received wisdom. Such paternalism was, and still is, a crucial ingredient in denying the subjectivities of the very users of the built environment.

However, the ideological nature of the aesthetic and the technical, of the architect as somehow a neutral arbiter, able and willing to provide for all, has been exposed by a range of writers who indicate how the institutional nature of the profession is dominated by a strand of conservatism which seeks to perpetuate ableist, masculine, values (Imrie, 1996; Laws, 1994; Rose, 1990). As Matrix (1984) and others have argued, built spaces in the postwar period have emphasized mobility over accessibility and have placed a premium on, for example, individuals owning a car. Indeed, designers tended to generate, and perpetuate, exclusive, segregated, spaces, primarily because of a stereo-typical conception of people as somehow being similar in their capacities both to get access to and to move around the built environ-ment. Yet, clearly, this is not the case and the myth of the 'normal person', of a white male, has been a powerful dimension of the design process, yet one which has had, and continues to have, clear racist, sexist, and ableist underpinnings. This, then, is far from designing for the subjective being, for human diversity, in the way which authors like Davies and Lifchez (1987) call for.

In particular it is clear that such exclusions were, and still are, enshrined and maintained by virtue of the institutionalized nature of the architectural profession (see Knox, 1987). A significant part of this relates to its wider governing bodies, especially the architectural schools and other regulatory bodies which have the primary responsibility for overseeing professional practices and conduct. Indeed a range of lit-erature indicates how the governing, corporate bodies, like the Royal Institute of British Architects (RIBA), have been complicit in reinforc-ing the elitist structures of architecture, and, as Lifchez and Winslow (1979) have argued, while the proportion of the population with disabilities grows, the architectural profession has been slow in taking account of the environmental implications of an ageing and/or increas-ingly disabled population – few practitioners, less than 4 per cent in the USA, even fewer in the UK, have a disability. Indeed, even where perspectives on disability are taught in architectural schools, they are still treated as an after-thought, an add-on and/or a special-interest subject, or what Davies and Lifchez (1987) have referred to as being underpinned by a 'system of indifference'.

The relative absence of corporate controls over architects, then, relates to some extent to the privatized nature of architectural practices. Yet, while disablist design can, in part, be understood as being per-petuated by the fragmentary nature of this system, a crucial aspect of our understanding also relates to the hierarchical and elitist nature of (privatized) clientist patronage that architects are locked into, and, crucially, to related systems of economic power. As Crawford (1992) notes, the peculiarities of the rise of the architectural profession left architects more or less wholly dependent upon a small group of clients who could afford to support them and their ambitions. Thus, while some architects gained status and economic remuneration, primarily by being sponsored by business and corporate capital, their autonomy was (and still is) heavily circumscribed by their clients (for an extended discussion of this see Crawford, 1992). As Crawford argues, 'architecture, a luxury rather than an indispensable service, remained within a pre-modern model of elite patronage, its provision of services primarily dictated by economic power' (1992, p. 31).

Indeed, as Crawford (1992) recounts, the dependence of architects on the wider corporate economy was a determinant of their loss of technical and economic control over building projects and, by the early 1950s, the combination of systems building, new technologies and the rise of the global economy was beginning to undercut both their status and their levels of autonomy (Knox, 1987; Sennett, 1990; Wolfe, 1981). As Sennett (1990) and others have commented, the estrangement of architects from the wider building processes was paralleled by the emergence of a division of architectural labour which drew increasing numbers of architects into managerial and bureaucratic roles, while reducing the amount of new building being commissioned through architectural practices (Knox, 1987). In this sense the extent to which architects, and other building designers, were exercising control over the built form was increasingly being challenged by a range of structural factors, and, as Crawford (1992) has noted, it is the materialities of the land market, or 'the actualities of the building industry, and the limits set by the clients paying the bills' (p. 38), which have become the dominant element in restraining the autonomy of architects and/or designers.

Thus, the emergence of corporate economics was, as Jencks (1987) points out, crucial in perpetuating the move towards technological standardization and scale economies in building design, while seeking to realize cost savings by utilizing cost-efficient building methods which made few concessions to the range of users who did not conform to the conception of the able-bodied client. For the modern corporation the idea that people were 'all of a type', that they too could be standardized like a piece of technology, was, in part, incorporated into the lay-out and design of the emergent workplaces, and, as Sennett (1990) has observed, modern buildings are less flexible than the 'rows, crescents, and blocks of the past', while the specific layout of the modern office environment is task-dedicated and more or less impossible to change towards alternative types of uses. In this sense those that were sponsoring the modern designers and architects, the corporations, were implicated in placing a demand for an ableist environment to cater for an able-bodied workforce.

Disabling ideas and the modern ideal in architecture

While the contemporary Western city is characterized by a pastiche, a constellation of diverse styles and forms, the dominant ideas and practices which have done most to shape it are clearly linked to modern aesthetic philosophies and socio-political institutions. For McGlynn and Murrain (1994) the rise of modern architecture was based on the advent of segregated and mono-functional forms, an aesthetic closely aligned to the rise of the corporate economy. Indeed the engineering aesthetics of the modern movement were, as Weisman (1992) notes, built upon an abstract, intellectual purity of rational, geometric, forms and a mass-produced industrial technology. Any sense in which it could relate to differences in body, human behaviour or access requirements were all but lost in a style that many have referred to as 'non-contextual' architecture, premised on forms which seemed to deny human subjectivity and the differences in bodily experiences and forms. In 1929, for instance, the English architect Eileen Gray characterized such non-contextuality in the following terms:

> this intellectual coldness which we have arrived at and which interprets only too well the hard laws of modern machinery can only be a temporary phenomenon ... I want to develop these formulas and push them to the point at which they are in contact with life ... The avant-garde is intoxicated by the machine aesthetic ... But the machine aesthetic is not everything ... Their intense intellectualism wants to suppress everything which is marvellous in life ... as their concern with a misunderstood hygiene makes hygiene unbearable. Their desire for rigid precision makes them neglect the beauty of all these forms: discs, cylinders, lines which undulate or zigzag, elliptical lines which are like straight lines in movement. Their architecture is without soul. (quoted by Nevins, 1981, p. 71)

In this sense modernism was founded upon the idea of the minimalist building and/or design bereft of (bourgeois) ornamentation, or, as Wolfe (1981) comments, buildings were to express function and structure and nothing else. In particular, the movement which grew up around such ideals, including the Bauhaus school, Les Congrès Internationaux d'Architecture, Archigram and the Ekistics school, asserted the importance of science and technology in the production of the built form, of the need to build inexpensively, to provide for all in the community. Its clarion call, originally espoused by the American architect Louis Sullivan, was that form should follow function, a maxim which many interpreted as the search for universal laws of human habitation and behaviour, of the possibilities of producing 'pure' design, singular styles and forms which were grafted from the essence of the human being. In this sense functionality was expressed as a means of maximizing building utility, premised upon the idea that human behaviour was wholly predictable and knowable, that human beings conformed to a type, to particular patterns of (able-bodied) normality in both bodily and mental terms. Thus human beings were, in this conception, reducible to a specific essence, an essence which, as we shall see, was the embodiment of ableist thinking.

In particular, the ableist nature of modernist ideas is revealed, in part, by its conception of functionality whereby there was a departure from seeking an individual or specific solution for what Sullivan (1947) termed 'a true normal type'. The search for such normality was evident in the thinking of one of the leading exponents of modernism, Le Corbusier, who believed that the propagation of universal properties in form-giving was an essential underpinning of the architect's mission, or, as he commented, 'all men [sic] have the same organism, the same functions . . . the same needs' (1927, p. 27). This search for normality, an inner essence, in people, provided the context from which a distinctively modern movement interpretation of 'form follows function' evolved, or, as Le Corbusier noted, 'the establishment of a standard involved evoking every practical and reasonable possibility and extracting from them a recognized type conformable to all functions with a maximum output and a minimum use of means and workmanship and material, words, forms, colours, sounds' (p. 27). The discovery of this 'standard', then, was at the root of the modern preoccupation with function, and, as Le Corbusier (1927) argued, the bare essentials of architecture are provided by aesthetic forms which he defined as being 'determined by the dimensions of man [sic] and the space he occupies' (quoted by Gardiner, 1974, p. 79; see also Sullivan, 1947). For Le Corbusier architecture could be defined only in and through the symbiosis between people and nature, and, as he commented, 'man must be rediscovered' (quoted by Gardiner, 1974, p. 79).

Yet this rediscovery was wholly based on a particular, ableist, gender-specific, conception of the person, an idealized man who was presented as the embodiment of normality. This embodiment of normality was expressed in a diagram conceived by Le Corbusier in 1925 called the Modular, a device which utilized the proportions of the (able) body to enable the architect to create the built spaces, or, as Le Corbusier argued, 'one needs to tie buildings back to the scale of the human being'. Yet, as Figure 9.1 indicates, the Modular presents an image of an upright person, muscular, taut, obviously strong, male, and displaying no outward sign of either physical and/or mental disability. It is the person for whom functionality in building design and form was being defined, a person who gained widespread acceptance in most elements of the modern movement and beyond. Such conceptions can also be extended to incorporate the possibilities that the denial of bodily differences was also premised on the idea of asexuality as the moral, or ethical, standard bearer of the emergent aesthetics of modernism. Indeed, as Batchelor (1994) comments,

> authentic modernism, predicated on the extent to which it excluded, was probably white, male, and uneasy with sexuality. Many modernists addressed the emotive, sensuous aspects of experience and the possibilities that these opened up in terms of modern architecture and design. But only certain forms were licensed. Others were regularly rejected as anti-rational, barbaric and representing a retreat to the primitive. (p. 115)

As O'Neil (1995) has noted, one of the ironies of the modernist project was the way in which its rationalism abstracted from the socio-political contexts of its practices, failing to communicate, or interact, with those who were the (often unsuspecting) recipients of the resultant built forms. As Knox (1987) has commented, how then could modernism ever hope to know of the subjective experiences of the users of the built environment when its philosophies more or less discounted the realm of the experiential, personalized, experience? As Wolfe (1981) and Knox (1987) have described, the leading exponents of modernism – Gropius, Le Corbusier, Mies van der Rohe, even its critic, Robert Venturi – asserted the 'special insights' of architects, of their privileged access to

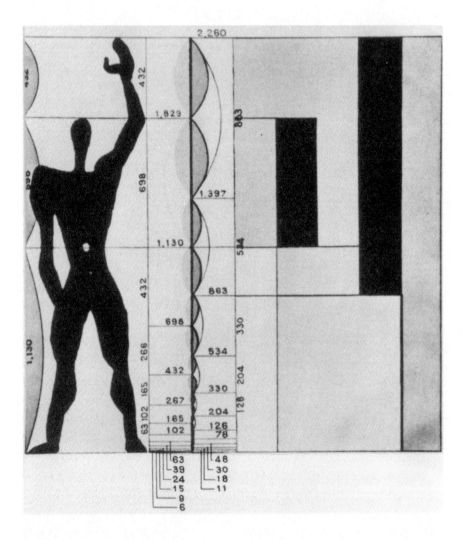

Figure 9.1 The Modular by Le Corbusier was devised in 1947. Modular man is 6ft tall and became a standard for architects and/or designers to build from. It seeks to present the human body as singular and universal, as a type. In this sense, it is insensitive to bodily variations.

knowledge. For instance, as Mies van der Rohe once replied, when asked if he ever submitted alternative schemes to clients, 'Only one. Always. And the best one that we can give. That is where you can fight for what you believe in. He doesn't always have to choose. How can he choose? He hasn't the capacity to choose' (quoted by Prak, 1984, p. 95). In this sense modernism was underpinned by a 'theory of technocracy, government by experts, rather than democracy, government by people' (Steinberger, 1985, p. 39). Consequently, the (claimed) intellectual purity of modernism descended into forms of what Knox (1987) has termed 'vain arrogance' or the perpetuation of an elitism whereby 'clients, other professionals, and users were systematically excluded and often patronised' (p. 369).

Not surprisingly, then, the abstractions of modernism, coupled with an elitist philosophy, were, in part, at the root of the estrangement of people from being able to influence the processes of production of the built environment. The emphasis on sameness, on uniformity, was problematical for its failure to differentiate between users and how places and spaces need to be multi-functional to cope with human diversity. In particular, commentators on the rise of the early, nineteenth-century, modern city refer to the onset of a placelessness, of an absence of variegated and differentiated spaces, of the dearth of place markers and/or signifiers (Giddens, 1991). In addition, a placelessness was seemingly underpinned by what Sennett (1990) has argued to be the modernist preoccupation with notions of functionality and wholeness which, as he suggests, generated conflicts between buildings and people, not the least of which is that 'the value of a building as a form is often contrary with its value in use' (p. 98). This observation prompted Sennett to refer to modernism as 'bequeathing the anti-social building' precisely because he saw the problems being generated by virtue of the irreducibility of human diversity to the types of environments which were being created.

Indeed, in terms of the legacies of the movement, of style and form, modernism has been characterized by designer ableism in a number of respects. As Moore and Bloomer (1977) have noted, for instance, in modern architecture the multiple changes of level 'have often been used to delineate and enliven space' yet in ways which elevate the aesthetic above the pragmatics of use (p. 4). Thus, the interplay between levels, connected by steps, is integral to a design which seeks to display divisible, yet interconnected, functional, spaces. Moreover, the

minimalism underpinning much modernist design does little to differentiate between walls, floors or furniture, while stairs, notorious
barriers to mobility and access, have often been given symbolic roles.
Indeed the main effect of the Bauhaus movement, one of the linchpins
of modernism, was to reduce space, to automate and to utilize standard, off-the-shelf materials, primarily in an attempt to persuade people
into using a certain kind of predetermined design. In this sense, bodily
differences were being denied, and architects and designers were seeking to standardize, and engineer, people's bodily interactions with the
built environment.

Emancipatory architecture and accessible environments

While modernist ideals are alienating and fundamentally ableist, the
possibilities for alternative ways of thinking and practising exist and
there are a range of socio-architectural practices based on a contrasting
set of ideas and philosophies about the interactions between humans
and the built environment. Perhaps the most widely espoused is that of
universal design, an approach to the construction of the built environment premised on, as Weisman (1992) calls it, a 'flexible architecture'
or one based on structures which are 'demountable, reasonable, multi-
functional, and changeable over time' (Weisman, 1992, p. 32). As
Weisman (1992) notes, the (modernist) construction of the built
environment conceives of spaces as somehow fixed and unchanging,
while buildings have tended to be (and still are) dedicated to single
functions, creating a form of stasis or unchanging places. However,
people and places are fluid, transformative, and multi-dimensional, yet
much architecture seeks to fossilize specific forms of social relations
while denying, even resisting, the dynamic nature of society.

The reactions against such conceptions represent one of the real
strengths and contributions of what some refer to as postmodern
thinking, that is, an emphasis on the vitality and importance of other
cultures and values over and beyond hegemonic discourses, and of the
need to generate political spaces for their articulation. In part, such
conceptions underpin universal design or the viewpoint which states
that environments should be sensitized to all users, that there is no such
thing as stasis in the built form, and that flexible building designs
should be utilized to permit people to transform the fabric of the places
and spaces that they interact with(in). Others see such principles as

being trans-generational while incorporating choice and alternatives in to the built fabric. Indeed, as Davies and Lifchez (1987) note, accessibility is much more than admittance to a building or a matter of logistics but is also a quality of (socio-psychological) experiences which modernist ideas did little to acknowledge. They comment:

> how one feels about a place, how one interprets it, or even whether one can adequately interpret it – these are all less quantifiable, but crucially important, aspects of accessibility. A place that supports people's activities and desires, permits them to be and do what they want, and causes them a minimum of pain, frustration, and embarrassment is more accessible than a place that confuses, harasses, or intimidates people. Many ostensibly accessible sites differ substantially in the quality of experience they offer. (p. 40)

Principles of design which reflect this wider conception of accessibility, while denying the stasis of the built form, are evident in a number of places, and especially in the Netherlands, Germany and France where a range of housing schemes have been developed with the objective of being adaptable to social change (see Daunt, 1991). Weisman (1992), for instance, cites the example of Stichting Architectin Research (SAR), a Dutch-based approach towards housing design premised on the idea that a dwelling represents much more than a physical entity but is a 'human act'. As Weisman recounts, the future tenants of SAR schemes are involved in designing their own living spaces and, in one instance, a family living in one of the housing schemes were allowed to lower the windowsills in their living area to provide their father with a view from his wheelchair. Likewise, one example of accessibility being wholly incorporated into a new building is the APL building situated in downtown Oakland in California. As Figure 9.2 indicates, accessibility for wheelchair users has been designed-in to the front entrance, yet, as the person responsible for access compliance commented,

> at the time of the original plans, the architects were insisting that the look of the building would be compromised by the front entrance access ways we were insisting on. They wanted it all in a side entrance and they see this as good enough but our attitude is that people with disabilities have the same rights as everyone else to go through the front door! (Gertner, 1994)

Figure 9.2 The APL Building in Oakland, California is a design success for disabled people. The pavement approaching the building has a deep pink colour to permit vision-impaired people to differentiate between the line of pavement going past the building and that directing individuals into the building. Entrances are also wide, with shallow gradients and well-positioned grab rails.

The conflict, in this instance, was the issue of the aesthetic versus the humane, of facilitating access for all types of persons, or prioritizing particular design aesthetics which, so APL claimed, were a necessity to the 'corporate image'. Yet, as Gertner (1994) argued, 'to see the two issues as separate, or in the way APL was presenting it, was crazy ... they've still got their image and we've got some access'. While all built forms are, to a certain extent, fixed, the APL building is interesting as an example of a design with removable internal walls and floors, while it incorporates induction loops and other technologies to facilitate movement around the building for different types of people with disabilities. However, its production occurred within the hierarchical relations of a corporate sponsor and a commissioned architectural practice and, as a range of researchers have noted, how far is it possible to produce sensitized design in a context where the social relations of building production are largely removed from democratic control and popular involvement (Davies and Lifchez, 1987)? As Davies and Lifchez (1987) have questioned, 'how ethical is it to practice architecture, to be a professional licensed to design buildings, without having first developed an intellectual and emotional understanding of people' (p. 35)? In this sense, Davies and Lifchez (1987) suggest that architects need to confront the social psychological context of design, of how it feels for the users and to acknowledge that there are no simple technical (design) solutions.

As O'Neil (1995) has argued, part of the problem of estrangement more broadly is related to the professionalization of a whole range of social activities, so maximizing the bureaucratic ethos and undermining the civic competence that many feel is a prerequisite of democracy. In this sense one way of returning knowledge and competence to the wider community is, as O'Neil (1995) argues, to institutionalize the 'transferability and thereby accountability of expert knowledge in order to raise the level of the well informed citizen or the need to create a pedagogy that will subordinate expert knowledge to the needs of political democracy' (p. 170). This, then, is one example of what Oliver (1992b) terms reciprocity, or a situation whereby the role of the architect is to be an enabler and educator rather than preacher or provider, with the resources of the design industry being placed at the disposal of local communities. Thus, to empower people with disabilities in the design process is a multi-faceted, multi-dimensional, process which, as a minimum, requires an engagement at the level of values and ideology, as well as the material base of building processes. Indeed, as Knesl (1984) notes, one needs to rethink radically the 'relationships between both the architect and the client and between the architect and the process of designing a building' (p. 4).

However, much more needs to be done in creating accessible environments, and, since the early 1980s, Western governments have increasingly acceded to the idea that inaccessible spaces and places in the built environment require some redress through the context of public policy. This is reflected, in the UK, by the emergence of new institutional fora for the development of access policies for disabled people while, in the USA, the drive towards barrier-free environments has been a staple part of institutional life since 1968. Likewise, in countries like Germany, the Netherlands, and Sweden, significant policies and programmes, aimed at creating accessible places for people with disabilities, have been an important part of their welfare states, yet most, if not all, responses have been piecemeal, *ad hoc*, and poorly resourced, while tending to be an add-on to social welfare policies rather than an integral and integrative part of them. Even at the supranational, European Union, level, the emergent policy frameworks have tended to emphasize socio-technical solutions towards access, as though a transformation in design, in and of itself, will provide the singular mechanism for overturning disabling environments.

That access policies and programmes should exist at all, however, is a recognition of the hostile and oppressive nature of the built environment, and, as Barnes (1991b) suggests, people with disabilities have made some gains in recent times. Such gains, particularly in the UK context, are encapsulated in a range of legislation which specifies that 'reasonable provision' should be made for disabled people's access while, since the late 1970s, systems of professional advocacy and representation have emerged as the state's response towards correcting the seeming powerlessness of disabled people and their exclusion from debates about the built environment (Oliver, 1990). In turn this has generated what one might term an 'access industry', with access officers and committees springing up all over the UK, co-ordinated, and orchestrated, by national access organizations. Yet the overwhelming impression is that the plethora of policies and programmes for access, particularly in the UK, are doing little more than reflecting and reproducing elements of state welfarism, the idea that what people with disabilities are receiving (yet again) is another form of government benefit (and, so some would say, a 'handout'). In this sense the position and status of architects, design professionals and others involved in the production of the built environment is little changed (see Imrie, 1996, ch. 5, for an extension of such debates).

Conclusions

As Davies and Lifchez (1987) have argued, access should not be viewed as a constraint on architectural design but should be conceived of as a 'major perceptual orientation to humanity' (p. 49). In this sense a range of authors note that design professionals increasingly need to reject the idea that there are technical solutions to socio-political problems, that there needs to be some kind of deconstruction of the ideological constructs that underpin the aesthetic ideals of design. Indeed many writers concur that there can never be a socially sensitive or just architecture given the present structural underpinnings of architectural practices (Knesl, 1984; Knox, 1987). As Crawford (1992) concludes, 'the restricted practices and discourse of the profession have reduced the scope of architecture to two equally unpromising polarities: compromised practice or esoteric philosophies of inaction' (p. 41). Yet, as Crawford suggests, such an impasse need not necessarily prevent architects from reconnecting their practices to social and economic questions, to issues, for instance, relating to the elderly, poor, people with disabilities, and the homeless. Unfortunately one still waits for such connections to be made.

Yet others are more optimistic in seeing the seeds of liberating environments and of the possibilities for non-ableist architectural practices. Hayden (1981), for instance, considers the elements of a transformative agenda which would challenge the socially oppressive nature of much past and contemporary architecture. She calls for a 'new paradigm of the home, the neighbourhood, and the city', one which describes, as a first step, the 'physical, social, and economic design of human settlements that could support, rather than restrict, activities of people with disabilities' (p. 7). Likewise Weisman (1992) locates the problematical aspects of access, of exclusion and segregation, in the comprehensive system of social oppression, not, as he puts it, the consequences of failed architecture or prejudiced architects. This is a crucial point because, in conceptual terms, it situates the actions and practices of agents and institutions in a wider framework of social structures, values and ideologies and avoids a reductionism which posits that people and/or institutions are somehow, independently, to blame for the perpetuation of disablist environments.

Acknowledgements

This paper is largely derived from chapter 4 of my book *Disability and the City: International Perspectives*, London: Paul Chapman Publishing and New York: St Martin's Press. I would like to thank the publishers for giving me copyright permission to reproduce sections of this chapter.

Further reading

Ghirardo, D. (ed.) (1991) *Out of Site: A Social Criticism of Architecture*. Seattle: Bay Press.

Imrie, R. (1996) *Disability and the City: International Perspectives*. London: Paul Chapman Publishing.

Weisman, L. (1992) *Discrimination by Design*. Chicago: University of Illinois Press.

10

Enabling Identity: Disability, Self and Citizenship

Nicholas Watson

Disabled people in Britain face discrimination and prejudice throughout their lives (Barnes, 1991b). People who are disabled are portrayed as tragic victims of some unfortunate accident or disease, as people who do not function normally. This has a number of implications. First, non-disabled people's perceptions of disability are based on stereotypic beliefs about dependency and helplessness. This can result in the creation of a barrier induced by a fear of contamination, of physical or psychic damage. People who have an impairment can act as a reminder of our own frailty, our own susceptibility to morbidity and mortality (Shakespeare, 1994c). Second, the rise of 'consumer society' and 'consumer behaviour', the genesis of 'commodity culture' with its focus on the body (Falk, 1994), can create anxiety in those who do not conform to cultural and social norms. These reactions serve to remind the disabled person that they are 'different' even if they see themselves as normal. So Goffman writes: 'the standards he [*sic*] has incorporated from the wider society equip him to be intimately alive to what others see as his failures, inevitably causing him, if only for moments, to agree he does indeed fall short of what he really ought to be' (1968b, p. 7).

This chapter focuses on the effects of chronic illness on self and identity. The notions of the self, identity and identification have recently re-emerged as central themes in sociology and social theory. This has been driven, in part, by a critique of essentialist, Cartesian notions of ethnicity, sex, class and nationality combined with a growth in psychoanalytical theorizing, especially in feminism (Hall, 1996). It is a contested area, and definitions of self, identity and identification vary. Here *self* refers to how a person thinks of themselves, and *identity* refers to how a person is perceived by others (Ball, 1972). However, it is not suggested that self has an *a priori* existence: it is not a psychological or biological entity, rather it is the way one sees oneself in relation to others (Mead, 1934), deriving from what Charles Taylor (1989) refers to as 'webs of interlocution' (p. 36). It is through language and interaction that we constitute and define the self. We cannot develop a sense of self on our own (Taylor, 1989). Our sense of self has a past and also an anticipated future.

Both Rose (1996) and Taylor (1989) have documented the recent upsurge in the individualization of the concept of the self. Rose attributes this to the growth in popular psychology and psychoanalysis. We are now held to be responsible for forging our own identity. The concept of individuality has taken precedence over social relations: 'It's as though the dimension of interlocution were of significance only for the genesis of individuality, like the training wheels of nursery school, to be left behind and to play no part in the finished person' (Taylor, 1989, p. 36). Linked to this concept of individuality has been a growth in the ideal of self-reliance, for independence. It is only by being independent that we can truly forge our own sense of self, our own identity. People who are not seen as being independent are in some way lacking; independence is seen as integral to our acceptance as responsible adults.

Interpreting disability

Social-model theorists argue that disability can best be understood as an interactive process, an interaction at both micro and macro levels. Oliver (1996) has described this as the hegemony of disability. Disability is not a pathological or medical problem, and research into disablement and social policies aimed at overcoming disablement should focus not on the disabled individual but on society (Oliver, 1993a). Attention should be at the interpersonal and institutional level. They argue that we already know that disabled people are stereotyped, that they lack cultural capital and consequently we do not need any more research into how disabled people cope with their impairment, the meaning that individuals ascribe to their impairment or how they organize their day-to-day lives. Disability is a structural issue, and, by removing disabling structures, disability itself can be eliminated. Finkelstein's article on the village is an example of this approach (1981a). It argues that disability is an arbitrary, group-based distinction, based on a fallacy that it is an essential characteristic. If discrimination were to be removed, disabled people would be free to choose the lifestyle they wish, unencumbered by stereotypes. Impairment is merely a biological description of the body and plays no part in determining a person's sense of self.

The social model is not without its critics, both from within the disability movement and from outside. Disabled feminists, such as Morris (1991; 1996), French (1993a) and Crow (1996), have argued that the social model, by excluding impairment, denies the personal. Critics of the social model from mainstream sociology, such as Bury (1996), assert that a refusal to link disability to impairment leads to relativism, and that the reification of structural barriers can serve to create a picture that is as incomplete as a traditional medical perspective. Pinder (1996) further argues that this approach is 'oversimplistic'. Bury (1996) goes on to say that it is through the sociological approach to researching disablement, namely qualitative interviews and relying on lay accounts, that a full picture of disability is emerging.

The recent collection *Exploring the Divide* (Barnes and Mercer, 1996) clearly demonstrates the theoretical gap that exists between these two positions. For mainstream sociology, the emphasis is on the meanings people attribute to their impairment, how they negotiate their daily lives and how they cope, or come to terms with, their impairment. By analysing interpretative accounts, chronic illness becomes what Bury has termed a 'biographical disruption' (1982). Sociological accounts of chronic illness concentrate on the way that people learn to live with chronic illness. The emphasis is placed on the meaning or consequences and significance of chronic illness (Bury, 1991), the uncertainty that having a chronic illness generates (Robinson, 1988) and attempts made to explain or legitimate the condition. They adopt what Gerhardt (1989) terms a negotiation model in which people with chronic conditions are characterized as struggling to be as normal as possible. Thus writers such as Charmaz (1983) can argue that chronic illness disrupts a person's sense of identity and sense of self-worth.

By adopting an interpretative analysis, viewing people with chronic conditions as agents, structural and contextual issues are often ignored. This ignorance results from the use of personal accounts which, it is claimed, provide personal meaning and insight into the experiences of chronic illness. It is this reliance on lay accounts that is problematic. As Mouzelis (1995) has pointed out, methods that focus on lay perspectives and micro sociology ignore the fact that people do not have equal access to 'economic, political and cultural means of production' (p. 16). People's accounts and experiences need to be contextualized, problematizing their views. There is no attempt to analyse what chronic illness or normality actually is, who defines chronic illness and what the implications of these definitions are. The 'webs of interlocution' from which we derive our sense of self are absent.

Disabled people are stereotyped as weak, pitiful, dependent and passive (Murphy, 1987), but these cultural perceptions are often absent in interpretive analyses. Morris (1991) puts this eloquently: 'The messages we receive are very strong and clear and we have little access to different values which may place a more positive value on our bodies, ourselves and our lives. Our self image is thus dominated by the non-disabled world's reaction to us' (1991, p. 28).

In the same way that micro sociology paints a reductionist picture of disablement, so a structural analysis runs the risk of reification. The social model portrays disablement as a universal experience; cultural factors are ignored in favour of class analysis (Shakespeare, 1994). It runs the risk of portraying disabled people as victims, not of their impairment but of a society that fails to include them. There is little room for agency or resistance. Further, issues such as gender, sexuality and race cannot be easily addressed within this model.

Gershick and Miller (1995), in their analysis of masculinity and physical disability, show that being disabled places an individual in an untenable position. A disabled man is not able to conform to the cultural demands of masculinity and gender identity, yet to be accepted within society he must have an appropriate gender identity. Their analysis is from both a structural and an agency perspective: the demands that are placed on men in contemporary society as well as the mechanisms used by disabled men either to meet or to challenge these demands. By adopting an interpretative and socio-political analysis of disability and masculinity they are able to address issues of identity and self without reifying either structure or agency. It is this approach that this chapter aims to emulate.

Method

The data for this chapter were collected as part of a study into people with physical impairments' ideas about health and health status. Each person was interviewed twice over a six-month period. Whilst the interviews were semi-structured, the object was to get people to talk as freely and openly as possible. Each interview lasted for approximately 90 minutes. All the interviews were tape-recorded for subsequent transcription and analysis. Thematic and subsequent inductive analysis following the usual guidelines for qualitative research (Lofland and Lofland, 1996) was aided by the use of NUD.IST software. The experiences of impairment and disablement are both public and intimate. It is only through people's stories and biographies that an understanding that unites the public and the private into a coherent entity can come into being. By an analysis of the particular, a picture of the general can emerge. Plummer's (1995) analysis of stories and narratives influenced the approach in this study.

Issues surrounding identity and self emerged as one of the most significant themes in the data, and it is this area that this chapter will concentrate on. The data from three individuals will be presented. All the informants have been given pseudonyms and their identity has been further protected by the removal of any non-essential information that may be used to identify them.

Joan

Joan is a 41-year-old married woman with two children. She was diagnosed with multiple sclerosis (MS) sixteen years ago, and lives in a flat within a complex specifically designed for disabled people. One of the most striking features of the interviews with Joan was the way that MS was central to all of the aspects of her life that she described. MS, and its attendant impairments, had taken over her sense of self: she no longer felt that she was healthy or that she had any quality of life:

> To me, to be healthy is to be walking . . . um, in my mind, I know it's a terrible thing to say, but people in wheelchairs should be allowed voluntary euthanasia. Because I certainly would. I think the quality of life has gone when you're in a wheelchair. I think, you know, personally.

She feels that, as an impaired person, she has no sense of worth. She described how she had become a burden because she was unable to help around the house:

I just have to get so much done for me, and I can't do ordinary things like changing beds. There's certain things I'd like that I can't do now, like when I go to bed, I can't manage to get myself from the chair into the bed, I have to get a help over. Well, actually, I've got a hydraulic hoist, you know? I think I'm a burden, I really do.

Joan also felt that her impairment prevented her from fulfilling her role as a mother and wife. Her impairment had, in her view, prevented her from doing 'so many things' with her children, and she talked about how her relationship with them had been affected. She talked about how she felt that she did nothing for her children, and was surprised when one of them commented on how much she'd miss her:

Something came up, I can't remember exactly, it was to do with road accidents and terrible tragic deaths and there was something on the news about a mum and dad both killed in a road accident and leaving four kids behind and she said 'Oh I couldn't cope if anything happened to you and dad, that would be terrible and my life wouldn't be worth living'. And I said 'Why not, I could understand about your dad because he does about everything for you but I don't do anything for you, so I don't know'. She said 'You do so, you are there, you listen to me, you can talk to me'. That is about all I do for them.

Thus Joan devalued what her daughters felt as important. Her impaired physicality and her inability to do what she considered to be the normal things in a mother-and-daughter relationship have become paramount. She explained how difficult it was for her to go shopping with her daughters, talking about problems with accessible toilets, not being able to get transport to and from the shops and the problems with wheelchair access in the city centre.

These barriers had also affected her relationship with friends to the point that she felt excluded:

I think an awful lot of people would be, you know, happy to take me along anywhere, but they say 'Oh, it's got stairs, or it's awkward', or 'You can't come 'cos it's not got a ramp and whatever, you can't come'. So I think . . . yes, I think that is what I mean, I feel excluded from things, yeah.

However, despite describing how this exclusion was the product of physical barriers, Joan blamed her MS: 'I think, if I wasn't in this goddamn wheelchair, I could, you know ... ' She further clarified the ambiguity between blaming social barriers and blaming MS when I asked her whether she felt that if these barriers were removed would she be any happier:

> I would feel bad about having MS, but for different reasons, just because I feel very bitter, I feel why me, why have I got it, there must be thousands and millions of others think that, although maybe they don't dwell on it. Maybe they accept it. I will never accept what I've got, I never have.

To her accepting implied 'making the best of it', something that she could never do. For Joan, to do that implied that she was accepting that she would never get better.

> Put it this way, I cannot accept what's wrong with me. I keep ... I keep having this imagination in my head and think, one day I'll be able to get up and start walking, and you know, I just can't accept it.

In her everyday life she met many disabled people who were managing their lives but was unable to identify with them. She described one person she knew, who was a wheelchair-user who worked and had what she termed a full social life, but she could still not feel that he led a full or worthwhile life. She talked about how she constantly thought about remission. Whilst she accepted that this may be 'a false hope, and would probably never happen', she could not accept the consequences of MS. When she was first diagnosed, and able to walk, she talked how she would be 'too embarrassed' to admit to anybody that she was tired or sore.

Similarly, she also told me about how MS had adversely affected her marriage. She revealed how her husband no longer talked to her, attributing this to her MS, although he himself denied that this was the cause.

> It's destroyed the relationship between my husband and I, because although my husband says that it's absolutely nothing to do with the MS, I feel it has, a lot to do with the MS, because he hardly even

talks to me now, apart from anything else, he just . . . no, he's feeling really depressed himself, and he says it's not my fault, it's his fault, but it's just . . . I think he feels really burdened 'cos of myself.

She felt that in part this was caused by her needing constant care, not allowing her husband any time for himself:

Um, in the way that I feel, well, one he doesn't talk much, and two, it's like his way, he just makes me feel hurried, he'll say 'Are you ready to go to bed? Do you want me to put the blanket on?' And I'll think, god, do you not even think . . . I know that's probably about half past ten at night, which isn't, I know, that early, but for me it is. And I think, oh, I just want to relax and read the paper, do whatever, you know? I just feel as though I'm always rushed away, as though it's like a relief to him to get rid of me to my bed so he can have time on his own, and either watch TV or whatever. You know, just to relax. And I can appreciate that he does need time to relax in, you know, to have his own time.

Her impairment affected her relationship with her husband. She no longer felt attractive and felt that she was unable to live up to what she perceived were her husband's expectations of what a wife should be.

Phil

Phil is 45 years old and lives with his partner. He also has a degenerative disease, FSH-muscular dystrophy, which was diagnosed in his teens. In contrast to Joan, having MD did not seem to be central to his life. He described his health as good 'apart from my breathing', ascribing this to always looking after himself and being free from illness. This enabled him to lead a 'quality life'. He felt that the issue of health was all in the mind:

I think it is all in the mind, quite a lot. I think if you've got a positive attitude, then I think that you can achieve an awful lot. I think you have to have a lot of drive . . . I think if you're a bit meek about things and a bit weepy and a bit wimpy, then I think you'll just shrivel up. I have a lot of imagination in my mind about things, and I tend to dress and I tend to look on life . . . as a normal individual although I know that I'm not, but I think I am sometimes.

Phil was determined that people were not going to see him as a stereotypical disabled person. He takes considerable care in his dress and appearance: he is always smartly turned out, he always wears a tie, describing himself as 'the vainest man alive'. He attributed this in part as a challenge to the way that many disabled people are dressed, describing how people in hostels are forced to wear tracksuits and often appear unkempt. He also felt that when he dressed smartly people treated him with more respect:

> I think appearance is very, very important, I'm competing with others ... It might be that I'm compensating for my weaker prob-lems; facially, physically that I can dress a bit smarter and detract from things. There have been many occasions when my partner has verified that ... when I'm in my suit people talk to me. We have had to go to odd things, a doctor or whatever, they are not fully taking into account the problems I've got, the physical problems. A lot of people don't ... for that sort of thing because I am creating this image like a bookcover. I think I look tidy and smart, the tie is dead right and I sit in a way – constantly occupy my mind with 'Am I sitting correctly?' 'Am I ... ' I am trying to look ... not sliding down with a double chin or whatever. Extremely vain, extremely aware of it, and it does succeed sometimes.

In this way Phil is challenging what he sees as societal attitudes to disabled people, an attitude that he had until his mid-thirties. Muscular dystrophy was never mentioned in his presence and he developed what he termed a 'hang-up' about the condition. He refused to listen to other people and wouldn't use a wheelchair or make any adaptations to his house or his life. He described how he used to feel that the day he needed to use a wheelchair was the day he ended his life. When he was 32 he fell and broke both his kneecaps and was hospitalized. During his rehabilitation he saw a video of himself walking:

> One of the things that hurt me really badly in the hospital was that they took a video of me walking and by that time I had reached the stage ... balance, which is a curved back ... with tummy hanging out because there are no tummy muscles there. I was standing up walking with this peculiar gait of slinging my legs round ... lean back and holding on to somebody's hands which by this time were above my shoulders. That was the most peculiar – I looked like

some zombie or a stick insect, I don't know. When I saw that video I crumbled, I couldn't believe it. I broke down in tears and was quickly put back in the ward. I really felt, oh, dear God.

In the hospital, through an informal network of support from other patients, he began to realize that 'I was screwing up because I was carrying on, not facing up to reality and what the future will really mean'. He learned to accept his impairment, started using a wheelchair, moved into an adapted house and got an adapted vehicle so he could start driving again, all things that he had rejected. Similarly he applied for and got benefit allowances, which he had refused to apply for in the past because 'I didn't want to be tied to the disability tag'.

Phil sees his acceptance of his impairment as central to his sense of self and well-being:

I think one should try and know what is ahead of you, having being prepared for things, for a progressive disease because that is the only way I can think of it, none of that I ever did. I never really planned my future, I never thought about the next move in my disability.

This is not to suggest that Phil accepts any deterioration in his body with equanimity, but that he has become used to it. As he says:

For years, I guess I have always said 'Look, I look much fitter. If things would stay at that level I could cope.' And then move on, and you just move with it and you have to adapt again. But again you would say . . . let's stabilize here.

His relationship with his partner is the most important thing in his life (although his car comes a close second!).

Senga

Senga is a 59-year-old woman with MS, which was first diagnosed in 1970. Her husband died five years ago and she now lives on her own in a flat in a complex for disabled people. She had recently moved to Edinburgh from a rural area where she rarely met or saw other disabled people. The two interviews with Senga were almost like interviewing two different people. In the first interview she described herself as being unhealthy, which was entirely due to her having MS:

> [Being healthy means] not having MS . . . there never was anything wrong with me and it was suddenly, it was as if my world had ended, I had MS. So to me it's a very difficult thing.
> *Do you think you are healthy now?*
> No, because I've got MS.

Later on in the interview she contradicted herself, saying:

> When somebody says, 'You're looking so well', I get a bit of a shock because I feel why should they pick me out because there's nothing wrong with me.
> *What do you mean by that?*
> Well when somebody, you know, because you're in a wheelchair, you poor soul, 'Oh you look so well', I think, 'Don't. There is nothing wrong with me, I'm perfectly all right.'

When I pointed this out to her she replied, 'I sort of feel I can't be healthy, or I wouldn't be the way that I am'. This contradiction between her being healthy and unhealthy ran throughout the whole of the first interview.

During the first interview Senga was very difficult to talk to, she felt that my questions were inappropriate, saying at one point 'I've never been asked such questions'. Her answers tended to be very short and it was an uncomfortable experience for both of us, so much so that I was surprised when she agreed to be interviewed six months later. She talked about how she had stopped going to parties and wouldn't go out, describing herself as a hermit.

> I got it in my head that I was something unclean, that I didn't want people to see me in a wheelchair. And it's quite strange, I was down at physio and I was saying this to one of the young men there, I said I've met women here and they've said 'You have so much confidence', and I said 'If they only knew that I keep creeping into my shell', and you see there were very few people in wheelchairs there, so really and truly, if you went into town, people looked at you. So I stopped going, I wouldn't go out.

She found it very difficult to accept that she was disabled and a wheelchair-user. When I asked her what image she had of herself she replied: 'When I think of myself, the only image that comes to mind is me walking and me running.' She talked about how she felt different to 'all the other poor souls' in the complex that she lived in, and was unable to identify with them. She had also tried 'every cure under the sun' including diet, medication and alternative therapies, although she had recently turned down the offer of hyperbaric treatment because she felt that she could not face the possibility of failure. She felt that, as a result of her past experiences and falsely raised hopes, in the future she would consent to treatment only if she knew that it would work. She described how she read all about her condition, her GP even commented to her that she knew more about MS than he did. She described herself as an expert on the condition.

Six months later Senga's whole attitude seemed to have changed. Although she herself felt that life was 'much the same' her responses suggest that quite a lot had happened to her. She talked about how she was 'getting more and more confident in myself'. When I asked her what had brought about this change she replied:

> I honestly . . . I don't know . . . this friend, she is a social worker and she has worked with disabled people and in that respect I am one of the luckiest people because if I didn't know her . . . she comes with me on all the holidays. And an aunt from up north did meet her she said it is because of her I'm the way I am. I don't think it is, it is as if coming here I've seen what other disabled people can do and it's as if they can do it, so can I. And that just started me wanting to go on holidays and go out because there was no way I would have gone to a pub, I couldn't believe, different people would say 'Tonight we will go to the pub for a drink' and I thought but you're disabled, you're in wheelchairs, how can you go to a pub and I discovered here everybody can do anything they want to do and that was it. That started bringing me out a bit.

She talked about how, through meeting other disabled people, she felt able to take control of her life. She described how she had changed in herself: 'It's as if for 25 years I've been dead and it's as if suddenly I'm coming alive again . . . I like myself.' She talked about how she used to be unable to think of herself as disabled and how 'I probably lived in a dreamworld then'. She used to feel 'As if I couldn't cope, life wasn't worth living . . . now I've discovered that I can manage or cope with all sorts of things, I just think it has all given me confidence.'

She also described how she no longer even bothered to read the MS Society's newsletter and had stopped reading about MS. When I asked her why, she replied:

> I suppose then I kept thinking I will read something that will be a cure and I suppose it finally hit me so far there isn't a cure, so. I just feel what is the point of reading through all this stuff.

This final comment sums up Senga's changed attitude to herself and her impairment:

> I was a poor disabled lady, but now I've discovered I wasn't a poor disabled lady after all, I was somebody and I could go where I wanted to.

Discussion

These data show how the experience of having a chronic illness can affect one's view of self. Joan is unable to accept chronic illness; she feels that having this condition makes her a burden, less of a person. She cannot identify as a disabled person, and feels that were she to do so she would be giving in to the condition. Being impaired is unacceptable. She could not be described as being in denial, for describing somebody in such language merely implies that she does not accept or agree with the analysis of her situation, and she is fully aware of the consequences of both her impairment and her disablement.

By contrast, Phil's sense of self appears to be unaffected by the presence of chronic illness. He still describes himself as healthy, an attribute that Crawford (1994) has described as central to the modern identity. He also challenges stereotypical views of disabled people by dressing smartly and sitting in a way that he feels allows him to be on equal terms with non-disabled people. Central to Phil's personal outlook on his life is acceptance of his impairment, something that Joan recognizes as important but appears unable to countenance. Similarly Senga, in her earlier interview, did not identify as disabled and it was only when she did so that she was able to come to terms with her condition.

What is interesting is the similarity between Senga's and Phil's analyses of how they came to terms with their respective conditions. Both were at one point unable or unwilling to accept that they had an impairment. This is evidenced by Phil's refusal to have the condition discussed in his presence, and his rejection of a wheelchair, and Senga's refusal to identify with other people who lived in the complex. However, it was through meeting other disabled people that they became aware of their own condition and how their attitude affected their sense of self. They no longer felt that they were something to be pitied. By meeting and talking to other disabled people, and seeing that they lived valued and creative lives, they were able to throw off their own beliefs and values around disability. Their self-image was no longer dominated by the perceptions of non-disabled people: they developed a self-identity through reflexivity, within what Giddens (1991) terms a collective context. Through interaction with disabled people they were provided with a narrative and were thus able to perpetuate a biography, the self being reflexively created into a self-identity. This involved the rejection of cultural and social stereotypes of disabled people. By meeting disabled people they were able to reject these constructions, replacing them with a more experientially based one. In this way they developed 'the capacity to keep a particular narrative going' (Giddens, 1991, p. 54).

Joan rejects the very idea of impairment. She sees it as an assault on her self and her self-identity. For her to lead a full and active life implies being able to walk and not have a chronic illness. Despite living in a similar situation to the other two informants and the positive comments of her daughters and her husband, she still feels that her life is worthless, that she has nothing to contribute to the day-to-day running of the family. Her disbelief of her daughters' comments is testament to this. An analysis of her interview from an interactionist, negotiation perspective would suggest that she is unable to cope with her condition, that she cannot come to terms with her impairment, and that the subsequent loss of self is a direct result of her impairment.

Rather than taking this line, it might be more beneficial to analyse societal attitudes to impairment and disablement and illustrate how these produce a culture in which disabled people find it impossible to accept their impairment. This implies moving beyond the social model, with its focus on the sociopolitical, to a more cultural analysis, such as that proposed by Shakespeare (1994). He argues that we need to pay more attention to the question of meaning and representation, moving beyond material processes and relations. We need to uncover 'the webs of interlocution' through which we develop our sense of self.

Disabled people face a daily barrage of images of themselves as other, as unworthy, as something to be feared (Morris, 1991). It is therefore not surprising that people such as Joan are unable to see their lives as worthwhile. As Kriegel argues: 'The world of the cripple is strange and dark and it is held up to judgment by those who fear it. The cripple is the creature who has been deprived of his ability to create a self' (quoted by Shakespeare, 1994). Thus it may be argued that Joan's sense of self is a reflection, a mirroring of societal views on chronic illness. Her sense of self has not been damaged because she has an impairment but because she has incorporated these views into her biography and this is reflected in her narrative. As Bourdieu (1984) argues, our world view is based on our social locations and social relations.

What is perhaps of more consequence to disability studies is the agency, or resistance, that is exhibited by Phil and Senga. By becoming part of a community of disabled people (by which I do not mean living in a complex designed for disabled people, but the sharing of ideas and experiences with other disabled people) and identifying as disabled they have, by integrating the individual and the collective (Shakespeare, 1996c), demonstrated the importance of identity.

Disability studies, with its concentration on disabling barriers, runs the risk of neglecting issues of identity. As Bailey and Hall argue:

> It is perfectly possible that what is politically progressive and opens up discursive opportunities in the 1970's and 1980's can become a form of closure – and have a repressive value – by the time it is installed as the dominant genre ... It will run out of steam; it will become a style; people will use it not because it opens up anything but because they are being spoken by it, and at that point you need another shift. (1992, p. 15)

Identifying with other disabled people rather than rejecting the label was what enabled Phil and Senga to resist their beliefs around disability. As recent developments in the gay, black and women's movements show, identity can become the basis for a political movement. Plummer (1995) has argued that it is through the sharing of stories that communities grow and a political sense of citizenship evolves. This citizenship can help people challenge the prevailing orthodoxies surrounding disabled people, and by reflecting on their own experiences and incorporating those of others they can begin to define their own identity.

Further reading

Crawford, R. (1994) The boundaries of the self and the unhealthy other: reflections on health, culture and AIDS, *Social Sciences and Medicine*, vol. 38, pp. 1347–65.

Crow, L. (1996) Including all of our lives: renewing the social model of disability, in J. Morris (ed.) *Encounters with Strangers: Feminism and Disability*. London: Women's Press.

Hughes, B. and Paterson, K. (1997) The social model of disability and the disappearing body: towards a sociology of impairment, *Disability and Society*, vol. 12, no. 3, pp. 325–40.

11

Body Battles: Bodies, Gender and Disability

Helen Meekosha

> The Anita Cobby file in the Fairfax library . . . is nearly as thick as a yellow pages phone book. There is no file, not even a single clipping, on Lorna Gibson. On May 30 (last year) [1986], Lorna Gibson was stabbed, asphyxiated, then mutilated by two brothers in Melbourne . . . Lorna Gibson . . . was intellectually disabled. (*Sydney Morning Herald*, 20 June 1987)

Violence against women with disabilities, violation of their bodies, murder, medical mutilation, enforced sterilization and abortion are not issues that attract media attention. Yet a vicious murder of Anita Cobby, a former (white) beauty queen, was barely off the front pages of the major Australian metropolitan newspapers in 1987. The mutilated beautiful body excites attention – the mutilated disabled body passes unnoticed. We need to question why some female bodies are more worthy of attention than others, some are a cause of celebration and some provoke disgust and are denied as important. These questions, rather than being marginal to contemporary difference theory, go to the heart of our understanding of the body in the social world.

In public discourse, as exemplified above, disability may be rendered invisible, as though the 'normal' mind cannot encompass a difference so profoundly embedded in its/our sense of the 'normal' and its silenced Others (those who are not part of the taken-for-granted everyday world of the dominant cultures). It is as though disabled bodies exist in spaces outside mainstream society. This chapter challenges contemporary theorizing on bodies, and offers an alternative framework for understanding both the multiple dimensions and the processes involved in disabled embodiment. It seeks to move beyond dichotomous binaries of nature/culture, body/mind and impairment/disability.

Nowhere is the problem more acute than in feminist discourses on the body, their claim to universality corrupted by their unselfconscious exclusion of disability from their world views. This chapter interrogates feminist engagements with bodies and looks at three broad dimensions that have developed in recent writings. I have labelled these as: objectified bodies, regulated bodies and bodies as texts. Based on this analysis an argument is developed for effectively gendering disabled bodies, exploring how feminist thought can be useful to an understanding of disabled embodiments. Two key ideas are proposed as a means of linking these two areas: that of normalization and that of regulation and surveillance.

Charting the concerns of disabled women

Even though disabled women may not have surfaced significantly in the feminist project, we/they have struggled to evoke their realities into the public world. Narratives of disability have been one way in which disabled women have sought to fashion spaces in which they can be heard (Browne *et al.*, 1985; Saxton and Howe, 1988; Keith, 1994; Barrett, 1995). These works movingly detail body/mind, spiritual and political struggles, but, while they have constituted a backgrounding of disabled women's lives and have helped create a community, these works show a limited engagement with broader disability or feminist theorizing. Storytelling has not been a sufficient strategy to move significantly either the broader disability literature or the concerns of feminist theory, to come to an engagement with gendered, disabled bodies.

On the other hand, rarely have these narratives been used by body theorists in developing theories of resistance to dominant social orders. The subjective stories or narratives of disabled women's (and sometimes men's) experiences together with new ways of theorizing disability can enhance the understanding of gendered relations. These stories go far beyond the simple media representations of suffering, overcoming or striving (Meekosha and Dowse, 1997); they constitute valuable material demanding interpretation and analysis. 'Silence is the condition of one who has been dominated, made an object; talk is the mark of freeing, of making one subject' (hooks, 1989, p. 129).

While disability studies has begun to emerge as a potential location for the intellectual and political work that is required, the struggle to establish the area and the paradigms of the social model seems to have consigned the more complex theoretical questions of gender, ethnic and class relations to the margins. Academic institutions have done little to encourage the employment and fostering of disabled academics – in particular disabled women; most academic conference organizers need reminding of basic access issues and rarely is disability seen as a legitimate part of the mainstream discourse. They have been silenced or neglected by omission (Newell, 1995; Chouinard and Grant, 1996).

Despite the questioning by contemporary feminism of the universality of the category of woman on the one hand, and the development of disability theory on the other, the terrain which might link these feminist critiques and disability has scarcely been charted and remains largely untheorized. Over the last decade disabled women have criticized the failure of feminist theory in broad terms to include disability, while the masculine bias of the disability movement and ungendered theorizing around disability issues have been highlighted (Wendell, 1989; Meekosha, 1990; Lloyd, 1992; Morris, 1993a; 1996). For the most part women are still 'added-in' to disability texts with special references to their particular issues (Swain *et al.*, 1993; Oliver, 1996; Christensen and Rizvi, 1996). Exploratory work by disabled feminists did not attempt inclusive analysis (Deegan and Brooks, 1985; Fine and Asch, 1988); distinct identity groups are often consigned to special chapters – for example age and ethnicity.

Feminist accounts of the disability relationship have tended to limit themselves to discussions of the Welfare State and the role of women as carers. The cared-for were rendered genderless and objectified, often given significance only through their role as the Other for the carer. Women with disabilities were subsumed under universal 'cared-for' in this debate, assumed as part of the 'burden' contributing to women's secondary or privatized status (Silvers, 1995; Braithwaite, 1990; Graham, 1993; Morris, 1993b). Where feminist analyses of disability have been attempted (as in Hillyer, 1993), they often leave unexamined the crucial relationship between the female carer and the disabled woman. While Hillyer's analysis is important for the perspective it brings to caring research, nevertheless it fails adequately to disengage the lives of the cared-for from that of the carers and the demands made by disabled women for more autonomy.

Re-envisioning the social to encompass a feminist concept of disability is no easy task. Women with disabilities working as academics may be reluctant to move into disability studies. Why teach about what may be perceived as the story of your own personal tragedy? Reconstructing subjectivity is risky business – we might be seen as spectacle (Bordo, 1993, p. 284). The late Irving Zola called this denial the structured silence of personal bodily experiences (1991), though Zola's dilemma is not easily resolved. For feminist disabled scholars it may be more appropriate to focus on gender or women's studies, rather than the too-often ungendered territory of disability studies.

Some feminist scholarship still appears hostile to the inclusion of disability within its frame of reference, as if the feminist project is being pushed one more step away from being able to speak with a strong political voice, particularly when the voice of the Other is not recognizable. Yet enabling the diversity and fluidity of gendered and embodied lives to be voiced will render feminism richer, more coherent and more relevant.

Complex social relations which characterize the contemporary world include dimensions of disability: an individual's impairment may be paramount or temporary and will always be part of an embodied identity; it will change as the individual engages with others in communities of sameness and communities of difference. At the same time a person's impairment will be influenced, read and constructed by various cultural, social, economic and political determinants as well as by their own experiences.

The location of feminist theory and the body

Feminist concerns with the body have encompassed a heterogeneity of discourses and issues. The traditional perception of women's bodies as subordinate and male bodies as superordinate became contested terrain. Initially critiquing the masculinity of the interests underlying claims to universality of human experience, feminist debates since the second wave have been concerned with contesting or overcoming the binaries of nature/culture, sex/gender and private/public. These debates have emphasized the body as the major site for ideological contestations. One such recent debate revolves around a feminist analysis of the emergence of cyborgs on the one hand (Haraway, 1990) and teratology on the other (Haraway, 1992; Huet, 1993; Lykke and Braidotti, 1996). Disabled bodies – central to both discourses – remain unexplored. For example, bodies that have been transformed by disease or accident, or those considered 'monstrous' as to be hidden from view, are not considered the proper territory of feminist scholarship. Similarly the inability to urinate, defecate and endure spasticity, nausea and pain – conditions that may require medical interventions, drugs or prostheses – is rarely analysed by body theorists.

Passionate, frustrated and agitated, Rose, dying of cancer, raged 'I need to invent colostomy ethnography' (Rose, 1995, p. 87). For her, changing body image had become an overworked cliché: she argued that we must address the resiting of bodily functions, both conceptually and physically. The lived or subjective experiences of women also include desire and emotion, issues hitherto the province of psychoanalysis and the mind. A proper focus of social analysis includes subjective experiences of suffering, pain, rejection, loss and grief, desire, joy and achievement. For some women, permission to celebrate or document these experiences creates a place of resistance to male hegemony, and constitutes women-centred worlds and spaces. For others this celebration is suspect, as it leads back to essentialism and biological reductionism. Debates contesting or claiming nurturing and caring as essential women's values provoke many opposing positions given different experiences mediated by race, class, religious beliefs, age and disability. Re-emerging in the writings of the eco-feminists and women embracing New Age politics, the nature/culture debate has not been resolved, though the complexities and contradictions inherent in simple dichotomies have become more apparent.

If biology is not destiny, then culture may be the determining context. If so, this means that all bodies are fundamentally culturally and socially determined and thus particular cultural forms determine the configuration of the body, the health and sickness of the body, the rise of distinctive illnesses such as cancer, heart diseases and eating disorders. Yet this position may just lead to another form of one-dimensional and essentialist explanations. Seen in this way, the body has been forced to vacate its residence on the nature side of the nature–culture duality and take up residence within culture (Bordo, 1993, p. 33). An example of this process can be seen in the repetitive strain injury 'epidemic' in Australia, the USA and the UK over the last decade, which has once again seen women and their injuries determined by their biology (Meekosha, 1986; Meekosha and Jakubowicz, 1991). Women have been more likely than men to develop symptoms

of repetitive strain injury, owing to their social and economic positioning in the labour force and their domestic responsibilities in the home;
yet arguments advanced by an army of lawyers, medical practitioners
and the media claim the injuries are psychosomatic and in particular
'hysterical' (womb-based) in origin and not physiological at all. The
injured women are then forced to 'prove' that the injuries are 'really'
physiological, caused by faulty ergonomics and poor work practices –
thereby forced into a mind/body and public/private separation. In
public imagery RSI has come to be closely connected with a view of
women which portrays them as essentially hysterical.

Understanding bodies as socially and culturally constructed has been
extremely useful in furthering an understanding of women's oppression. But there are limitations to this approach. Indeed rather than
speak of dichotomies at all, we might more usefully appropriate Grosz's
imagery of a Möbius strip which 'has the advantage of showing the
inflection of mind into body and body into mind, the ways in which,
through a kind of twisting or inversion one side becomes another'
(Grosz, 1994, p. xii). The juxtaposition of the mind and the body is
indeed a site of struggle in itself, as will be argued in relation to
disability. How do we account for the multiplicity of meanings given to
bodily adornments and alterations – fashion trends, cosmetic surgeries,
mutilations – by women in different cultural settings? If the body is
socially constructed how do we, individually and collectively, exercise
any power over this social construction?

Feminist debate about bodies has ranged from the strategies necessary to gain control over our own bodies, such as struggles over
reproductive rights, through to the tension expressed between the
semiotics and the symbolics of different bodies. Insisting on women's
'control' over their own bodies challenged this perspective as part of the
process of liberation, seeking autonomy from and questioning male
hegemony. 'Deviant' female bodies have increasingly become foci for
examination, as have queer and/or sexually transgressive bodies. Feminist discourses demand that the body should be seen as a sexed body,
that the subjective experiences of sexuality, of child bearing and rearing
are legitimate and affirmed. Acknowledging personal experiences and
taking bodily control within a political context became central to the
revived feminism. Desire and eroticism are a central part of these
analyses, yet rarely do they consider the disabled body worthy of
examination. Sexuality is also part of the disability experience, even if

repressed, violated or denied (but see Shakespeare *et al.*, 1996 for a first attempt to bring these issues together).

AIDS or eating disorders such as anorexia nervosa – conditions that go to the heart of contemporary topics of desire and sexuality, conditions that create texts that can be 'read' off the body – have become important topics in cultural and social analysis (*Media Information Australia*, 1994). Yet little work has been done away from these 'afflictions of the hitherto "normal"' – the engagement seems to be with the physical and/or psychic trauma resulting from an able-bodied person being forced into another social or physiological space. There appears to be an unacknowledged resistance to applying similar analytic approaches to those whose lives have always been in that 'other space' – those born with impairments. Gendered and disabled bodies are fundamental to contemporary social analysis for they offer a site for examining the major contradictions of the social, psychological and political.

Objectified bodies

Female bodies have been understood as objectified bodies. An understanding of the body as central to women's oppression has revealed the processes by which women's bodies are given shape by medicine, fashion, the health and fitness industries and the media. The interweaving of patriarchy (in the form of the male gaze), the state and bureaucratic control renders women subordinate through bodily policing. Bodies are not 'natural', but socially produced, reproduced and culturally inscribed (Turner, 1996). Legislation regulating abortion, state intervention in birthing practices and IVF, control over biotechnology and the human genome project all have major ramifications for women and raise issues about the appropriation and control of bodily processes.

Second-wave feminists of the 1970s began to argue that female bodies were commodities – to be sold in the market place. The value of women's bodies as property could be seen as determined by the market under capitalism. Exploitation of their bodies allows for the sale of commodities and they are used to market products as diverse as soft drinks and cars: here sexual desire is being sold. Women are often willing accomplices in these processes of appropriation. These processes have provoked dissent between feminists – some who view much advertising using female bodies as demeaning and others who suggest that this form of feminist censorship denies women's sexuality and their active engagement in the consumption of advertising (Lumby, 1996). Disabled women's bodies are used to evoke pity and the charity donation, and increasingly as potent symbols of unexpected strength to sell products such as soft drinks (Meekosha and Dowse, 1997).

As in classical art, women's bodies may be featured as dismembered parts. Yet this dismembering is not related to the disabled body. It is not grotesque, it is the eroticization of body parts: the viewer is asked to consider the whole perfect woman, to fantasize the whole from the perfect parts. Understanding the world of fashion, style, weight control, sport and health and fitness regimes for women calls for an understanding of both the controlling and the normalizing aspects of these practices. The objectified female body can also be understood as a machine: a breeding machine reproducing the species, a machine from which profit can be extracted in the labour market, or a machine which can be tuned and retuned in gyms and health centres.

There are parallels between the embodiment of disability and the embodiment of gender. Women's bodies and disabled male bodies are reduced to their biological (lack of) functioning; as deficient, as not able-bodied males. They have been subject to abuse, invasion, remodelling under the surgeon's knife, regulation, medicalization, normalization, state intervention and rendered the Other *vis-à-vis* both non-disabled male bodies and (sometimes) disabled male bodies. For disabled women, the oppressor may at times be another woman acting as colonizer, regulator or controller.

The less nationally or geographically specific experience of disabled women can be illuminated by the more specific experience of colonized women. An understanding of the use and abuse of colonized women's bodies, for example Aboriginal women in Australia, provides one key to unlocking the ideologies and intentions of colonialism (Pettman, 1996). Aboriginal women were sexually exploited, raped, used as a free supply of domestic labour, as means of 'breeding' out the race and by way of controlling the male Aboriginal population. In the USA and Europe objectification of the racialized body impacted with the disabled body in freak shows and medical discourses at the turn of the nineteenth century. Often disabled bodies were racialized – presented as tribal – while the racialized, but non-disabled bodies were presented as freaks of nature. At these points the discourses of race and disability collided in teratology (Bogdan, 1987).

Regulated bodies

With the rise of civil society, new freedoms and citizens' rights have emerged, but at the same time new disciplinary regimes constitute individuals as citizens through regulation of bodies. Thus, modern institutions of prisons, hospitals, schools, factories and the armed services form the individual as prisoner, patient and so on in time and space. Moreover citizens are also engaged in a process of self-surveillance. So issues of power have become much more diffuse (Foucault, 1977).

For example, women's fitness magazines inculcate an unrealistic body ideal in women (Duncan, 1994). Here control is more subtle than overt: women can be active participants in their own domination. Workout books and videos represent this form of self-surveillance. But women are also active in constructing their own bodily meanings. Fitness and exercise can also be understood as women taking more control over their bodies. From sexual desire to bodily adornments to health monitoring, some women are increasingly in a position to exercise more choice and power. So while the body has been and still is central to women's oppression, it can also be viewed historically as subject to a multiplicity of changes through time and space.

At the same time the interests of dominant social and economic institutions, from multinational cosmetic, pharmaceutical and fashion companies to global media institutions, are invoked as responsible for the domination and invasion of women's bodies. So are we in any position both to act on our own bodies and to take control of the processes of bodily domination? Can we intervene in the process of social construction or reconstruction? Using Foucault's notion of self-surveillance to understand women's collusion with the normalizing and homogenizing processes of body invasion is useful. But this under-standing then suggests the question: What leads women to take both individual and collective political action against these processes? More-over, if all bodily experiences are socially constructed, what is left of the biological experience? How are we to explain the subjective experience of bodily processes and functions? Are all our experiences simply mediated through culture and society? If so, we 'have no direct, innocent or unconstructed knowledge of our own bodies; rather, we are always reading our bodies according to various interpretive schemes' (Bordo, 1993, p. 289).

Bodies as text

Bodies can be described as texts in which we can read the ideological assumptions of the social system: texts for understanding social institutions, social discourses and social forms. Bodies have been used as metaphors for describing the social and political world. Thus, in nineteenth-century England, images of inmates of Bedlam with their distorted and typically grotesque bodies were used in popular cartoons to signify political life – the asylum as the microcosm of the world (Gilman, 1995). In the twentieth century cancer and AIDS are often exploited as contemporary societal metaphors (Sontag, 1991).

Women's bodies may be used to signify 'natural inequalities' in the social world, but while healthy and beautiful female bodies (white) signify the reproduction of the dominant race, disabled women's bodies signify the opposite – dangerous reproductivity or lack of fecundity or ability to reproduce and hence ugliness. Adornments, tattoos, mutilations and so on, often associated with 'primitive societies' and currently fashionable in Westernized societies, all make statements about how the bearer relates to his or her social world (Mascia-Lees and Sharpe, 1992). For some women bodily alterations are the result of current ideologies about women's role and appearance and the demands of consumer capitalism; for others fashion can be used to parody and resist dominant ideas about women's subordination.

At a different extreme, female genital mutilation carried out on girls globally can be viewed as control of sexuality. While it is demanded by male fears and desires it is carried out by women (Walker and Parmar, 1993). Bodies-as-texts analyses can also be applied to disabled women – understanding the mutilation and invasion of their bodies reveals societies where those with less than perfect bodies are often subject to dehumanizing, degendering and devaluing processes (Meekosha and Jakubowicz, 1996). There is a danger of seeing the individual as being without agency if the body is seen only as a culturally inscribed text. The body as a passive entity upon which power stamps its own images can undermine the feminist project of both re-evaluating women's experiences and challenging oppressive practices. Women are not simply victims of wider social forces; they make conscious choices with regard to desire, sexuality, medical intervention and so on. Women can resist or collude in normalizing bodily practices, and at times both processes may be at work. Agency and control are key issues for understanding both the potential for body freedoms on the one hand and state and societal interventions and controls on the other.

Towards a gendered theory of disabled bodies

'We all have bodies, but not all bodies are equal, some matter more than others: some are, quite frankly, disposable' (Braidotti, 1996, p. 136). While the language and theory of much feminist work fail to take into account the intersection of gender and disability, the use of the language of disability by feminist writers – such as claims that women are 'disabled' by their capacity to reproduce or 'handicapped' by their subordinate status in society – demonstrates an ignorance of the growing political importance of women with disabilities and the centrality of disability to an understanding of the body. Declaring female embodiment as a barrier to equal participation in society raises insurmountable problems and contradictions for disabled women. For instance, and apparently totally unselfconsciously, Grosz in the opening sentence of her book *Volatile Bodies* (1994) argues that the body has been a conceptual 'blind spot' in contemporary feminist theory – *blind* being used as an adjective of denigration.

In August 1968, at the 'No More Miss America' demonstration, the position paper 'outlined a complex non reductionist analysis of the intersection of sexism, conformism, competition, ageism, racism, militarism, and consumer culture as they are constellated and crystallized in pageant' (Robin Morgan quoted by Bordo, 1993, p. 19). The intersection of disability and sexism was absent from the feminist agenda of the 1960s, and beauty pageants globally have been and still continue to be organized by charities to raise money for people with disabilities. Opposing beauty contests and 'personality' pageants has largely faded from the political agenda and become associated with an earlier and more austere feminism. Yet these pageants represent a process of policing the female body and are central to the oppression of women with disabilities (even though some in Australia are now won by men!).

Some disabled women have argued for an analysis of double discrimination, disadvantage or oppression (Deegan and Brooks, 1985; Lloyd, 1992), while others have argued for a subgenre to be established within feminist studies (Thomson, 1994). But disabled women's bodily experiences are simultaneously mediated through class, racial, religious or ethnic identity and age. Attempts to develop feminist and gendered theories of disabilities to date have tended to assume the experience of white heterosexual women. The double or multiple discrimination approach is limited – it suggests a layering of discrimination on to a female body. The experience of disability must be moved from the margins of feminist theory to the centre – a movement that has the potential to transform both the centre and the margins: to transform conceptualization of the normal female body. We need an interrogation of feminist theory of the body from a disability perspective as well as a feminist interrogation of disability theory.

How could feminist thought be useful to disability?

A gendered theory of disability starts from the premise of questioning the unproblematized normal female body. Clearly a return to disability as biology and some essentialist notion of the disabled body as deficient is neither theoretically useful nor politically strategic. Uncontrollable biology has been the excuse for gendered harm done to disabled women in the form of forced sterilizations and hysterectomies. Yet the socially constructed disabled body does not adequately account for the totality of the trauma and suffering of impairment, the subjective experience – for example negotiating pain, spasticity, incontinence and the iatrogenic effects of drugs and appliances (Crow, 1992; French, 1993a).

The social-constructionist approach to female embodiment suggests that 'it is not biology per se but the ways in which the social system organizes and gives meaning to biology that is oppressive to women' (Grosz, 1994, p. 17). Disability theorists, following feminism's rejection of biology as the determining factor in the making of the gendered or racialized body, have similarly rejected biology as the determining factor in the making of the disabled body. They have questioned the dominance of the medical and rehabilitation paradigms which seek to transform and normalize, indeed 'cure' the disabled body. Arguing that the disability/ability dichotomy as grounded in biological functioning or lack of functioning is fallacious has been a significant political and theoretical advance. But social constructionists of disability tend to assume a fixed embodiment – a fixed, static disability. This approach raises a number of issues, in particular for women with disabilities, who are more likely than men to experience degenerative conditions such as multiple sclerosis and arthritis. So, for example, socially constructed disability does not explore a changing body image or identity and functioning. Here the disabled woman must continually renegotiate the relationship between body, self *and* socially constructed disability.

The social-constructionist view of disability is in danger of maintaining dichotomies of nature/culture and mind/body; denying human agency in dealing with impairment. Focusing only on the disabling affects of a prejudiced and discriminatory society with a political project geared to changing institutions, beliefs and practices leaves the impaired body as untouched, unchallenged: a taken-for-granted fixed corporeality. Changing body identities remain unexplored as do notions of 'passing'. Many disabled people search for solutions which may improve or remove their impairment to improve their bodily functioning to achieve harmony between body and mind in distress. This is not simply because people with acquired disabilities feel alienated from or confined by their bodies. It reflects philosophical inheritances of the constraints of the mind/body opposition.

The rigid dualism of either a socially constructed disability or a disability grounded in biology is being disputed in the subjective discourse – the lived experience. Charmaz's and Rose's descriptive accounts of the daily experiences of people living with chronic pain and illness and increasing disability moves into the realm of cultural analysis where the experience faces personal interpretation and processing into a system of meaning and what Rose calls the 'agon' of daily life (Charmaz, 1991; Rose, 1995). Conceptions of embodied subjectivity hold promise for valorising disabled people; disability as bodily deficit becomes undermined.

Rather than positioning those whose narratives seek to resist or moderate disability status (see for example Monks and Frankenberg, 1995) in opposition to those proposing a socially constructed disability, a political project that transforms both meanings attached to disability and the disabled body itself, takes us beyond crude dualisms. The embodied experience of disabled people leads to contesting normalcy on many fronts – sexuality, political representation and power, the meaning of work, medical practices – as well as contesting the very meanings of body identity.

Associations of women as nearer to nature and more in touch with the body are paralleled in the public imagination of disabled people. The work of feminists of colour has similarly highlighted the physicality of racist discourses, where black bodies are symbolized as animalistic. Thus, women or disabled people or racialized (black) people find themselves on the same side of the (wrong) divide. Bodily control or fear of difference and allusions to uncivilized nature must be seen as common themes in the history of oppressed peoples.

Normalization of disabled female bodies

Both state regulatory institutions and patriarchal structures are involved in the normalization of the disabled female body. Divergent contemporary theories of normalization are rarely together in an examination of the disabled body. The Foucauldian theory of normalization emerges out of cultural and social theory, while in mainstream rehabilitation theory models of normalization and social role valorization used extensively in the USA and Australia focus on integration into the wider society of people with disabilities (Wolfensberger, 1970; 1995). Understanding the impact of these 'training models' clarifies the processes of normalizing the disabled body.

A Christmas appeal letter from the Multiple Sclerosis Society of New South Wales featured a woman – Anna – who wants to be 'tied to the kitchen sink' – given the opportunity to be a 'normal' housewife. Here, according to the Wolfensberger model of normalization, opportunities are being opened up, while a Foucauldian analysis suggests a policing of the disabled body. Anna is being normalized into a housekeeping and caretaking role: cooking and home maintenance; this role reflects a crucial characteristic of the normalization discourse – 'the conservativism corollary'. A different reading would suggest that Anna is being 'helped' to internalize the dominant ideologies of female subordination and exploitation characteristic of patriarchy. 'Emphasizing similarities to the able-bodied ... does not challenge the able-bodied paradigm of humanity' (Wendell, 1989, p. 117).

The deficient female body is also subject to medical intervention. Some have argued that all female bodies are 'disabled' by their deficiencies. The American Society of Plastic and Reconstructive Surgeons stated that 'There is a substantial and enlarging body of medical opinion that these deformities [small breasts] are really a disease' (quoted by Danek, 1992, p. 8). Is elective cosmetic surgery a process of control, colonization and normalization or freeing up and liberating the body? Surgical interventions such as breast augmentation, nose reconstructions, face lifts and tummy tucks may reduce the female body to a machine – the inferior or primitive parts of this machine are thus transformed into a 'femina perfecta' (Morgan, 1991, p. 30). The many disabling and dangerous effects of such surgery have been noted, and many entrants into the Miss America Quests have undergone cosmetic surgery (Morgan, 1991). Entrants in beauty quests are on an assignment – status, power, privilege and the raising of funds for charities for disabled people.

Disabled women are confronted with rehabilitative or corrective surgery: to correct facial disfigurements, to provide artificial prostheses, to straighten deformed body parts, to insert cochlear implants. These processes may be performed under the guise of indispensable medical treatment, but are in fact often designed to normalize the less than perfect body – to make it more attractive and pleasing, to fit dominant conceptions of attractiveness and desirability. Morgan argues against engaging in cosmetic surgery, a political programme of refusal, but also suggests a feminist programme of appropriation for healthy [sic] women to use cosmetic surgery as a means to parody and protest in order to make women 'ugly' and participate in Ms Ugly competitions. Yet she does not expect women who are 'immobilised bodily through physical weakness . . . [to] engage in radical gender performatives of an active public sort, by which the feminist subject is *robustly* constituted' (Morgan, 1991, p. 45) (emphasis added).

This bizarre form of political action, which could be dismissed as utopian fantasy – the ultimate form of body politics – nevertheless raises issues about body ideals for disabled women who see opportunities for their social advancement by engaging in processes of normalization (including cosmetic surgery) which may lead to greater integration or equality. What is the price of such integration?

Regulation and surveillance of disabled female bodies

Disabled women, in greater numbers than disabled men, have been incarcerated in prisons, hospitals, nursing homes and a multitude of institutions. Seen as having no useful role in society and as a burden, they are often warehoused. Disabled and elderly women constitute the majority of residents of nursing homes (Australian Institute of Health and Welfare, 1993, p. 236).

Denial as sexual beings, while being subject to sexual assault and other forms of violence, has ensured a more compliant female population. Forced sterilization and abortion parallel the ideologies and practices of eugenics directed against racial minorities and colonized women, also seen as deficient and unfit to breed. Sterilization, a process of degendering and desexing of disabled women, has taken place in the context of both menstrual management and limiting or preventing the fulfilment of reproductive and mothering roles.

Scott *et al.* (1993) have argued that for some disabled women an impaired ability to evaluate potential threat and to protect oneself against attack makes them more vulnerable to rape. Women suffering from mental illness or developmental disabilities are particularly vulnerable to repeated sexual assault. Research suggests that this situation is compounded in the USA for women of Hispanic origin.

Actual or threatened mutilation and wounding as a form of punishment has long been practised by men against women, and serves as another form of regulation. Although it is a practice now extinct, Lewis (1990) details a practice amongst Tungaru of Micronesia where it was culturally acceptable for a woman's husband to bite off her nose, making her unattractive to other men, in the case of conjugal jealousy. Hatred against the Other is expressed by marking, damaging or violating the body of the Other. Domestic abuse and violence can result in permanent or temporary physical and psychiatric disabilities.

Surveillance of female bodies occurs in public as well as in private spaces. Male comments made to women in the street are a form of harassment and invasion of private space. Disabled women are considered fair game to a variety of inquisitorial comments, remarks and unwanted physical contact. Men traditionally have used public space as if it were their home territory (Gardner, 1980), while women often regard the city streets with fear. For women with disabilities new possibilities have been opened up for 'independent' living in the community. But from moving from the regulated and disciplining world of the institutions, the experience of deinstitutionalization has heralded new forms of normalization in the community.

Conclusions

The process of disabled embodiment can be understood only within historical, cultural and class contexts, along with the gendered and/or racialized body. If the body is a site of political struggle, disabled women are involved in multiple contests which may result in unexpected alliances with dispossessed Others.

First, in the academy, the struggle to position disabled bodily experiences within feminist discourses must be recognized. Second, disabled women, while severely medicalized and normalized, are also agents in their own right, fighting on both ideological and material terrains: for the right to parent, to be accorded bodily status beyond that of burden, arguing for acknowledgement of bodily desires and beauties that do not conform to Western ideals of the feminine. Third, the disabling effects of bodily interventions and conditions that are more likely to affect women than men – early and unnecessary hysterectomies, the effects of drugs more readily administered to women, the connections between socially induced illnesses such as anorexia and later disabilities, and the disabling effects of cosmetic or medical interventions – are all areas for further research. Here feminist interrogation of science, technology and medicine must be of assistance in further elucidating the interconnections between gender, bodies and disability. Finally, utopian technologies should be examined for their liberatory potential as well as exposing their dangers as tools of domination.

> We are *dis-abled*. We live with particular social and physical struggles that are partly consequences of the conditions of our bodies and partly consequences of the structures and expectations of our societies, but they are struggles which only people with bodies like ours experience. (Wendell, 1989, p. 117)

Note

This chapter is dedicated to my precious friend and support person, Pam Benton, who lost her own body battle with cancer on 28 February 1997. In November 1995, sitting on the beach in Coledale, New South Wales, she persuaded me to write again.

Further reading

Davis, K. (1997) *Embodied Practices: Feminist Perspectives on the Body*. London: Sage.

Wendell, S. (1996) *The Rejected Body: Feminist Philosophical Reflections on Disability*. London: Routledge.

12

Understanding Cinematic Representations of Disability

Paul Darke

Cultural, cinematic, images of marginal(ized) social groups – gays, ethnic minorities, women and the disabled – provide an opportunity to identify and deconstruct many of the nuances, trends and the stereotypes constructed in them. Such images offer a measure by which we can identify shifts in social attitudes towards marginalized groups, and an indication of particular sites of resistance to change. Consequently, images matter; for the disabled, images of themselves are especially important as they are presumed by virtually all critics and audiences to be essentially self-evident in the truths they reveal about impairment, the 'human condition' and, as such, disability. In fact, they are as socially constructed, illusionary and functional as any other images (be they of the oppressed or not). Thus, after a brief résumé of other disability imagery writing, I will concentrate on revealing the specificities of a newly identified genre: the *normality drama*.

Disability imagery writing has, to date, been fairly limited in both quantity and scope; with most writing (populist or academic) concentrating on the identification of types and stereotypes – taxonomies of impairment imagery – and arguing that such images fail to represent the reality and/or the social constructionist element of impairment as disability. Longmore (1987), Klobas (1988), Barnes (1992a) and Norden (1994) all detail stereotypes of disability cultural imagery in British and American media: stereotypes such as the 'noble warrior', the 'charity cripple', the 'curio', the 'freak' and the 'Pollyanna'. Each writer's stereotype label(s) is/are different, as is the number identified, but all share a feeling of persistent 'disapproval' of whatever they see. Other writers, notably Schuchmann (1988), on images of Deafness, and Morris (1992), on images of disabled women, follow a similarly taxonomical methodological approach and, as such, have been equally reductive. Cumberbatch and Negrine (1992) have carried out an interesting statistical analysis of images of disability and although it was primarily of television imagery its lack of disability theory does not weaken its significance in identifying the prevalence with which disability is represented either in a medical context or as something which one 'bravely' overcomes in the struggle to be 'normal'.

Norden (1995) is significant in that, in identifying specific stereotypes and their prevalence in different cinematic eras, he has shown how the socio-political and economic factors in any given nation and period are key factors in what types of stereotypes are prevalent in particular cultural images. For example, he argues that following the Second World War images of impairment were more normalizing and 'rehabilitative' owing to the high number of returning disabled veterans (and, significantly, the war experiences of the writers and directors of such images); he then goes on to show how many of the writers and directors of such normalized images of impairment were key targets of the McCarthy witch-hunts, which when combined with the national fear of the Cold War (difference) meant that images of impairment soon resorted back to being of a more 'freakish' nature.

Davis (1995), writing about images of Deafness on film and in the canons of English literature, has tried to get away from mere classification and has moved on to the identification of the social, national and political significance of such images to argue that they, in total, are the result of the social construction of normality; a construction that has resulted in the need for the construction of abnormality as a means of social, national and political order. For example, Davis persuasively demonstrates how sign language was marginalized in the eighteenth century as a means of maintaining clearly defined national cultures and boundaries in the face of the threat of the potentially universal language of Sign. Hevey (1992) has tried to show, somewhat confusingly in many instances, the role charity images have had in the perpetuation of the disablement of impaired people; arguing that they tap into, amongst other things, a 'normal' psychological fear of bodily decay and death. The problem with criticism which advances a generalized psychological rationale for a presumed negative imagery of impairment is that it fails to account for the fact that not all societies and people see impairment as essentially negative. Equally such criticism reinforces the ideals of there being a normal psychological state of mind; as dubious an argument as that used to justify the falsehood of the normal body.

One of the key problems with 'disapproving' disability imagery writing and the simple identification of stereotypes (which are, in fact, social archetypes; an identification that is no less constructed but which explains their persistence and resistance) is that it falls into what Macheray (1978) labelled the 'normative fallacy'. It is a fallacy to argue that there is a 'true' way in which certain images can represent impairment and disability; apart from the fact that there is no universally 'true' way anything can be represented, it is even more pernicious that most disability imagery writers insist on more 'normalized' images of impairment: images which they consider to be 'positive'. I would argue that such images validate not difference but normality, the very illusion at the heart of the oppression of disabled people. It is quite bizarre that disabled writers argue that images which negate difference in favour of normality and conformity are 'positive'. One suspects that such a perspective reveals more about the writer's social and attitudinal position than it does about disability.

Fortunately writers, some of those already discussed and new ones, on disability imagery are beginning to move away from simple classification and disapproval and on to a more synthesized way of looking at images of disability which is multi-disciplined; many writers now combine cultural, literary, feminist, sociological, discursive and disability theory (in any combination) in a significantly more coherent and astute manner which is revealing more of their meaning, as well as their number, power, pleasure and coherence. It is often written that disabled people are not represented on film or on television, that they are invisible; the opposite is true. As Norden and Davis have shown, they are everywhere in cinematic and literary forms and in large numbers; Davis even goes so far as to argue that the notion of abnormality is in every thing, if not in actuality. Where I disagree with many of the writers, and Davis in particular, is that the use of abnormality in cultural imagery (primarily in films) is not haphazard, it is quite coherent; nor is it the by-product of the social construction or illusion of normality. Quite the opposite: abnormality is used in cultural imagery to define the parameters of normality, not vice versa; it creates the simulacrum through which most apparently 'normal people' live their lives. Thus, there is a coherence, I feel, to disability imagery that has been ignored through a failure to see the role abnormality plays in creating normality; through creating the illusion of normality out of the apparent reality of abnormality. The easiest and most coherent way to carry out such a social construction is in the most pleasurable and entertaining form of the genre.

The normality genre

When one thinks of a film genre it is usually Western or film noir, or perhaps even horror films, not a normality drama; a genre, I will argue, that specifically uses abnormal – impaired – characters to deal with a perceived threat to the dominant social hegemony of normality. The normality drama follows its own genre conventions: a physically or mentally impaired character is represented to reinforce the illusions of normality: a normality exhibited either in a film's non-impaired characters or by the impaired character's rejection of their impaired self.

Equally the normality drama initially, and superficially, represents disorder and chaos – abnormality – so that order and stability can be created in the denouement of the narrative thrust; thereby providing both entertainment and a simple resolution to the highly complex social 'problem' of abnormality and disability. Even though the resolution for a normality drama's central abnormal character can vary in a range of specific narrative actualities (ranging from suicide to integrated normalization to an acceptance of segregation), the model of disability followed is always within a medical-model paradigm; logically so, if the discursive aim of the drama or narrative is constructed (either consciously or subconsciously) in order to reinforce and reaffirm the perceived social supremacy of normality. The key elements of a medical-model representation of disability concentrate on impairment (abnormality) as an individual, pathological, problem to be either overcome or eradicated; the social elements of impairment (i.e. disability) are almost totally absent. Thus, such representations are often very literal and place the impaired character in a medical (hospital) setting even though they are not 'ill' or dealing with a specific medical issue. Equally one of the least problematic ways in which to individualize an impairment narrative is to produce a story that claims to be based on, or from, a 'true story', or a simple biopic (such as *My Left Foot, Born on the Fourth of July* and *The Story of Alexander Graham Bell,* amongst hundreds of others) – though even then the narrative is often more false than true in even the simplest facts, as Custen (1992) and Darke (1994) have shown in biopics in general and in disability biopics respectively.

Along with references to other writers on genre, my key textual reference is, ironically, Rick Altman's seminal work on *The American Film Musical* (1987). In this classic text he gives a definitive breakdown of the elements that make up a genre, in general, when he writes that they are: dualistic; repetitive; cumulative; predictable; nostalgic; symbolic; and functional. Other elements are also at play in the genre, as Altman (and others) show, and I will deal with them below, prior to a detailed utilization of Altman's theory: i.e. the role of the audience, and the capitalist film industry's necessity for genres. My use of Altman's work, on the Hollywood musical genre, is ideal as it is an examination of a genre, and this is the irony, that it is unique in its exclusion of either physically or mentally abnormal characterizations. I would argue that such an exclusion is mainly due to dance being culturally perceived as, to paraphrase Irene Castle (cited by Cohan and Hark, 1993), the pure language of the body; a language that is so ritualistic and socially exclusive that to incorporate or include the mute bodies of the impaired would create such an anomie in the genre that its entertainment value would decrease and initiate a generic cachexy. This is not to say that dance and impairment do not go together – the mixed-ability dance troupe CanDoCo have shown that not to be the case – only that the generic expectations that are ideologically embedded in the musical genre are the antithesis of equality in difference; the musical is dance's apotheosis: equality in uniformity and conformity or, to use a musical phrase, harmony.

Not all films that have an impaired character in them are normality dramas; the normality drama specifically revolves, narratively speaking, around a central or key character with an impairment and their experience, and that of those around them, of that impairment. Prime examples are films such as *My Left Foot* and *Annie's Coming Out* (cerebral palsy); *Passion Fish*, *The Waterdance*, *The Raging Moon* and *Born on the Fourth of July* (paraplegia); *Breaking the Waves* and *Whose Life Is It Anyway?* (quadriplegia); *Children of a Lesser God* and *Johnny Belinda* (Deafness); *Pride of the Marines* and *Torch Song* (blindness); *The Best Years of Our Lives*, *Johnny Got His Gun* (amputation/war injury); *The Elephant Man* (bodily deformity); and *Rain Man* and *The Eighth Day* (mental impairment).

Many other films, which may also be members of other genres but which also deal with a significant character's experience of impairment, can be included in the normality drama genre; for example *Moby Dick* (amputee); *Freaks* (deformity/restricted growth); *The Story of Alexander*

Graham Bell and *The Tingler* (Deafness); *Monkey Shines* (quadriplegia); *Midnight Cowboy* (limp due to TB); *The Small Back Room* (amputation due to war injury); and *The Hunchback of Notre Dame*. A full list would run to hundreds of films, covering a wide range of impairments over a considerable period of time, drawing on many other different generic forms, from all over the world. It is quite surprising that no other film-writer has yet seen a genre form where there is so obviously one; though this may be partly explained by the placing of many normality dramas in the genre of medical drama (a literalization of the medical model of disability makes the point less open to misinterpretation); but it is equally likely to be due to the tendency in film criticism to see impaired characters on film as self-evidently abhorrent and/or as archetypal truths about the 'human condition'.

There are other films, that often fit in to other genres (especially horror films, for example), which represent their impaired characters so superficially that they are merely skimpily drawn stereotypes who are simply adding a touch of generic colour; 'types' which give atmosphere and draw a line of simple classification (Dyer, 1993) between who is good in the narrative and who is bad. As, for example, in the Western *The Good, the Bad and the Ugly* (an amputee) or the horror film *I Don't Want To Be Born* (a character of restricted growth). Equally such films' abnormal characters place disability within the medical model, and they reinforce the film's normal central character's (heroic) normal-ness, but their marginalization within the narrative ensures that they remain ciphers rather than anything of intentional wider social sig-nificance; their symbolic nature is directed to that individual film's resolution rather than a wider social resolution. The normality drama's impaired central character has a much wider social significance in that they offer a clear solution to a wider social, non-narrative-specific situation – the classification and taxonomy of disabled people's relative worth, and of each specific film's definition of good or bad normality and abnormality. As Neale (1980) has written, genre specificity does not have exclusive use of an element but greater use of specific ele-ments; it has a greater degree or prevalence of an element. The normality drama is not the sole user of any given normal or abnormal elements – in this case impairment – but it uses them in a more detailed, developed and distinctive manner. For example, in a medical drama genre film, such as the Dr Kildare series of films of the 1940s, the doctor's life is the key element in the narrative even though he may deal with one or many impaired, though more often 'sick', characters; the impaired character is supernumerary or functional in the narrative to push it along.

Many films of the normality drama genre are, wrongly, attributed to the genres of the medical drama, or the realist chronological tradition of the classic Hollywood narrative (Bordwell and Thompson, 1993), or labelled as mere melodramas. Again this is partly explainable by the failure of film writers in the past to see representations of impairment as anything other than axiomatic truths. Part of the problem of genre analysis is that early definitions of what a genre is were, and often still are, fairly vague in themselves and have an emphasis, simply put, on repetition of style, function, content and narrative situation; views which range from the work of Aristotle to Todorov to Fry and most other literary critics (cf. Dubrow, 1982; Palmer, 1978). Though Fry does provide a useful insight into the cultural significance and nature of genres when he writes that a genre is a series of echoes across the space between texts, perceived by the reader if he is sufficiently 'cultivated' (cited by Palmer, p. 124); echoes, in the normality drama, of an audience's social culturation into the medical model of impairment perspective that views disability as abject and abhorrent, and which equally valorizes normality.

Todorov made an equally significant point when he wrote that 'for there to be a transgression [in a genre text], the norm must be apparent' (cited by Dubrow, p. 100). Todorov's insight provides us with the answer to the question of why I call the genre the normality drama genre rather than *impairment*, or *disability*, or *abnormality* genre. What is at stake in films that have, superficially, impairment or disability as their central theme is not the impairment or the abnormality but the degree to which it can either define or validate its opposite: normality. Thus, when in a film such as *My Left Foot* (the story of Christy Brown) the key character triumphs over the personal tragedy of their situation, two explicit generic themes are clear: first, that the state of abnormality is nothing other than tragic because of its medical implications; and, second, that the struggle for normality, or some semblance of it in normalization – as represented in the film by the other characters – is unquestionably right owing to its axiomatic supremacy. The same is true of a film like *Whose Life Is It Anyway?*, even though the finale is quite different: a film in which a newly impaired character with quadri-plegia fights for the right to die and succeeds. Here normality is

validated by the tragedy of having an impairment along with a perceived inability to achieve any degree of normalization; thus, again,
normality is reinforced as superior and abnormality is made abject in
comparison through the representation of all the other 'normal' characters in the drama. The point of the drama is about the relative worth of
being, or striving to be, normal rather than abnormal; the logical
corollary is that the audience leave satisfied as their own attitudes and
conformist lives are validated at the expense of that group who are as
equally marginalized in society as they are in films (Barnes, 1991b;
1992a). Thus the genre is more properly a normality drama rather than
an abnormality drama as its specificities are driven, and determined, by
normality rather than vice versa.

Two other points need to be made to clarify why disability criticism
of normality dramas is often reduced to naive whingeing over a film's
negative or positive representation of disability and the use of stereotypes or archetypes. Often disability film criticism is highly reductive
and examines the impaired character in isolation from the rest of the
characters in a film – an error as, if my hypothesis is right, they are given
their relative worth in comparison to the film's other characters, both
normal and abnormal, only in order to define and validate normality.
Concomitantly, on that basis, they can never be positive because they
are rooted within a medical-model paradigm and merely there to
valorize what they are not. The call for positive images (which is in
reality a call for only pseudo-normal images of abnormality) is not only
a retrograde step but positively damaging to the valuation of difference
(the disabled) in the future. The call should be for the valuation of
difference (abnormality) in itself, as only then will the illusion that
normality is a reality be laid to rest. Equally the reason why so many
disabled people can enjoy a normality drama and its use of impairment
stereotypes is because, as Oakes *et al.* (1994) have clearly shown,
stereotypes do reflect inter-group relations. Such an argument does not
mean that stereotypes or archetypes are true in any literal sense; it
merely stresses that stereotypes reflect the realities of social interaction
between the group that creates a stereotype and the stereotyped. In
investigating impairment stereotypes we should move away from discussing their relative accuracy, as they are not accurate and that is not
the point; the only way that we, as the disabled, can either challenge or
appropriate those images is by showing how they reflect the realities of
social integration and how that subsequently denigrates the stereotyped

(the disabled) and validates the stereotypers (the non-disabled). Arguing for more normalized images of disabled people not only plays into the hands of the normality drama and its ideological thrust but it also detracts from identifying that the stereotypes do reflect a real social reality: the negation of the abnormal in the process of perpetuating a fantasy of normality.

Before going into a detailed appropriation of Altman's work to justify my stance that there is a normality drama genre I will quickly mention the audience/industry capitalist paradigm (cf. Neale, 1987); a paradigm which, I would argue, supports my contention of the identification of a new genre for most films about people with impairments. An appreciation of the audience/industry paradigm provides an understanding of the resilience of the genre in the face of the call for change by the politically active disability lobby and the emergence and acceptance of the social model of disability. The audience/industry-paradigm argument is that, owing to the needs of production capital, genres are essential as they virtually guarantee a level of return on initial investment capital as they are a tried and tested box-office performer; similar films have been made in the past and performed well. Thus genres usually go in cycles as they appear to be a proven way of increasing potential capital investment returns. For example, the gangster films of the 1930s, film noir of the 1940s, the musicals of the 1950s, the exploitation films of the 1970s, the explosive blockbusters of the 1980s and the costume dramas of the 1990s: genres which often remake similar stories over and over again until they make the genre nothing other than repetitious, eventually killing its profitability.

Genre films provide a less risky capital investment opportunity as – and this is the audience's part in the paradigm – paying customers have shown repeatedly that they are likely to go and see a specific genre's films consistently; after all, we all say: 'I love Westerns'; 'Those gangster films are the best'; and 'Give me a good comedy any day'. The audience's investment in the film – buying a ticket – is equally secure if they know the boundaries of the picture by its inclusion in a generic type; thus the audience's desire for generic classification is as essential as it is for the capitalist investors in its production. Neale (1980) writes that 'genres are not to be seen as forms of textual codification, but as systems of orientation, expectations and conventions that circulate between industry, text and subject' (p. 19). Significantly Neale has left out one key circulatory element that I believe is essential to an understanding of all genres, and not just the normality drama, and that is the role of society in the making and reception of any genre film. We do not consume or interpret cultural artefacts, such as films, in a vacuum as individual subjects but as social and cultural beings with many shared views which we bring with us as our social baggage: a baggage which not only effects our readings but affects our cultural sense of self, and the place of the self, in any given society. Thus, for a largely 'normal' audience viewing a normality drama, an able-bodied audience's cultural and social baggage will be almost exclusively rooted in the socially hegemonic interpretation of impairment as a medical and individual 'problem' to be either overcome or eradicated (Oliver, 1991; 1996), along with a belief in normality.

Genre films are as reassuring to the capitalist production system as they are to the audience; you know what you are paying to see before you have even seen it, even though you may not know the exact story or the twists it may make along the way (if you do, then it becomes boring and 'played out'). Equally they are entertainment and, as Dyer (1992) has written, entertainment provides simplistic answers in the simplistic world of the cinematic experience; the complexities of the real world are supplanted by a cinematic one and made manageable for the audience. The representation of impairment in a normality drama is no different: it provides a simplistic answer to a socially complex issue in a rarefied world where problematic nuances are erased in favour of obdurate simplicity. The normality drama obviates disability – the societal and audience's role in the oppression of the impaired – from the narrative to a clearer and less messy paradigm rooted in the socially prevalent interpretation of impairment that currently exists: a medical model that individualizes (another generic tendency as identified by Hill, 1986) and perniciously offers itself up as an arbiter of truth.

The audience of a normality drama will, by and large, consider itself to be 'normal', and, as such, will seek solace (and perhaps even a cathartic or Rabelaisian (Bakhtin, 1984) experience) from a film that reinforces the everyday 'common sense' (which Gramsci (cited in Forgacs, 1988) has shown to be an equally bourgeois social construction) that the audience will bring to a film about an individual with an impairment. The fact that Western culture rhetorically perpetuates, primarily in its cultural artefacts, the illusion of disability as a personal tragedy or triumph story, rather than a socio-economic and political issue, serves only to encourage film-makers and film audiences to make and interpret a (any) film in such a light. The normality drama genre fulfils both the audience's expectations and needs as well as the industry's need for reduced risk; there can be no other reason for the success of the genre over the entire history of cinema (cf. Norden, 1994; Barnes, 1992a; Longmore, 1987; and, in relation to literature, Davis, 1995); especially if considered alongside the cyclical nature of many other genre forms (see above). Equally the normality drama reassures the industry and audience that impairment is interpreted both by themselves and society at large in the correct way: the medical way. The cultural knowledge an audience, primarily in Western culture, brings to a normality drama defines both the ideological intent – and, as such, any possible interpretation – of the genre and the way in which it is constructed (to the extent that it would be illogical and irrational to expect it to be any other way).

If we accept the existence of the normality drama as a prevalent and widespread genre then we can start to understand the desire to interpret the narratives and form of the genre as indicative of some psycho-social human attribute predisposed to make the impaired the 'Other', or 'dustbins of disavowal', and 'liminal' beings (cf. Morris, 1992; Hevey, 1992; Fiedler, 1978; Murphy, 1987; and summarized in Shakespeare, 1994c). There is no essential need on behalf of the 'normal' for the impaired to be disabled; what there is, though, is a desire to rationalize culturally the social disablement of the impaired on behalf of individual society's members and society as a whole – bringing us back to the stereotypes of impairment reflecting a social reality. Consequently cultural images rationalize the social construction of marginalized groups as Other, liminal or abject; they are not essentialist psychological acts but attempts to rationalize in cultural artefacts those social constructions that seem 'true' but which are mere construction. Thus exclusively medical-model cultural representations of impairment are not due to a 'normal' person's psychological imperative to see them in that way by either film-makers or a film's audience; they are socially constructed and mediated artefacts re-presenting society for society in an entertaining and socially accessible and soothing (ideological) and reinforcing form (i.e. the normality drama).

Disabled people are not represented as liminal in any essentially psychological sense, but as a reflection of their social liminality: neither allowed full citizenship nor completely socially excluded. Thus, they are culturally represented as the Other for exactly the same social reasons: the validation and reinforcement of normality. The nature of entertainment and the generic form makes it easy to see cultural (primarily cinematic) representations of the impaired as dustbins of disavowal but this is also a misinterpretation as it presumes that – owing to their apparently verisimilar representations – such representations are about either the experience or the interpretation of impairment or abnormality. They are not; they are about the social valorization and definition, in a clear and simple way, of normality; it does not matter that normality (or abnormality) does not exist (Canguilhem, 1989) in any psychological or essentialist real way; what matters is that it exists as a social construct, within an almost total consensus, in a largely medical-model nexus.

The stereotypes and archetypes that cultures utilize of impairment in their numerous acts of disabling rebarbative sophism (cf. Barnes, 1992a; Norden, 1994; and Schuchmann, 1988, in relation to images of the Deaf) are intended as socially positive acts in the creation of the illusion of normalcy; an illusion at the root of the medical model which, owing to the non-existence of normality, makes the use of abnormality take on a significance it would not otherwise have. The medical model of social interpretation is about the struggle to define the norm, not the abnormal; thus, the cinematic equivalent is concerned with the struggle to define, and advocate on behalf of, the normal (that which the audience believes itself to be, or struggling to be). The elusiveness of a definitive normality means that the abnormal are press-ganged into the service of the medical model of interpretation and disability – which, in cinematic terms, means the continued omnipresence of the normality drama.

Altman's seven genre characteristics applied to the normality drama

A genre is dualistic. Altman argues that genres set up a binary opposition of cultural norms to values that threaten those norms: they 'oppose cultural values to counter-cultural drives' (Altman, 1987, p. 331). The normality drama does this – epitomized in Hollywood's normality dramas of the post-Vietnam-War period, films such as *Cutter's Way*, *Coming Home* and *Born on the Fourth of July* – by creating within the narrative a choice for the central character between fighting to regain (if the impairment is acquired) – or gain (if it is congenital, as in *My Left*

Foot) – some semblance of normality. A normality as represented in the decency and support of those characters who exist around, and for, the impaired central character. Thus many of the disabled characters in such narratives are bitter, frustrated and unfulfilled and either anti-social or asocial. A narrative is set up so that any specific disabled character's anti-social or anti-normal tendencies must be overcome so that the film's finale of the integration of the impaired can take place (or even the segregation if the anti-normal elements of the impairment cannot be overcome, as in *The Raging Moon* or *The Elephant Man*).

Thus the affirmation of conventional cultural norms over and above any validation or tolerance of significant degrees of difference is stated in a drama that clearly expresses impairment and 'normality' as mutually exclusive, and in opposition, in the scheme of cultural values as expressed in the film. In this genre order, normality and individuality are affirmed at the expense of an acceptance of difference or social diversity expressed and defined earlier in the narrative of any individual normality drama. A particularly insidious way in which many normality dramas make explicit this point is by having a 'good cripple' and a 'bad cripple' in the same film – as in *My Left Foot*, in which other people with cerebral palsy are clearly shown as less 'valid' than Christy Brown by their inability to become as normal as Christy; thus he gets special, individualized, treatment at home. The scene in *Born on the Fourth of July*, where the main disabled character visits a group of drop-out disabled vets in Mexico who use prostitutes, acts in a similar way; our 'hero' returns and becomes a valid member of society: he is, thus, the 'good cripple' who reinforces the norm rather than the values represented by the drop-outs in Mexico. From what I have written it is easy to identify that the cultural norms validated in many normality dramas are those of the status quo as typified by white bourgeois behaviour and morality.

A genre is repetitive. Altman writes of the genre film that 'each new film varies the details but leaves the basic pattern undisturbed' (1987, p. 331). As I have argued, the pattern that remains undisturbed is the validation of the supremacy of the normal at the expense (or destruction, as in those normality dramas that also constitute part of, for example, the horror genre) and negation of the abnormal (the impaired and disabled). The way in which many normality dramas are also members of other genres is clearly indicative of the way in which they vary the detail (horror – *The Mummy*; medical – *Whose Life Is It*

Anyway?; social realist – *A Day in the Death of Joe Egg*; Westerns – *The Proud One*; period – *The Elephant Man*; and comedy – *Dumb and Dumber*).

A genre is cumulative. Altman writes that 'each sequence contributes to the desired overall effect, which is more important than any single dialogue, character or action' (p. 331). The point of this element comes back to my earlier point that one cannot look at an image of disability in isolation from the rest of the characters in any film. This is especially true of supposedly 'positive' images of disability because, even though one image may be superficially 'better', or more 'accurate', than another one, in comparison to the other characters within that narrative the impaired character is still a comparatively second-class citizen in the world of the film. *My Left Foot* is, as always, a prime example: Christy Brown may well be a writer, relatively wealthy and happy, but he is not seen as sexual in any way nor does he have any children – a cultural norm of the film – in the narrative as his peers have.

A genre is predictable. Altman argues that the pleasure of the generic narrative is 'not so much a question of novelty as it is one of affirmation' (p. 332). When one sees a normality drama it is a certainty that the abnormal character will do his or her best to overcome their bodily or mental impairments; if they fail to overcome it they will at least have done their best. Normality dramas do not challenge cultural norms, they reaffirm them both in their predictability and in the specificities of their narratives. The normality drama is predictable within the narrative but also, significantly, in generic total; as all previous normality dramas have reaffirmed a certain set of perceived shared cultural norms (normality as superior to abnormality), the pleasure of, and the reason for, watching them is that they guarantee that reaffirmation over and over again. That is the reason for the success of superficially depressing films such as *My Left Foot, The Elephant Man, Born on the Fourth of July, The Best Years of Our Lives* and many hundreds of other normality dramas.

A genre is nostalgic. For Altman the 'genre film perpetuates the notion that the past was somehow more complete, more rewarding, more exciting than the present' (p. 332). Altman does not simply mean that all genre films take place in the past – though many do for the purpose of clarity – he means that the morality, or even the ideological standpoint, of the film may be atavistic. Prime normality drama examples of this are the pro-assisted-suicide/euthanasia films *Whose Life Is It*

Anyway? and *A Day in the Death of Joe Egg. Whose Life Is It Anyway?* is set in an ultra-modern intensive care unit where people with quadriplegia are 'saved' and 'treated', an activity the film decries in favour of simply letting (encouraging) people with severe disabilities die as they would have done *in the past* prior to the development of the medical technology used to keep such 'vegetables' – to use a term frequently utilized in the film – alive. The point is that, in these normality dramas, apparently severe impairments are beyond normalization and, as such, are represented as a threat to normality; thus they (the disabled in such a position, the film argues) wish to be able to die or be killed for the benefit of society to remove the burden that they are made out to be; independent living is not an option in these films. *Joe Egg* is less subtle; it simply mocks the current possible ideals of the integration of the disabled by stressing the futility of such a course of action as both unrealistic and burdensome. It then highlights the 'right' course of action – as the film labels it – that Hitler and the Third Reich (one presumes in the good old days of absolute medical hegemony as in 1930s Germany) took in the management of the disabled: mass forcible euthanasia. Even a film that does not seem to be literally nostalgic – *The Waterdance* for example – often is in how it treats the acquisition of the impairment or the significance of it.

A genre is symbolic. Altman writes that 'the genre film cries out for wider interpretation' (p. 333). The normality drama, by its affirmation, and construction, of normality over and in comparison to abnormality raises the question of what it is to be normal and abnormal: alive. Thus the symbolic nature of the normality drama, and most other genre films for that matter, is often viewed as being about the 'human condition' or the tragedy of human existence. Thus they often create heroes, or anti-heroes, and role models as examples of what to do when we, as members of the audience, face real-life impairment or abnormality scenarios or situations. In the case of the normality drama the role model tells the audience they must try to reassert, and regain, as much of their normality to be valid human beings: i.e. overcome what is represented as the personal tragedy of disability. Many of these normality drama films end with a cure: *Monkey Shines*; *Blink* and *Night Song* (as in many normality dramas about visual impairment); and *Extreme Measures*. Conversely, if one cannot be normalized in a satisfactory way one should be altruistic and remove the burden from society by asking for, or advocating and seeking, death as a merciful release for everyone concerned – as in *The Elephant Man, Joe Egg, Whose Life Is It Anyway?* and *Duet for One*.

A genre is functional. Altman states that the 'genre film asks the questions and solves problems [*that is its function*] which society has thrust aside because it refuses or is unable to handle them. The first step in understanding the functional role of a Hollywood genre [*any genre*] is thus to isolate the problems for which the genre provides a symbolic answer' (p. 334, my italic insertions). The advancement of euthanasia and assisted suicide in the face of impairment is a good example of a subject that society fails to deal with in any coherent sense but which is dealt with in many normality dramas (as stated above); in normality dramas there is no equivocation on what should be done (as abnormality is represented as inherently abject). The entertainment element of the genre (any genre) means that it simplifies and eradicates any thing or nuance that might cloud an issue or make a specific narrative's point seem questionable. The normality drama is no different: it ignores the disability movement's demands, and new insights on the social construction of impairment as disability, in order to erase any doubt that its view, the medical model, is the right view. This is seen in *Whose Life Is It Anyway?*, when independent living, an equally valid alternative to life-long hospitalization, is never raised; if it were it would undermine the narrative, and the ideological thrust, of the entire film.

Conclusion

If we accept my argument of the existence of the normality drama, following on from the above, it is apparent that the question, or issue, that the genre deals with in a clear and concise manner – which is unambiguously a negation of ascribing any real social or individual value to the impaired or abnormal, and which society at large equally refuses to address – is: Why does society disable the impaired and the abnormal in the way it does? The normality drama provides the answer in a consistent, seemingly logical and rational way, and in an apparently truthful form and manner while remaining entertaining. The normality drama's function is to state that society does what it does because the impaired and the abnormal are not normal: conversely, the depiction of the abnormal Other reinforces the normality of the audience itself.

Further reading

Norden, M. (1995) *The Cinema of Isolation: A History of Physical Disability in the Movies*. New Brunswick, NJ: Rutgers University Press.

Pointon, A., with Davies, C. (eds) (1997) *Framed: A Disability Media Reader*. London: BFI Publications.

Schuchmann, J. (1988) *Hollywood Speaks: Deafness and the Film Entertainment Industry*. Chicago: University of Illinois Press.

Part Three

Debates and Dialogues

13

Multiple Oppression and the Disabled People's Movement

Ayesha Vernon

The hegemonic discourse is an established concept of 'normality'. In Western society this is defined as being 'able-bodied/minded', white, male, heterosexual, young and financially secure. Consequently, disabled people are rendered Other ('abnormal' and inferior) to non-disabled people (Shakespeare, 1994c), Black people to white (Miles, 1989) and women to men (de Beauvoir, 1949). Thus, those who deviate from the established norm in more than one way – for example, disabled Black people – are rendered multiply Other (Vernon, 1996d).

The social model of disability, which locates the problem of limitations experienced by people with impairments in society, rather than with impaired individuals (UPIAS, 1976; Oliver, 1990), has led to increasing research documenting the extent of disadvantage experienced by disabled people both socially and economically (Barnes, 1991b). The experience of disablism has been compared to the experience of racism and sexism (Abberley, 1987; Baxter, 1989). More recently, questions have been raised about disabled people who experience racism (Begum, 1992b; 1994a; Confederation of Indian Organisations, 1984; Sharma and Love, 1991; Stuart, 1992; 1994), sexism (Fine and Asch, 1988; Hanna and Rogovsky, 1991; Lloyd, 1992; Lonsdale, 1990; Morris, 1989; 1991; 1996), heterosexism (Corbett, 1994; Hearn, 1988a; 1988b; 1991) and ageism (MacFarlane, 1994; Zarb and Oliver, 1993).

It has been argued that disabled Black people experience a 'double disadvantage', that of being Black in a racist and disabled in a disablist society (Confederation of Indian Organisations, 1984). Similarly, disabled gay men and lesbians have talked of experiencing 'dual oppression' (Hearn, 1988a; 1988b; 1991). Hearn reported that her lesbianism is negated on account of her being rendered asexual because of her impairment – which is a common experience of many disabled people whatever their sexuality (Shakespeare *et al.*, 1996). Corbett (1994) argues that disabled gay men and lesbians experience a form of 'double invisibility' because they feel that 'I am invisible in the lesbian and gay community as a disabled person, as lesbians and gays are in the straight community and I feel I am invisible as a lesbian in the disability community' (p. 355). MacFarlane (1994) states: 'becoming an older person is one thing, but becoming an older disabled person, especially, a woman, is quite another issue'.

Recently disabled Black people have applied the concept of 'simultaneous oppression' to their own position, rightly arguing that previous analyses of their experience, which were additive, have been inadequate (Begum, 1994; Stuart, 1993). Simultaneous oppression, in this instance, refers to the fact that disabled Black people's realities are shaped by racist and disablist structures at the same time. Stuart (1993, p. 99) assumes the primacy of racism in the experience of disabled Black people when he concludes that their experience is 'distinct' from that of white disabled people. However, racism is neither more nor less prominent than disablism in the experience of disabled Black people (Vernon, 1996b).

There are important similarities as well as differences in the experience of all disabled people regardless of 'race', gender, sexuality, age and class. Henderson (1992) describes the position of Black women as follows:

> Through the multiple voices that enunciate her complex subjectivity the black woman not only speaks familiarly in the discourse of Others but as Other she is in a contestorial dialogue with the hegemonic dominant and subdominant or ambiguously non-hegemonic discourses. As such, black women enter into testimonial discourse with black men as blacks, with white women as women, and with black women as black women. At the same time, they enter into a competitive discourse with black men as women, with white women as blacks, and with white men as black women.

Similarly, disabled Black people struggle altogether with disabled white people against disablism while they also struggle against the racism of white disabled people and as Black Other, they struggle altogether with

Black non-disabled people against racism while they also struggle against the disablism of Black people. The same is true of disabled women's and gay men's and lesbians' experience in that they, too, struggle altogether with other disabled people against disablism while they also struggle against the sexism and heterosexism of other disabled people as, indeed, they do in mainstream society which is a commonality they also share with non-disabled women, gay men and lesbians, older people and those from the working class. In other words the reality of being rendered a multiple Other results in shared alliances as well as oppositional interests between different groups of Others.

A fundamental dilemma rooted in oppression is that there are very few pure oppressors or pure victims. Even those who are themselves oppressed often consciously and unconsciously engage in the oppression of others who deviate from the established norm in a different way from them. Hill-Collins (1990), writing in the American context of Black women's experience, captures this reality succinctly for all oppressed groups when she uses the term 'bothstand conceptual stance' to refer to an analysis of a situation in which

> all groups possess varying amounts of penalty and privilege in one historically created system. In this system, for example, white women are penalised by their gender but privileged by their race. Depending on the context, an individual may be an oppressor, a member of an oppressed group, or simultaneously oppressor and oppressed. (p. 225)

The same is also true of disability, age and sexuality (Vernon, 1997a). Thus those who are a multiple Other are also frequently an Other within an Other (Vernon, 1996d).

Furthermore the experience of simultaneous oppression is not unique to disabled Black people. Disabled women also have to contend with the simultaneity of disability and gender stereotypes (Fine and Asch, 1988; Lloyd, 1992; Lonsdale, 1990; Morris, 1991). Similarly, disabled gay men and lesbians, older people and those from the working class all experience the simultaneity of disablism and heterosexism and/or ageism and/or classism. However, the concept 'simultaneous oppression' is inadequate in explaining the day-to-day reality of those who are rendered a multiple Other as it overlooks the complex and often variable interaction between different forms of social oppression (Vernon, 1997a). Disability, 'race', gender, sexuality, age and class are not invariably experienced at the same time on a daily basis.

Oppression is rife in all human encounters (Brittan and Maynard, 1984). Hence the stigma (Goffman, 1968b) of being impaired and Black and/or female and/or gay and/or older and/or working-class interacts in variable and complex ways in shaping people's daily experience so that they do not only experience the simultaneity of institutional discrimination prevalent in our society against all oppressed groups. We live in a society which is implicitly hierarchical with one dominant group and several subdominant groups who define 'normality' according to their own interests so that there are degrees of 'normality' within one established norm (Hill-Collins, 1990). For example, being heterosexual is 'normal' as opposed to being gay and consequently the privilege of being heterosexual applies to all – men and women, white and Black, non-disabled and disabled people, etc. The same is also true of disability, 'race', gender, age and class. Thus disabled Black people, women, gay men and lesbians, older people and those from the working class (as well as non-disabled people with multiple stigmatized identities), all experience oppression singularly, multiply and simultaneously depending on the context (Vernon, 1996a; 1996d; 1997a). For example, when a disabled Black person is in the company of non-disabled Black people, s/he may experience disablism but not racism. Similarly, when s/he is in the company of white disabled people, s/he may experience racism but not disablism. And, in the labour market, s/he may be refused a job because of the perceived stigma of impairment or 'race' or both.

Therefore the experience of disabled women, Black people, gay men and lesbians, older people and those from the working class is beyond simple parallels. It must not be assumed that, for example, disabled Black people's experience is one of racism plus disablism or that disabled women's experience is sexism plus disablism. Often a combination of two or more stigmatized identities can exacerbate the experience of oppression so that it is more than disablism and sexism and/or racism and/or heterosexism put together (Vernon, 1997b).

Hanna and Rogovsky (1991) talk of disabled women experiencing a form of 'double handicap plus factor' on account of their being female in a patriarchal society, being disabled in a disablist society and being disabled females. As Lonsdale (1990, p. 83) has commented:

women (like men) want to confirm that it is the society which disables and oppresses. But for the women, the discussion is not confined to the modes of economic and social discrimination identified by disabled men. Disabled women are concerned to explore questions of sexuality, and sexual identity to challenge stereotypical images of child bearing and motherhood. Women are simultaneously expected to be sexual play things, responsive, caring and good mothers, physical disability represents a threat to these expectations and roles.

Thus impairment, which is a precondition (although not an inevitable one) of disability, settles upon anyone, but the effect on any individual is very largely modified, minimized or exacerbated by who that person is in terms of their 'race', gender, sexuality, age and class.

Multiple oppression refers to the fact that the effects of being attributed several stigmatized identities are often multiplied (exacerbated) and they can be experienced simultaneously and singularly depending on the context. It also takes account of the fact that the experience of disability or any other form of oppression may be modified by the presence of some privileged identities (for example, being of higher social class status or male).

Disabled people's movement under attack?

In recent years there has been a number of polemical writings expressing a general dissatisfaction that the differing experiences of disabled women (Lloyd, 1992; Morris, 1991; 1996) and disabled Black people (Hill, 1994b; Stuart, 1993) are overlooked by social model theorists because of an overwhelming desire to proclaim commonality in the experience of disablement. For example, Morris (1996) has commented:

> the experience of disabled women has been largely absent from feminism's concerns and within the disabled people's movement has tended to be tagged on as a special interest . . . Our encounters with both groups have often made us feel powerless for we have either been treated as invisible or our experiences have been defined for us. (p. 1)

Campbell and Oliver (1996) assert that the disabled people's movement has not so much ignored these issues out of a deliberate attempt to marginalize the experience of any one group. Rather it has been a 'pragmatic decision' to concentrate on an issue which has been so completely overlooked by other social movements – namely, how society disables people who have impairments. This may, indeed, be the case. However, it is also true, as Morris (1991, p. 178) points out, that 'Disabled people and their organizations are no more exempt from racism, sexism and heterosexism than non-disabled people and their organizations ... both women and ethnic minorities are distinctly under-represented and issues around racism, sexism and sexuality have tended to be avoided.'

Similar critiques also exist with regard to other social movements, particularly the feminist movement (Adams, 1994; Bhavnani and Coulson, 1986; Carby, 1982). Barnes (1996b) has responded to the criticisms made of the disabled people's movement by asserting that

> We live in a society centred around patriarchy, inequality and elitism, and it is inevitable that these traits should be present in our own organizations. But in my experience the British disabled people's movement has done far more than most to address these issues ... the movement has, in fact, been dominated by women ... women have held and continue to hold key posts in most of the organizations up and down the country. (p. 56)

However, the real concern is not whether the disabled people's movement has enough numbers of disabled women or Black people in its organizations. Although, if they are grossly under-represented in proportion to their representation in the surrounding community, then that should also be a legitimate cause for concern. It is the fact that in all the numerous discussions and textbooks on disability, issues of 'race', gender, class, sexuality and age have been either omitted as irrelevant to disabled people's lives or added on as an optional extra.

Hill (1994) argues that disabled Black people should 'keep faith with the Black voluntary sector' rather than with the disabled people's movement. However, this is far from satisfactory (Vernon, 1996b). The assertion that pragmatism dictates a need to concentrate on one oppression at a time is also prevalent in the Black community where the sole emphasis is on overcoming racism, as Macdonald's (1991) experience of his family's reaction demonstrates: 'to fight for the rights of black people is one thing; to fight for the rights of disabled people is something else, there is not enough time and energy to fight two different wars.' Such attitudes present a real dilemma for those who are rendered a multiple Other because, if you cannot be sure that the other Xs, Ys or Zs are going to accept or understand the extra dimension of your additional identity as a V or a W, which aspect of your identity do you prioritize and which do you leave out? The experience of those who are subjected to several forms of oppression cannot be compartmentalized as though they are quite distinct and separate from one another.

Barnes (1996, cited by Campbell and Oliver, 1996) has commented:

> The politics of disablement is about far more than disabled people; it is about challenging oppression in all its forms. Indeed, impairment is not something which is peculiar to a small section of the population it is fundamental to the human experience. Disability – defined by the disabled people's movement as the social oppression of people with impairments – on the other hand, is not. Like racism, sexism, heterosexism and all other forms of social oppression it is a human creation. It is impossible, therefore, to confront one type of oppression without confronting them all and, of course, the cultural values that created and sustain them.

This is indeed true. The politics of eradicating any oppression must take into account the whole oppressive nature of society and challenge all forms of social oppression, not least because of the mutual supporting interaction between different ideologies of oppression (Miles, 1989; F. Williams, 1995), but also because individuals are seldom affected by only one form of oppression.

However, the reality is rather different in that the politics of disability has only ever focused on disablement (the oppression of people with impairments). This is not unique to the disabled people's movement. The fundamental problem is that each oppressed group is really focusing only on a single system of oppression, the nearest to its heart, believing it to be the primary cause of all human suffering. An example is the feminist analysis of patriarchy seeing men's domination of women as the primary oppression and Black people seeing racism as the primary oppression etc. (King, 1988); therefore, overlooking the significant feature of human oppression which is the interlocking of the different ideologies of oppression (Hill-Collins, 1990), especially because individuals seldom fall into one neat category (for example, disabled women, Black middle-class men).

The experience of multiple oppression is treated as though it is an issue which concerns only a minority of disabled people. However, the majority of disabled people inevitably consists of disabled Black people, women, gay men and lesbians, older people and those from the working class, all of whom experience the negative effects of being rendered a multiple Other in consequence of deviating from the established norm in several ways. Consequently they are rejected for several reasons and from several quarters including those with whom they share some commonality (Vernon, 1996d). For example, Dragonsani Renteria, a deaf lesbian from the Hispanic community, has succinctly captured this reality in her poem 'Rejection' (1993, p. 38).

Thus, whilst disability may be the only aspect of disabled white heterosexual men's experience of oppression, the same cannot be said of disabled Black people, women, gay men and lesbians, older people and those from the working class. They can point to no single source for their oppression. For them the potential for discrimination is greater in all situations because of the increased likelihood of one or another aspect of their stigmatized identity being an 'undesired differentness' (Goffman, 1968). Their experience is commonly characterized by multiple rejections, discriminations and fragmentation of their identity even within the equality movements, including the disabled people's movement.

Despite some obvious differences between the experience of disabled Black people and white people, as well as between disabled women and men, etc., there is one critical similarity in the experience of all disabled people arising from the stigma of impairment which often overrides all other boundaries of 'race', gender, sexuality, class and age (Vernon, 1996d).

Because of this, the social model of disability has significance for all disabled people despite the fact that for many disabled people it does not account for the whole of their experience. However, the fault does not lie with the social model of disability, which is an excellent framework for ultimately eradicating the oppression of people who have impairments and, as such, must remain non-negotiable. Rather the problem lies in how the social model is being applied. That is, if the ensuing discussion does not take account of the fact that for the majority of disabled people their experience of oppression is shaped by additional dimensions of their lives, then the application of that methodology needs to be examined, for it represents only a partial picture. For example, if disabled people achieve full civil rights (enshrined in an anti-discrimination legislation which the disabled people's movement is tirelessly campaigning for), we will no longer be barred from entering public buildings, travelling on public transport, denied a job or educational opportunities on the basis of our impairment as we are now. But those of us who are Black, female, gay, etc. will continue to be denied jobs and experience (or live under a constant threat of experiencing) verbal and physical abuse.

There is an underlying assumption which is that the other experiences of disabled people such as racism, sexism and heterosexism are taken care of by other social movements. This would be true. Except that disabled people, because of the stigma of being impaired, are also excluded from the movements of 'race', gender and sexuality. Therefore it is all the more important that the disabled people's movement should not exclude or marginalize the experience of disabled people who are a multiple Other. Furthermore it is all the more important that the experience of disabled Black people, women, gay men and lesbians, older people and those from the working class is fully integrated to take account of the fact that the experience of disability is often exacerbated by the interaction of other forms of oppressions. The politics of eradicating disability, therefore, must take into account the whole oppressive structure of our society and be careful to challenge all forms of oppression wherever it is found. It is not enough merely to acknowledge that, because inequality is rife in society at large, it is inevitable that disabled people will have absorbed these practices too. To do so is to condone and perpetuate all forms of inequality. As Read (1988) points out, in a society that is riddled with oppression there is no neutral ground.

Further reading

Begum, N., Hill, M. and Stevens, A. (eds) (1994) *Reflections: The Views of Black Disabled People on their Lives and Community Care*. London: CCETSW.

Hearn, K. (1991) Disabled lesbians and gays are here to stay, in T. Kaufmann and P. Lincoln (eds) *High Risk Lives: Lesbian and Gay Politics After the Clause*. Bridport: Prism Press.

MacFarlane, A. (1994) On becoming an older disabled woman, *Disability and Society*, vol. 9, no. 2.

Stuart, O. (1993) Double oppression: an appropriate starting point?, in J. Swain, V. Finkelstein, S. French and M. Oliver (eds) *Disabling Barriers – Enabling Environments*. London: Sage and Open University Press.

14

Still Out in the Cold: People with Learning Difficulties and the Social Model of Disability

Anne Louise Chappell

During the last three decades people with learning difficulties have travelled a long way, yet no distance at all. Thirty years ago many people with learning difficulties were neglected in isolated long-stay hospitals. Now they are neglected by the social model of disability which ought to promise them so much in terms of its analysis of their experiences and its strategies for change. This chapter seeks to examine the position of people with learning difficulties within the social model and the reasons for the continuing marginalization of learning difficulty.

For several years the apparently progressive potential of the normalization principle dominated the learning difficulty agenda. Public questioning and criticism of normalization emerged only at the end of the 1980s and early 1990s (see Brown and Smith, 1989; Baxter *et al.*, 1990; Bayley, 1991; Chappell, 1992; 1994a). This critical scrutiny of normalization and challenges to its dominance over community care debates should be regarded as positive steps for people with learning difficulties. Furthermore the emergence of the social model of disability means that there exists a theoretical tool which could assist people with learning difficulties, not just in a struggle for better services (the primary concern of normalization) but for full economic, social and political inclusion in society.

The promise of the social model

However, it is necessary to examine the implications of the social model of disability for people with learning difficulties. There are important questions concerning the continued marginality of learning difficulty within the sociology of disability. The disability movement comprises people with physical or sensory impairments, people with mental illness and people with learning difficulties. Clearly this includes people with a very wide range of impairments who, traditionally, have been classified by the medical model of disability and, therefore, have been defined as having little in common.

There is also great diversity among disabled people on the basis of age, gender, ethnicity, class or sexuality. The concerns about marginality within the social model do not apply solely to people with learning difficulties, but also to disabled women or older disabled people and so on. As Morris argues in the context of the experiences of disabled women: 'within the disabled people's movement, [gender] has tended to be tacked on as a special interest' (1996, p. 1). My worry about the position of learning difficulty within the social model, however, is that it is almost entirely ignored – it hasn't yet even attained the status of a 'special interest'. The danger is then that the analyses which emerge from the sociology of disability are theoretically flawed and their explanatory power is weakened.

In the early 1990s it seemed hopeful that learning difficulty could come to figure more prominently on the agenda of the social model of disability. The analysis of disability presented by the social model is that disability is a social construct created by a range of historically and culturally specific factors. It is the social and economic structures of a particular society which create disability through processes of prejudice, exclusion and discrimination. This explication of disability can apply equally to the experiences of people with learning difficulties or physical or sensory impairments. A brief look at the history of disabled people in Britain points to certain key events which led to the emergence of the long-stay institution:

- the rise of capitalism in Western Europe
- the expansion of state activity into new areas of economic and social life and the emergence of professionals
- the growing influence of eugenicist ideas about the quality of the population.

These factors all combined in the late nineteenth and early twentieth centuries to identify disabled people as a social problem. This was the impetus to develop a system of lifetime segregation for disabled people, regardless of the nature of impairment.

As I have indicated, the social model attempts to encompass the experiences of all disabled people. In so doing it challenges the traditional separation of disabled people from each other. To apply the social model to physical or sensory impairment, but not learning difficulty, seems to me to be akin to suggesting that the analyses of society offered by feminism are applicable only to white women, and that the neglect of the experiences of black women within much feminist writing is because patriarchy has no explanatory power for them. Having said this, nevertheless, the question remains as to why learning difficulty is neglected within the analyses of the social model. What appeared to be the promise of the sociology of disability does not seem to have materialized. The experiences of people with learning difficulties remain as marginal as ever.

My reasons for this worrying conclusion are twofold. First, an examination of the literature produced by writers and academics associated with the disability movement reveals that there is little usage of literature produced by writers concerned with learning difficulty to develop their arguments. The debates about disability appear to be continuing on two parallel tracks with comparatively little cross-fertilization of ideas. There are some exceptions to this general rule. For example, in 1994, Mike Oliver presented a conference paper which used the social model to apply a materialist critique of normalization although, as far as I know, this paper has not been published. Jenny Morris's book *Encounters with Strangers: Feminism and Disability* (1996) includes a chapter about The Powerhouse, a refuge for women with learning difficulties who have experienced physical or sexual abuse. Yet these tend to be the exceptions, and much literature is produced which utilizes the social model but says nothing about learning difficulty. Thus Oliver's sketch of some of the key literature associated with the social model (Oliver, 1996) mentions no writers or debates which are specific to learning difficulty.

Second, the experiences of people with learning difficulties are generally omitted from much of the disability literature, even when those experiences are central to the arguments presented by the author. It appears the best that people with learning difficulties can expect is an implicit inclusion in any writing about disability. Thus some of the arguments emanating from within the social model are assumed to refer to *all* disabled people, when in reality they do not. Such arguments clearly are very partial.

If we accept the premise that the social model of disability can and should include learning difficulty, there is a need to examine why learning difficulty remains so marginal to debates within the disability movement. There are, I think, a number of possible explanations.

Focusing on the body

Much of the disability literature tends to define impairment in terms of the body. There is nothing intrinsic to the word 'impairment' which suggests physical rather than intellectual imperfection. However, the *usage* of the term often suggests that this is so. For example, a perusal of debates about disability and culture illustrates this, because it is images of disabled people which are being examined.

Furthermore there are occasions in the literature where 'able-bodied' is used as the opposite of 'disabled' (for example, French, 1993a). Barnes (1996c, p. 43), for example, writes of the material and cultural forces 'which created the myth of "bodily perfection" or the "able-bodied" ideal'. This would be fair enough if the chapter clearly were about physical or sensory impairment, but it is entitled 'Theories of *disability* and the origins of the oppression of *disabled* people in western society' (emphasis added). The use of the term 'disabled people' should include people with learning difficulties, but often it does not, and their experiences remain hidden.

Hevey (1993) also focuses on physical or sensory impairment in his discussion of the cultural representation of disabled people. He argues that the representation of impairment is based on gazing on the body and portraying this in cultural terms. Bodily imperfection (Oedipus and Richard III are oft-quoted examples) becomes a metaphor for a serious character defect, which entails his (usually his) eventual downfall. Thus, as Hevey argues: 'The history of the portrayal of disabled people is that disabled people are portrayed as flawed able-bodied people' (1993, p. 118). Such an analysis may well be applicable to people with physical or sensory impairments. However, for people with learning difficulties it is more problematic. Here the body is not the site of the impairment: the impairment may not be immediately apparent and nor may it be associated with any physical imperfection.

A similar problem emerges concerning the question of the sexuality of disabled people. The literature here tends to use as its starting point the conventional assumption that disabled people are asexual. This stereotype is assumed to refer to *all* disabled people. Yet for people with learning difficulties there is more than one stereotype of their sexuality. There certainly exists a view that people with learning difficulties are eternal children who never develop an adult sexuality. However, there also is a strong historical association between learning difficulty and powerful images of a very threatening and promiscuous sexuality which must be restrained.

Thus a key factor in the segregation of people with learning difficulties in the early twentieth century was their supposedly threatening sexuality. As Williams (1989) points out, not only did people with learning difficulties fail as workers, they failed as *parents*. Eugenicist concerns of this period were underpinned by fears of trade competition, the struggle for imperial expansion and the immigration of Jews from Eastern Europe. The labelling of people with Down's Syndrome as 'mongols' underscores the link that was made between racial and intellectual inferiority (Booth, 1987).

Such concerns focused attention on people with learning difficulties and the way that their supposedly uncontrollable sexuality, promiscuity and high fertility threatened the moral fibre of society. In particular, it was people with mild or borderline learning difficulty who were seen as being especially dangerous. Their impairments were unrecognizable to the untrained person and, if unchecked, they would be able to merge into wider society and spread their pernicious immoral influence.

It was for this reason, Gelb argues (1987), that the American psychologist Goddard adapted the European Binet test, which attempted to classify different degrees of learning difficulty, so that it was deliberately harsh at the upper end of the scale. The express purpose of doing this was so that the test would pinpoint those with a presumed mental age of 12 years who were defined as having a mild learning difficulty and retarded moral development. At the same time, pseudo-scientific studies were made of the genealogy of so-called deviant families in order to demonstrate that idiocy, moral degeneracy and criminality were all hereditary. The sexuality of people with learning difficulties, therefore, appeared as socially dangerous and this was part of the impetus behind their segregation from society under the terms of the 1913 Mental Deficiency Act.

This is not to suggest that all writing on disability and sexuality excludes learning difficulty. Shakespeare (1996a), for example, notes the vulnerability of people with learning difficulties to sexual abuse. Obviously this is a very serious matter which must be discussed. Nonetheless, it accords with the more general view expressed in the disability literature that disabled people are stereotyped as sexually passive and powerless and it is this which makes them vulnerable to abuse. It does not explore the possibility that some people with learning difficulties may be stereotyped as sexually predatory and dangerous (that is, stereotyped as *abusers*) and experience discrimination on those grounds.

The meaning of impairment

A new area of debate which has been emerging in the disability literature seeks to examine the 'reality' of the experience of impairment. Some writers and academics associated with the disability movement have indicated a concern that the definitions presented by the social model deny that impairment has any relevance. That is, there are no limitations imposed by impairment which cannot be removed by what French refers to as 'social and environmental manipulation' (French, 1993a, p. 22). This debate is sensitive because of the danger that it will be used to reassert individualistic models of disability in which impairment and disability are synonymous (Oliver, 1996; Crow, 1996).

My concern about this debate is its assumption that impairment is located in the body. As Crow argues, 'impairment means the experience of our bodies can be unpleasant or difficult' (1996, p. 209). It is the bodily pain of impairment that is referred to and the body which must be theorized. If the view is accepted that the meaning of impairment must not be denied and that it warrants examination, then this is an important issue for people with learning difficulties too. Yet what happens to the analysis if impairment is located in the intellect? Without the inclusion of the experiences of people with learning difficulties, any analysis of the meaning of impairment will be incomplete. Moreover, the question of impairment raises issues which relate to the limitations faced by people with learning difficulties to ensure that their experiences form a central part of the agenda of the social model. Are these limitations socially driven or impairment-driven or both? I will return to this point a little later.

The personal is political

One of the most important features of the emergence of the social model has been the relevance of personal history and experience to the writing that has been produced. Writers such as Mike Oliver, Jenny Morris, Sally French, Lois Keith and Paul Abberley, to name a few, have theorized their personal experiences as disabled people to develop political insights into the meaning of disability. In taking such an approach, writing about disability reflects the feminist principle that one's personal experiences do not take place in isolation from wider social, economic and political structures. The personal also must be theorized.

However, the experience of writers and academics who have written about disability in this way is physical or sensory impairment. It is this that has tended to shape the analysis which has developed. For people with learning difficulties, the issues are more problematic. While it is possible to call to mind a number of people with physical or sensory impairments who research, write and publish (whether based inside or outside academia), I can think of none who have learning difficulties.

Why should this be? Is it simply another manifestation of the discrimination that is meted out to disabled people? Does it mean that the intellectual and academic environment should be manipulated (to use French's phrase) so that people with intellectual or developmental impairments can participate? Should we be seeking to undo the emphasis on presenting material in a theoretical way, if it precludes people with learning difficulties? What would this mean for the development of disability theory?

Or is the nature of intellectual or developmental impairment more likely to create restrictions on the ability of people with learning difficulties to gain positions (for example, as researchers) where they can present their own theorized accounts of the world in the way that people with physical or sensory impairments have been able to do? How does this fit into calls to re-examine the meaning of impairment? To paraphrase Liz Crow (1996), external disabling barriers may create social and economic disadvantage, but the subjective experience of the intellectual or developmental impairments of people with learning difficulties is part of their everyday reality.

I am not suggesting that people with learning difficulties are not capable of articulating their experiences or do not recognize prejudice and discrimination when they encounter them. It is clear that many do. However, these views and experiences have not been conveyed in the disability literature to the same extent as those of people with physical or sensory impairments. Neither have they been conveyed without the involvement of non-disabled people as 'allies', 'supporters' or 'facilitators' (and I would identify myself as someone who has taken this approach).

The obvious danger here is that non-disabled sympathizers will assume a dominant role. For example, in some self-advocacy groups attached to day centres, staff may begin as facilitators with the intention of supporting the self-advocates. Yet they end up dominating proceedings so that meetings become an opportunity for staff to justify the operation of the service and pay lip service to the principle of self-advocacy. If people with learning difficulties do require allies to enable them to convey their experiences in a way which is acceptable to researchers, examiners, editors, publishers and other gatekeepers, how should the integrity of their accounts be safeguarded?

Disability theory: avoiding the errors of the past

Presenting the arguments along the lines of this chapter should create a sense of *déjà vu*. Any reading of the history of second-wave feminism makes it clear that the first feminist literature which emerged in the early 1960s, with its idealist emphasis, claimed to articulate the experiences of all women. With hindsight we can recognize that this was not the case.

The experiences of white women (*vis-à-vis* their place within the family and their relationships to the workplace and the Welfare State, for example) are quite different from the experiences of ethnic-minority women. Similarly, disabled feminists (Morris, 1991; Keith, 1992) and non-disabled feminists (Walmsley, 1993) have exposed the partiality of the conventional feminist wisdom on informal care, by highlighting the way that feminism has ignored the experiences of disabled women and relegated them to the status of 'the other'.

Is this the destiny of people with learning difficulties within the social model? Is it inevitable that their views and experiences will be ignored, marginalized and rendered largely invisible? How much more literature will be produced that begins by using the term 'disabled people', but gradually lapses into the term 'able-bodied people'? How much more theory will develop that fails to include and explain the experiences of people with learning difficulties?

Conclusion

The sociology of disability (underpinned by the social model of disability) has been one of the most significant intellectual and political developments of the last ten years. It has transformed the meaning of disability, at a personal, intellectual and political level, for many people. As Oliver (1996) points out, this transformation is a continuing process.

So, while it is important to recognize achievements, it is necessary also to raise concerns about the direction of some of the debates in the sociology of disability and point to new pathways for debate. Much of the content of this chapter has been shaped by a sense of frustration at the continued exclusion of people with learning difficulties from the analyses of the sociology of disability. They are located currently in the backwaters of disability studies. Their experiences and aspirations should take their rightful place in the mainstream of debates about disability.

Yet the problem of marginality requires a shared response. Part of this responsibility rests clearly with people who are committed to the social model and interested in learning difficulty. However, to strive to embrace all disabled people within the social model is also a wider collective responsibility. It is my hope that writers in the disability movement keep the question of learning difficulty in their minds and ask themselves whether the empirical or theoretical work in which they are engaged is solely about physical or sensory impairment (if it is, this must be made clear) or about *disability*. If the latter, the analysis must address the question of learning difficulty.

Note

A full version of this paper was presented at the *Disability and Society: Ten Years On* conference, Ashford, Kent, 4–6 September 1996.

Further reading

Atkinson, D. and Williams, F. (1990) *Know Me As I Am: An Anthology of Poetry, Prose and Art by People with Learning Difficulties*. London: Hodder & Stoughton in association with Open University Press.

Chappell, A. L. (1992) Towards a sociological critique of the normalization principle, *Disability, Handicap and Society*, vol. 7, no. 1, pp. 35–51.

Goodley, D. (1997) Locating self-advocacy in models of disability: understanding disability in the support of self-advocates with learning difficulties, *Disability and Society*, vol. 12, no. 3, pp. 367–80.

15

Disability Discourse in a Postmodern World

Mairian Corker

The social model of disability separates disability from impairment, and then attributes the creation of disability to the dominant socio-cultural environment. In the Western world this environment is largely an oppressive one which views disability as deviance, damage, dependence – the so-called 'sick role' – and perpetuates labels and stereotypes which stigmatize, disempower, deskill and marginalize disabled people. These frameworks for interpreting disability and giving it meaning or discourses are not, however, the only frameworks which exist, nor do they necessarily reflect the characteristics of Western society as we know it today. In some societies (see, for example, Connors and Donnellan, 1993; Ingstad and Reynolds-Whyte, 1995), disabled people are considered to be no different from anyone else, and in others we are revered, even given God(dess)-like status. There is also historical reference to disabled people forming alternative, sometimes separate communities, formed around a distinct collective social identity, which is sometimes presented as a direct challenge or alternative to the identity imposed by the dominant culture (Groce, 1985; Padden and Humphries, 1988).

Anthropological evidence generally supports the idea that culturally embedded discourses construct the dominant experience of disability within a given culture, time or social context (Davis, 1995; Barnes, 1996a), and that this construction is reinforced by and interpreted through social practices and social structure. The role of discourse in the construction of disability has not, however, been given prominence within current debates on disability. This is perhaps because discourse is caught between:

- the top-down view of the relationship between the individual and society as framed by the social model of disability, which leaves discourse as a side effect of social structure so that it cannot therefore be the focus of social change, and

- methodological individualism which cannot accommodate any kind of social constructionism, and therefore ignores discourse altogether.

However, it may be important for disabled people to consider the implications of restricting the role of discourse in this way at a time when tensions within disability dialogues and theory are beginning to show themselves.

In this chapter I explore the contribution which a post-structuralist framework might make to our understanding of disability in society, with particular reference to one group of people – deaf people – who have become marginalized both from disability discourse and from the multitude of discourses which make up the social world. At the same time I would wish to emphasize that deaf people are not the only group of disabled people who have become marginalized from disability discourse, and the frameworks which will be presented in this chapter may be of relevance to the way in which the movement sees its relationships with other marginalized groups, for example people with learning difficulties (Brechin and Walmsley, 1989), people who wish to see more emphasis on the relationship between impairment and disability (French, 1994; Crow, in Morris, 1996) and people who are marginalized by virtue of multiple 'Others' such as disabled black and ethnic-minority people (Stuart, 1992; Vernon, 1996a), disabled women (Begum, 1992a; Morris, 1996) and disabled gays and lesbians (Hearn, 1991; Corbett, 1994; Shakespeare *et al.*, 1996).

The postmodern world

The idea that disability is socially or culturally created seems more at home against the scenery of the cultural and intellectual movements of postmodernism and/or post-structuralism, since these are the movements within which social constructionism has taken shape. Postmodernism challenges the idea that there can be an ultimate truth about reality which can be discovered through reason and rationality, arguing that such an approach was more appropriately placed in the context of mid-eighteenth-century thought. The postmodernist movement rejects the dominant belief of Western cultures that the world can be understood in terms of underlying structures, such as the economic structure exemplified in the work of Marx and the psychic structures of Freud and Piaget, along with the supposition that such structures can be explained by all-embracing grand theories or metanarratives. In a sense, then, social model discourse operates through postmodernism in its rejection of the 'ultimate truth' of the individual view of disability (see Oliver, 1996). But postmodernist critiques seem also to be at the roots of current challenges to the essentialist nature of the social model itself (Shakespeare, 1996c). Further, the tenets of postmodernism are relevant for contemporary research in the human sciences since it is advocated that there cannot be 'pure' measures of people's contexts and characteristics as, inevitably, to arrive at 'purity' involves the distorting practice of filtering out the normal social context of a person's life. This reflects to a certain extent the view of disabled researchers such as Abberley (1991) and Barnes (1996b) in their exposition of participatory or emancipatory research.

However, in its emphasis on pluralism and individuation, which are seen as the dominant characteristics of the postmodern world, postmodernism rests uneasily within disability discourse. Pluralism is the co-existence of a multiplicity and variety of context-dependent ways of life, whereas individuation refers to the multiplication and segregation of roles, including cultural roles, available to, and to some extent forced upon, individuals. These characteristics are inherently difficult for oppressed communities already threatened by fragmentatory discourses, structures and practices. Indeed, in relation to sociology and disability, Barton (1996, p. 9) refers to the need to 'guard against . . . the regressive relativism of particular forms of postmodernism', and Riddell (1996), in the same volume, says that 'postmodernists question whether it is possible to sustain accounts of oppression since it is impossible to establish one account of events as being superior to another'. Nevertheless, pluralism and individuation do seem to have relevance in the context of current tensions within disability discourse. Oppression has manufactured the community of disabled people as a community of 'unrelated strangers', largely without the benefit of a relationship based on collective co-operation and trust – a community reminiscent of the *Gesellschaft* tradition which began around the time of the industrialization of the Western world (Tonnies, 1957). But as the world population has exploded, it has provided more of each possible variety of individual. This, together with a parallel growth in the density and globalization of different channels and forms of communication, has, paradoxically, made it easier for individuals to form recognizably distinct groups (Simon, 1996) based on different kinds of relationships.

The evolution of meaning

The increased visibility of pluralism in human populations also means pluralism of ideas, intellectual trends, identities and cultures, each of which demands speaking rights or 'warrants voice' (Gergen, 1989) by grouping around different discourses. Post-structuralism is an important part of postmodernist philosophy, so important in fact that the terms *post-structuralism* and *postmodernism* are often used interchangeably. Post-structuralism, however, deals specifically with language and discourse and, as such, is bound up with issues of meaning, representation and identity. Its main premise is that meaning can never be fixed because human discourse is constantly evolving and therefore continually engaged in creating new meanings. Because of the unbreakable links between language and meaning, explanations of the social world lie 'not inside individuals, but out in the linguistic space in which they move with other people' (Burr, 1995, p. 40). Words, signs, pictures, books, jokes and so on change their meaning over time, from context to context and from person to person. There is, moreover, a great deal of evidence for this when we look at how the structure and meaning of language has changed and is still changing.

These changes are evident in the disability field, where the recent work of Jenny Corbett (1996) is particularly significant. She says:

> Language reflects conceptions of reality, or truth. As such, I feel the term 'special need' is no longer useful or constructive. To me, it is reflective of professional ownership where medical and educational definitions dominate the discourse. It jars uncomfortably with the discourses in the disability movement where new languages and metaphors are emerging in a creative burst of pride and assertion . . . if we are able to 'move through' identities, we can also adopt a similar approach to the use of special language, [one which] will make all language special. Thus 'special' becomes normality. (pp. 32–3, 101)

For example, the original meaning of the term *deaf* – 'wholly or partially without hearing' – placed the concept firmly in the auditory sphere. Its common association with the terms *dumb* or *mute* established and reinforced phonocentric links between audition and linguistic competence. The meaning of *deaf* was then broadened to refer to any person who, regardless of whether they could hear or not, ignored, refused to listen to or comply with something or someone, and, likewise, *dumb* became equated with stupidity. Now *deaf* has two context-specific uses. The first, *deaf* (hearing impaired), is used mainly by professionals working with deaf people and in the disability field, and the second, *Deaf*, is used within that group of deaf people who see themselves as a linguistic minority group, and their allies.

In a similar way, the meaning of a simple phrase such as 'Does s/he take sugar?' will be different when addressed to children, adults with limited or no direct experience with children or disabled people, parents of disabled children and disabled people themselves (Burr, 1995), and the dominant culture continues to legitimate the term *disabling* in the context of 'disabling unexploded bombs', for example, but is unable to accommodate its use in the context of disabling people.

Discourse and power

However, it must be remembered that new meanings do not simply replace old meanings. Meanings tend to exist alongside each other, largely because, in addition to their definitive role, they delineate the boundaries between things and people, their relationships to other things and other people – and so the process of defining is bound up in 'matters of identity' (Turner, 1994; Corker, 1996), and therefore, with action, political or otherwise, which is taken:

> The major rejection of Deaf people as a linguistic minority group has come from people who believe that Deaf people should primarily be regarded as disabled people and treated as such. Once considered 'disabled' we can be thought about as imperfect members of a hearing society rather than as competent members of a different linguistic society . . . The lay person's attitudes affect how we are regarded and responded to in society. The views that professional service providers hold about us affect how our autonomy is respected, how we are provided for, the educational

opportunities we have access to, and how opinions about us are transmitted in society. (Ladd and John, 1991, p. 11)

Moreover, some meanings persist when words or signs become attached to particular meanings and so may appear 'fixed' in that relationship (Saussure, 1974). So the vast majority of people still define deafness as impaired hearing, use the term 'deaf' in its wider sense and, along with many deaf and disabled people themselves, do not make a distinction between impairment and disability. For example, Harlan Lane (1995, p. 179) says that 'In ASL, the sign whose semantic field most overlaps that of the English DISABILITY can be glossed in English LIMP-BLIND-ETC.', but this sign does not include deafness because, in Lane's view, Deaf people do not regard themselves as disabled.

Language, then, is not a system of signs with fixed meanings with which everyone agrees, but a site of variation, contention and potential conflict. As such, language is about power relations and politics, because discourses compete with each other on many different levels and in many different contexts. The post-structuralist view of power, as epitomized in the work of Michel Foucault, is that it is held by those who are able to draw upon discourses which allow their actions to be represented in the light of 'knowledges' currently prevailing in society – knowledge is power over others and the power to define others (Foucault, 1972; 1977). Thus the availability of different discourses is critical to understanding meaning in context, and to power, because 'knowledge' refers to the particular construction that has received the stamp of 'truth' or 'normalcy'. In Western society this is 'individual, liberal humanist' discourse, which is central to our present social and economic organization.

The individual construction of disability is legitimated within this discourse, and so brings with it the potential for acting in one way rather than another and for marginalizing alternative ways of acting, such as those framed by the social model of disability or the linguistic-minority construction of deafness. This is clearly expressed throughout the work of many deaf and disabled academics and activists referred to in this chapter in a number of ways. But, significantly, it also forms the sub-text of Lane's article, referred to above. After an initial solitary reference to the 'social construction' of disability (1995, p. 172), without citing the origins of this approach in the disability world, nor its relationship to the social model, he devotes the rest of his article to reinforcing the idea that the linguistic-minority construction is different from the disability construction, through continuous reference to the individual construction of disability. In a sense, then, he selects particular discourses on deafness and disability which are not directly comparable. In doing so he successfully emphasizes his main premise that Deaf people are not disabled, and so justifies Deaf people's claim to the right to co-exist as a minority group which advocates special measures, a share of available resources and, in Britain, a high degree of dependency on the dominant culture for its livelihood (Kyle, 1991).

But this brings us to another important element of post-structuralism, which stems from the work of Jacques Derrida (1974; 1978; 1981). Derrida's concept of 'différance' emphasizes that a particular discourse has meaning only in relation to other discourses – the identity of something is as much a function of what it is not as what it is. So to describe oneself as Deaf means that one is not hearing (or deaf), but it also means that being Deaf is defined in relation to hearingness (or deafness) – the changing meanings of the term 'deaf' described above signify different relationships to hearing and different kinds of linguistic and cultural representation. This is why Lennard Davis says that, on the one hand, 'the term "disability", as it is commonly and professionally used, is an absolute category without level or threshold. One is either disabled or not' (1995, p. 1) and, on the other, that 'normalcy and disability are part of the same system' (1995, p. 2). These two perspectives epitomize the struggle between structuralism and post-structuralism, which, like normalcy and disability, exist alongside each other.

However, when Davis, as a hearing person with Deaf parents (1995, p. xix), says of his wish to be hearing that 'what I was fleeing was not deafness per se, but the deafness constructed by the hearing world', and this flight led him to the understanding 'that deafness was a category of oppression' – a path which Lane (1992) describes as an 'extrapolative leap' of the imagination – his meaning is somewhat different to that which is implicit in disabled people's use of social-model discourse to locate disability in society. The effect of the conflict between linguistic-minority discourse and medical discourse for deaf people, for example, is ultimately fragmentation which, in turn, produces further categories and further conflict. The process is circular. For hearing people, on the other hand, the effect is to manufacture a division between the 'positive, proud Deaf person' (whom they revere and see as a legitimate area for 'academic' and 'socio-cultural' study) and the 'negative, impaired deaf person' (whom they pity or reject in line with Western society's 'individualistic' discourse). Thus their positions and their power within both discourses are maintained. This echoes Derrida's (1978) belief that the widespread use of the language of otherness in anthropological discourse to describe the West's encounter with non-Western cultures, or with anything which is 'other than' the dominant beliefs and values of Western culture, tends to keep the dominant discourse intact. This to some extent reflects Liggett's (1988, p. 271) reference to the dangers of a minority-group approach which reinforces a particular constitution of disability. However, in my own work, where I have compared social-model disability discourse with linguistic-minority discourse, both of which are couched in the language of otherness, I have, unsurprisingly, come up with a completely different perspective on the relationships between Deaf and disabled people (Corker, 1997).

The application of a post-structuralist framework suggests further reasons why the separation of Deaf discourses from disability discourses in this way is worrying. First, as individuals, we are constantly subject to an interplay of different discourses, each with its own structure of rights, obligations and possibilities for action, and each carrying identity and power implications. The restructuring of meaning depends to a very large extent not only on how people 'position' themselves in relation to alternative discourses but also on whether all discourses are available and accessible to all people. Class, age, gender, ethnic origin, sexuality and disability can all be linked to restrictions on the kind of person we can claim to be, and this is as true within our communities as it is within the dominant culture. It is significant in this context that groups of disabled people who are most marginalized from the disabled people's movement, or who are more likely to withdraw from both the dominant culture and the movement into alternative communities, are those groups for whom language is critical in some way.

The post-structuralist view of development is one of a process of becoming more and more sophisticated in one's ability to produce accounts by using the linguistic and accounting rules of one's culture. Harré (1981) sees this ability as developing, at least in part, through the social interaction between young children and the adults around them.

This, again, emphasizes that language is not just a descriptive tool – we use it and do things with it to achieve certain effects, and so language itself is a means of exercising political expediency.

Using this kind of developmental framework we can ask further questions about the apparent gulf between knowledge of social-model discourse in the Deaf community and Deaf people's well-documented experience of disability as social oppression. For example:

> When they use an interpreter, how do Deaf people know that the interpreter's voice-over of their signing is correct? Have they ever wondered, but could not know for sure, whether poor interpreting voice-over was to blame when communications with a hearing person did not go well? Does it worry these Deaf people that an interpreter may do a poor voice-over at an important meeting, such as a job interview? (Reid, 1994, p. 19)

This is an important example, because it demonstrates another way in which hearing people maintain their power within both discourses, but it has different implications for the form that this power takes. There has been much evidence to suggest that signed discourses and spoken discourses are not fully translatable because signed discourses originate in the visual–spatial realm and spoken discourses in the oral–aural realm. This means that translating from English to French, for example, is a completely different exercise from translating from English to BSL (British Sign Language).

There is also a great deal of evidence for the huge barriers experienced by many deaf children to learning a language which gives primacy to the oral–aural realm, and to the transmission of culturally relevant linguistic and accounting rules when most adults in the child's immediate social world are effectively from an 'alien' (hearing) culture. If a deaf child learns his or her first language primarily through the visual–spatial mode, this will, as Ladd and John (1991) implied above, serve them well in social situations with other sign language users. However, if a Deaf person is subsequently unable to learn the language of the dominant culture fully, and cannot therefore draw upon a range of alternative discourses, the skills of the interpreter in the above situation will be irrelevant because language is not just about words or signs, it is about their meaning in a whole variety of contexts. A fair proportion of this meaning, as I have suggested, may not be translatable

– for example, hearing idioms and non-manual signs – but, if a Deaf person has only one meaning for a particular term within their linguistic repertoire and especially if this meaning is part of the dominant discourse and so imbued with cultural value judgements, it is this meaning which will be understood, irrespective of whether translation is accurate.

This may seem to reinforce a view of the Deaf community as a closed culture where only limited transfer of information can occur with the dominant culture, and what transfer there is is largely dependent on how hearing people act out their role as mediators between discourses. Within the community there is a hierarchy which is structured around the links between discourse and power. Leadership status is conferred on Deaf people with high linguistic competence in both their own language and the language of the dominant culture, and it is these 'educated' or 'professional' Deaf people who often shape the dominant discourses within the community, not always in a way which is representative of the range of views within or outside the community. However, developing competence in the language of the dominant culture, like competence in any language including BSL, requires contact with this culture. For many Deaf people in Western society a great deal of this contact will have been oppressive and, as a result, they have tended to position themselves in opposition to discourses of 'hearingness'.

From a post-structuralist perspective, however, it stretches the imagination a little to view Deaf culture as a separate culture which is not related in any way to the dominant culture (Turner, 1994). Indeed the work of a number of Deaf activists (see, for example, Ladd and John, 1991; National Union of the Deaf, 1992; Dimmock, 1993) reinforces the alternative view that the beliefs and values underpinning Deaf culture risk becoming equivalent to a kind of 'inverted audism':

> As we struggle to agree on appropriate names, we must ever be aware that labels exclude and that rather than defining ourselves we may actually be reducing ourselves only in a different way ... As a cultural description, Deaf captures the experience of an identifiable group, but when it is used to question, invalidate, or trivialize the authenticity of someone else's cultural experience it can in itself be an oppressor's term. (King Jordan, 1992, p. 69)

This is similar to the 'inverted racism' inherent in some sections of the Black community (Katz, 1996), and the belief of some social-model theorists that the 'truth' of disability lies exclusively in economic and social oppression which institutionalizes and reifies disability, and which therefore inverts the structuralist underpinnings of the individual model of disability. That being said, these issues must be emphasized in the context of deafness primarily because a great deal of attention is paid within deaf education to the structural elements of language and the means of articulation, whilst comparatively little is given to the functional aspects of language and what Foucault (1972) describes as 'the archaeology of knowledge'.

Celebrating marginal discourses

Thus post-structuralism highlights the inherent difficulty with essentialist notions of disability, whether they stem from 'bottom-up' or from 'top-down' ideas about the individual and society. It seems to be saying that the individual/society dichotomy is itself a construction, one way of thinking about the world, but not necessarily a way we have to be committed to. Ultimately disability discourse originates in our varied responses to Western culture and we thereby influence it, though not necessarily through the kind of social relationships and power structures that we would wish for. We are not separate from it because 'we never actually see "society" on the one hand and "individuals" on the other' (Burr, 1995, p. 104). Discourses are built on the relationship between us and society, and new discourses, as we have seen, have evolved and will continue to evolve from our resistance to inappropriate and irrelevant meanings. Foucault saw power and resistance as the two sides of the same coin, arguing that the power embedded in one discourse is only apparent from the resistance embedded in another.

It is precisely because disabled people – and our allies in different ways – have resisted or defied disablist oppressors that the nature of power in relation to disability has shifted from what Foucault called sovereign power, where rulers and their officials could engage in eugenics, genocide or forced institutionalization of disabled people (Barnes, 1996c), to the more subtle disciplinary power which is exercised through the production of discourses which are used to control disabled people by making it appear that it is for our own good.

Many disabled people still freely subject themselves to control through the scrutiny of others, especially 'disability experts' and 'the media'. But we also exercise self-discipline through internalizing our oppression. Indeed, the discourse of internalized oppression is very much like sexuality discourses, which, though widespread, were driven underground by the surveillance of the Catholic Church's 'confessional'. Internalized oppression is marginalized by Western culture and, sometimes, by the disabled people's movement. But whilst Western culture says 'disabled people must cope with internalized oppression because we are our disabilities' and the movement says 'we must hide it because we can't effect political or social change if we don't', our lack of power is reinforced. Social control is achieved by imposing an artificial division between nurturant social network support, on the one hand, and economic resources and political action or action facilitating support, on the other (Cutrona and Suhr, 1994).

It could be argued that there are historical precedents for the view that there can be strength in social diversity and individualism as well as in the collective pursuit of a political goal, and from this knowledge there has arisen an awareness of ourselves as part of a social and cultural ecosystem. The relationships between the individual and society, like those between power and resistance and between different meanings for linguistic terms, are an interactive web in which we are all caught. This, in my view, is reason enough for us to begin to move away from the 'either/or' logic of essentialism.

The disciplinary power used by Western society in the continued oppression of disabled people is, paradoxically, evidence of its lack of power, since oppression is used when the limits of power or social control have been reached. Instead of seeing the post-structuralist tenets of pluralism and individuation as a threat, it is worth remembering that the prefix 'post', in the context of post-structuralism, means 'coming after and adding to' rather than 'rejecting' (Burr, 1995, p. 39). Post-structuralist discourse on disability does not 'reject' the social model. Rather it suggests that, since disability is now located in a postmodern world, it is appropriate to begin to look at the relationship between the individual and society rather than to focus on the individual or society. As such it can bring marginalized voices to the fore in a positive way, and use the diversity in our own communities to work directly against the categories which the dominant culture uses to divide us. It aims to render social control through disciplinary power useless, and so begin the next wave of change.

Further reading

Corker, M. (1997) *Deaf and Disabled or Deafness Disabled: Towards a Human Rights Perspective*. Buckingham: Open University Press.

Davis, L. J. (1995) *Enforcing Normalcy: Disability, Deafness and the Body*. London: Verso.

Lane, H. (1995) Constructions of deafness, *Disability and Society*, vol. 10, no. 2, pp. 171–90.

16

The Sociology of Disability: Towards a Materialist Phenomenology

Gareth Williams

> We all live our lives in bodies of a certain sort, whose possibilities and vulnerabilities do not as such belong to one human society rather than another. (Martha Nussbaum)

Within sociology there is a tradition of linking humanistic methods to left-wing ideology or at least left-leaning sentiment. Since Howard Becker, if not before, being on the side of the victims of society's vicissitudes entailed a methodological stance that purportedly reduced the distance between the researcher and the researched – where the researched were those groups pushed to the margins of social participation and economic security. Doing life histories and participant observation, in particular, was seen as a way of getting inside the lives of other individuals and different ways of life with a view to 'telling it like it is'. Anthropologists and devotees of what was then called the 'new journalism' provided the model for this kind of work, and sociologists who were fed up with trawling government statistics or constructing yet another mindless attitude scale warmed to it.

During the 1960s and 1970s this approach to the sociological craft suggested the possibility of developing forms of knowledge that avoided the pitfalls of both grand theory and abstracted empiricism. Being rooted in some kind of substrate of people and places, it held out the promise of a theoretical discourse with a human face. In advocating data collection that was flexible and responsive to the needs and views of the people being researched, it offered the hope of a form of sociology more alive to the dynamics and contexts of human life than the conventional survey method or the quasi-experimentalism of social psychology.

Some people were troubled about scientific legitimacy but, as Peter

Worsley has argued in a recent interview, people flocked to do sociology in the 1960s and 1970s almost because it was 'not a proper intellectual discipline' (British Sociological Association, 1997, p. 7). Twenty years ago the American sociologist Peter Berger argued:

> Sociology, greatly to the surprise of its older practitioners, has acquired the reputation of being a liberating discipline . . . All this is very recent indeed. Only a few years ago most outsiders, if they thought about the matter at all, visualized the sociologist as a dry character, with an insatiable lust for statistics, who at best might dig up some data of use to policy makers, and at worst (in the words of one malevolent commentator) would spend one hundred thousand dollars to discover the local whorehouse. (Berger, 1979, p. 11)

Humanistic, radical, sceptical and critical sociologies emerged out of this ferment of politics and ideas. The civil rights movement, the women's movement, the gay liberation movement were all part of a context in which the 'scientific study of society' could no longer be undertaken with quite the same academic control over production that had once been the case. In a sense you could say that during that period Western society went from being some kind of organizational pact to being a ferment of movements of opposition. Then came the disability rights movement, with its critique of the way in which disabled people were oppressed: denied citizenship, respect, and resources. Disabled people began to suggest that not only were they *badly treated* by society – refused access to education, employment, housing and other areas of social and economic life – but that the way in which disabled people were 'helped' by those professionals who were, on some views, the defining feature of postwar British society was itself disabling.

Initially, sociologists in their liberationary mode were very much in tune with this movement. They too had been increasingly concerned about the nature of professional power and the uses to which it was put (Gabe *et al.*, 1994). They too had begun to see the role of medicine as being both less effective and less beneficent than the profession itself claimed. The movement from medical sociology to the sociology of health and illness was itself partly an attempt to augment sociology's own autonomy in relation to health matters. Medical sociologists increasingly were less tied to the apron-strings of medical research and more willing to stand back and put medicine itself – the techniques, the knowledge, the profession as a whole – in some kind of proper context.

One feature of the process by which this transformation was undertaken was political in the sense that it was a way of critiquing the authority of the medical profession. Another was the ferment in methodology and epistemology. Medicine was fundamentally positivist in its orientation to the world. Doctors worked with what was to them a clear separation of subjective and objective knowledge, personal opinion and scientific fact. Those sociologists who worked within this paradigm – sociologists *in* medicine rather than *of* medicine to use Robert Straus's classic distinction – were those abstracted empiricists who took for granted the objective nature of the phenomena of ill-health, and whose underlying assumptions were fundamentally functionalist and normative. That is, while affecting a stance of value-neutrality, they actually operated on behalf of the values, interests and powers of the medical and political establishment.

Defining disability

At the outset many sociologists worked happily alongside medical and other scientists working within this scientific orthodoxy. As Mike Bury (1996) has argued, the field of disability research and policy in the immediate postwar period was conspicuous only by its absence. Social scientists working within the growing fields of social medicine, social policy and rehabilitation in this period began to make a contribution to researching the social aspects of chronic illness and disability relating to injury. Most of this work was concerned with the prevalence of disability, but it was hampered by a lack of any clearly agreed definition or approach to measurement. It was this intellectual concern that drove the work that culminated in the development of the International Classification of Impairments, Disabilities and Handicaps (ICIDH), published by the World Health Organization in 1980.

The outstanding characteristic of the work that developed during this period was its attempt – without malice, but with the professional paternalism typical of its time – to shift medical and governmental thinking away from an exclusive focus on an anatomico-pathological analysis of a breakdown in people's bodies to a wider understanding of 'disability' (the terms used varied) as representing a much broader spectrum of personal and social needs. Arcane as some of the discussions about definition may seem, they provided the basis for a much more realistic assessment of the prevalence of disability and an argument for increases and shifts in forms of provision. In the period up until 1979 disability was part of the wider discussions about the strengths and weaknesses of the Welfare State.

For a whole range of epidemiological, economic and policy reasons the attempt to find a satisfactory socio-medical definition of disability underpinned this enterprise. Against the dominant biomedical model, it was argued that the differences between the impairments arising out of clinically different diseases or accidents were less important than what they shared in terms of their psychological, social and economic consequences. In part this was a recognition of the limited impact that much disease-based rehabilitation had on the lives of those people going through long periods of treatment. What was important for someone with multiple sclerosis, it was argued, was not so much the nuanced variation of the unfolding of disease in different cases, but the broad impact of living with such symptoms on global areas of social life: work, education, family, sex, identity, self-esteem and so on.

The growing involvement of social scientists in this area also began to open up different ways of looking at disability. Although many of the social scientists working in the area shared the dominant interests and assumptions of the experts in rehabilitation and public health with whom they worked, they also brought with them a set of theoretical and empirical approaches to thinking about social phenomena that were radically different. The work of Goffman (1968b), on stigma in particular, had a significant impact not just on what social scientists thought mental and physical illness were but on the legitimacy of different ways of researching and writing about them. The 'symbolic interactionist' approach in which Goffman can be located included a notion of individual roles and identities that was seen to be highly relevant to the way in which sociological research on disability might be conducted.

Exploring the meaning of illness

As Bury (1996) has noted, sociologists became increasingly interested in the 'meaning' of chronic illness and disability. While by no means all of this work shared any obvious links with Goffman, the focus on disability as an emergent property of social relationships has characterized sociological studies of disability. The method and style of these studies vary, but the work of Blaxter (1976) in Britain and Glaser and Strauss (1975) in the USA provided some kind of paradigm for the work which was to follow. What these and other studies attempted to do, very successfully in my view, was to take the idea that chronic illness and disability were in some sense social phenomena unfolding over time, and explore their meaning through the experiences of people who were ill and disabled. Sociological concepts of 'career' and 'trajectory' helped to shift thinking away from the functionalism of the 'sick role' to something more dynamic, subjective, and 'meaningful'.

The depth of the exploration of meaning varies depending on the extent to which the analysis focuses on one or other of two senses of meaning identified by Bury (1991). Bury argued that the meaning of an illness can be defined in terms of its 'consequences', which refers to the impact it has on practical aspects of the person's roles and relationships in everyday life; or in terms of its 'significance', which relates to the cultural connotations, the symbols and significations, surrounding different sorts of illness and disability.

Both these forms of analysis of the meaning of chronic illness and disability have the notion of embodied experience at their centre, but, rather than attempting to define functional incapacity or activity restriction in biomedical terms, they explore the ramifications of the experience from the point of view of the person affected. In other words, while the biomedical model has disease or dysfunction at the centre of its picture, the sociological perspective focuses on illness as something whose meaning and reality vary depending on the biography of a particular individual and the circumstances in which they find themselves.

Instead of using socially oriented measures of disability as a means of estimating the prevalence of need, this work typically used qualitative methods as a means of exploring the experience of need with relatively small numbers of people. In other words, once we know that there is in the non-institutionalized population a certain number of people who are disabled in some way, the questions then become: What is life like for people with these chronic health problems, and what kinds of services need to be developed to offset the disadvantages they face? These studies, while undertaken for the most part by people who were 'not disabled', were genuine and incisive attempts to unlock the nature of disabled people's experiences and realistically locate them in the context of 'daily life'.

As with the development of socio-medical approaches to conceptualizing and measuring 'disability', these studies provided an important counter to the dominant research models in rehabilitation. These latter purported to measure 'activities of daily living' but in a mode that was both so clinical, so positivistic and so abstracted that daily living seemed to bear no relationship to what people with chronic illness and disability were experiencing. In line with the positivistic underpinnings of medical science the emphasis of traditional assessments is on some universal definition and measure that can be applied by appropriately qualified people without reference to the disabled person's own perspective, the roles they occupy, the relationships in which they are embedded, the circumstances of their milieux or the wider political context of barriers, attitudes, and power. The work of social scientists in this area attempted to bring back into the analysis some degree of personal experience and social structure.

The attempt to understand the meaning of experience by looking at it in its context lies at the heart of the medical sociological project. For sociologists this development was part of a development from the critique of positivism, and an attempt to define a sociological approach to illness liberated from the dominance of biomedicine. The focus on chronic illness and the experience of disability associated with it can be seen as an attempt to move away from the rehabilitation models which were rather static, in addition to their being reductive and focused on the mechanics of functional limitations and activity restriction. While the experience of 'adaptation' to a limb amputation or some other trauma-induced impairment clearly has its own dynamics, influenced by personal, situational and treatment factors, chronic illness adds a new dimension of enormous variability and unpredictability.

Moreover the experience of different chronic illnesses is – to tempt tautology – clearly a very different experience. While disability might have certain common features, sociologists have been interested in both subjective variation in responses to the 'same' illness and impairment and variation in the meaning (in the second of Bury's senses) of different kinds of symptoms in society. Explorations of breathlessness, raging skin, inflamed joints, heart problems, end-stage renal failure and many others have allowed sociologists and anthropologists to explore

the seemingly infinite permutations of the experience of being physically different in a highly normalizing society.

Some of these sociological analyses are phenomenologically 'deep' or
'thick', others are more inclined to skate over the surfaces of meaning,
but nevertheless deal with the interaction between symptoms and
situations. The hallmarks of this kind of work are, therefore, its focus on
the symbolic and material interaction between the individual and
society, and the interpretative processes whereby individuals construct
meaning from their experiences. Disability as a social reality of people's
experiences is caused neither by the externalities of the environment
nor by any 'facts' of biological trauma or deterioration, but emerges out
of the relations between persons and society.

With this shift in focus from the individual with an impairment to the
meaning-giving nature of interaction there comes a shift in the nature of
the intervention that may be appropriate. If the problem is not the need
of the individual to adapt to the impairment, but rather the complex
process of negotiating the interactions out of which daily life is created,
then the role of professional experts as people who do things to the
impaired body is clearly limited. Much more important may be a
supportive milieu of lay people who can help the individual renegotiate
their place in the world (Williams and Wood, 1988).

The perils of solipsism

The notion of re-establishing a place in the world is at the heart of some
of the more phenomenologically thick analyses of the meaning of
chronic illness and disability. These too may concentrate on the interactions within the mundane world, but there is a sense in which the
purpose of these interactions can be interpreted as having rather more
transmundane qualities. Such analyses lead us away from the empirical
features of the impaired individual's interaction with the material world
back into the individual's 'self' and 'body'. The focus of the problems
shifts from interactionism to the exploration of the lived body, the body
incarnate, drawing its theoretical inspiration less from symbolic interactionism and more from philosophical phenomenology. There is less
exploration of the interaction between the person and society in the
presence of the disruptive effects of chronic illness, and more searching
the constitution of the self in the presence of a disordered body.

Some of the most powerful phenomenological analyses come from individuals, usually middle-class and often academics or writers themselves, who have tried to explore autobiographically the depths of their own experiences of cancer, neurological disease, heart attack or whatever else. The best of this work gives pre-eminence to the ill person's perspective, emphasizing the 'illness' (the social experience) above the 'disease' (the physiological processes). However, the aim within this project to attempt 'to consider illness stories as embodied also deconstructs the distinction: the illness experience is an experience in and of a diseased body' (Frank, 1995, p. 187).

In much of this work the storied or narrative nature of illness and disability is emphasized. The exploration of the experience of illness becomes a vehicle for exploring basic questions about the nature of the self in the world, the fundamental meaning structures in a person's life. The danger in much of this work, however, is that it loses sight altogether of the structures which make the experience take the shape it does. History and even biography are dissolved by the heat of a phenomenological analysis which burns ever more deeply into the reality of self and world. What started out as a sociological analysis becomes part of a quasi-religious or spiritual quest for the truth which illness is supposed to reveal. So profound is the truth of illness that even the person experiencing the illness is merely a vehicle for allowing the body to speak of its suffering: 'The body is not mute, but it is inarticulate; it does not use speech yet begets it. The speech that the body begets includes illness stories; the problem of hearing these stories is to hear the body speaking in them' (Frank, 1995, p. 27). While Christian theology and the learning of other world religions certainly provide rich languages for exploring questions of ultimate concern – life and death, suffering, guilt and redemption – they can also limit the experience of illness and disability to a personal quest for meaning and truth. The politics and history of illness and disability become marginalized, and the realities of cuts in the budgets for health and social care become forgotten.

Renewing the sociology of disability

There is no neutral language with which to begin the process of discussing chronic illness and disability, and language itself is central to any discussion of how we approach the problem of dealing with 'disability'. Disability is fundamentally a problem of representation in a number of senses: there is no language to talk about it that is untainted; the language and categories we use influence the definition and measurement of 'the problem'; and there is continuing dispute about who are the legitimate representatives of the experience and reality of disability in the modern world.

I have tried to show how sociologists have responded to the limitations of traditional rehabilitation perspectives on chronic illness and disability. They have done this by emphasizing the need to move away from professional definitions of impairment and disability in order to explore the ways in which people with chronic illness and disability themselves define their situations. Using various forms of qualitative method, they have attempted to reconstruct from people's own accounts of their experiences the reality of chronic illness and disability as something which emerges out of the relationship between the person and social structures.

However, I have also indicated how the relational can at times slip into a phenomenological analysis in which the individual or even the body returns to the centre of attention, albeit constructed in a discourse somewhat different from that employed within biomedicine. While explorations of the lived body can illuminate experiences of extreme situations, once detached from the political economy and history of disability and its relationship to state and society, they are sucked into the vortex of subjectivity. The consequence of this is that what began as an attempt to see chronic illness and disability as the product of the complex relationships between individuals, milieux and social structures becomes an exploration of the quintessence of illness and its consequences for identity.

This is in stark contrast to the work of many disability theorists in Britain and elsewhere for whom the prime mover in causal terms is most certainly not the illness, nor the individual in a state of tragic adaptive 'failure', but the oppressive society in which disabled people live. If disability is seen as a personal tragedy, disabled people are treated as the victims of circumstance. If disability is defined as social oppression, disabled people can be seen as the collective victims of an uncaring, discriminatory society (Oliver, 1990).

Both medical sociology and disability studies have in different ways attempted to develop a critique of such traditional models of the relationships between disability and the environment in the context of the experience of individuals in relation to their milieux and the wider structures. In that sense they are both a critique of positivism, but they vary in the emphasis which they give to subjectivity and structures. Let me contrast two quotations in order to give a flavour of the difference between some medical sociology and the work of disability theorists:

> Certainly physical dependency, if not also social and economic dependency, can result from illness. (Charmaz, 1991, p. 80)

> Dependency is created amongst disabled people, not because of the effects of functional limitations on their capacities for self-care, but because their lives are shaped by a variety of economic, political and social forces which produce it. (Oliver, 1990, p. 94)

I would agree with the argument that the 'social model' represented here by Oliver is not a sufficient explanation of the oppression experienced by disabled people (Crow, 1996). It seems to me that the oppressive quality of everyday life for many disabled people is unquestionable, and the origins of much of this oppression lie in the hostile environments and disabling barriers which society (politicians, architects, social workers, doctors and others) erects. However, there are three reasons why the processes whereby discrimination takes place are often extraordinarily subtle. First, most disability in modern societies emerges from chronic illness, and illness, unlike ethnicity or gender, emerges slowly over time. Second, someone who is able-bodied is only temporarily so. Disability is therefore a category theoretically open to everyone, and, as populations age, one that becomes a more likely endpoint for any given individual. Third, disability is, at some level, undeniably to do with the pain or discomfort of bodies, and this is a dimension of the oppressive quality of chronic illness and disability for large numbers of people.

What is needed is an interactionist analysis within a materialist framework or, in Shakespeare's (1996c) terms, an approach which recognizes both unities and differences in experience. The fact that disability is profoundly influenced by both social forces, such as class, and differences in the subjective experience of bodily impairment, means that the nature of oppression in relation to disability is not easy to see or articulate, and people speak in different voices. As Irving Zola, the American sociologist and disability activist, argued:

One of the features of oppression is the loss not only of voice but of the tools to find it . . . It will take us time to speak out, to learn what we have lost, to articulate what we need. But as I have tried to state here and elsewhere, the numbers trying to speak out are ever growing and the chorus of voices is increasingly diverse. (Zola, 1994, p. 65)

In place of the monochrome languages of the 'medical model' on the one hand and the 'social model' on the other, we find in Zola's work, and in some of the more recent developments in disability studies and the sociology of health and illness, a willingness to examine disability from many points of view, and a desire to understand the contribution the different voices have to make to our discussions. In the context of an occasionally intolerant debate over the correct language to use in talking about disability, work such as that by Irving Zola persuades us that it is possible to be politically engaged while remaining free to explore the darker phenomenological waters of people's experiences.

Further reading

Bury, M. (1996) Defining and researching disability: challenges and responses, in C. Barnes and G. Mercer (eds) *Exploring the Divide: Illness and Disability*. Leeds: The Disability Press.

Charmaz, K. (1991) *Good Days, Bad Days: The Self in Chronic Illness and Time*. New Brunswick, NJ: Rutgers University Press.

Frank, A. (1995) *The Wounded Storyteller: Body, Illness, and Ethics*. London: University of Chicago Press.

Zola, I. (1994) Towards inclusion: the role of people with disabilities in policy and research in the United States – a historical and political analysis, in M. H. Rioux and M. Bach (eds) *Disability Is Not Measles: New Research Paradigms in Disability*. North York, Ontario, Canada: Roeher.

17

Activists and Academics: Part of the Same or a World Apart?

Penny Germon

A s an activist within the disabled people's movement, I have been
part of a highly organized struggle for civil and human rights
throughout England, Scotland and Wales. At the core of the movement
are the local organizations run and controlled by disabled people. What
these organizations and their members have in common is the agreement that our 'problem' is not ourselves (our impairments) but the
institutionalized discrimination we face every day of our lives. It is this
oppression, interwoven into the fabric of society, that organizations are
set up to challenge. Disabled people's organizations have two main
aims: to promote equality and anti-discriminatory practice in services,
in policy development and in legislation so that disabled people can
fully participate in all aspects of political, social and economic life;
and to facilitate the empowerment, self-determination and self-
organization of disabled people.

Parallel to the remarkable growth of disabled people's organizations
and the promotion of the social model has been the development of
disability studies as an academic discipline. Disability theorists have
taken a significant profile within the movement and within academia:
their contributions have included new literature which tells a new story
about disabled people.

This chapter explores the relevance and relationship of disability
theorists to grass-roots organizations of disabled people. I am not
writing on behalf of anyone, I am writing and reflecting my own
thoughts and experiences as a paid activist with seven years' experience
of development work with disabled people and being part of the local
and national network of disabled people's organizations.

Setting the scene

> One distinguishing feature of the Black feminist thought is its insistence that both the changed consciousness of individuals and the social transformation of political and economic institutions constitute essential ingredients for social change. New knowledge is important for both dimensions to change. (Hill-Collins, 1990, p. 110)

Since the publication of *The Politics of Disablement* (Oliver, 1990) there has been a steady stream of books and publications about disability written from the social-model perspective (Shakespeare *et al.*, 1996; Oliver, 1990; 1996; Barnes, 1990; Barnes and Mercer, 1996; Morris, 1991; 1993; 1996; Campbell and Oliver, 1996; Barton, 1996). For an activist starting out in the latter half of the 1980s such books were in short supply. The main source of reference, recognition and analysis were informal gatherings in the pub with a hard core of activists and articles which appeared in *Coalition*, the magazine of the Greater Manchester Coalition of Disabled People (GMCDP).

As a new worker for an organization run and controlled by disabled people I had responsibility for 'facilitating the empowerment and self determination of disabled people' and for building the public profile of the organization across the local authority, the voluntary sector and among disabled people. I was concerned to understand 'the social model' and how this would apply to the people I was working with. I believed I had a responsibility to my comrades to get it right. Ultimately, the social model, or disability equality perspective, provided me, a development worker, disability equality officers in the local authority, the management committee of the Coalition and all future workers with our frame of reference.

To be an activist therefore required an understanding of the theory of disability as well as the practical implementation of the theory and its relation to the lives of disabled people. It is difficult to state categorically where we were learning from at that time and to what extent disability theorists helped us. We did draw on *The Politics of Disablement* and a number of articles in *Disability, Handicap and Society*. Not all of us read these books but relied on others drawing on them in debate. It felt like our very own local debate which was, in the broadest sense, reinforced by the books and articles, by other disabled people's experiences, but also it made sense in relation to our own experience.

The variety and breadth of literature now available make an exciting and essential contribution to the movement. These books for me are all worth celebrating. They reflect a remarkable achievement on the part of the authors but also the movement. At long last our history is being re-written. Decades of received wisdom about the lives of disabled people are being challenged. Perhaps even more significant is that disabled people, at whatever their stage in their 'journey', have access to research and literature which reflects our experience not as sad pathetic victims but as a powerful force denied social, economic and political participation in mainstream life. As Ken Davies recalls, 'I was like many Disabled People who knew there were issues, who knew there was discrimination and prejudices, who felt very angry about them, but actually had not discovered the literature that defined them and had not discovered any forum in which to project them' (Campbell and Oliver, 1996, p. 117). Reflecting on his own experience Ken clearly makes the link between the ideas, theories and broader picture reflected in literature, and implementing or 'projecting' ideas and analysis with others in self-organized groups. Like the women's movement, disabled activists have recognized the need for theory to inform practice. 'Feminism is for us both theory and practice, a framework which informs our lives. Its purpose is to understand women's oppression in order that we might end it' (Kelly *et al.*, 1994, p. 28).

Exploring the relationship

In the closing paragraph of *Understanding Disability: From Theory to Practice* (1996) Mike Oliver reflects on the role of 'intellectuals' in the movement drawing on Foucault's assertions of the intellectual performing a role as 'citizen' in connecting the personal and the political and 'illuminating the interweaving of sectional and societal interests'. Mike goes on to say:

> Such a task was undertaken by those people with impairments who produced the *Fundamental Principles of Disability* while struggling to achieve their own individual and collective liberation. *Such a project provides the criteria against which I would ask you to judge this description of my own intellectual journey.* (1996, p. 170) (emphasis added)

The invitation to judge Oliver's work in this context sets the scene for the debate that follows. It also provides a very suitable criterion for evaluating the work of all academics and the work of the many organizations, activists, freelance consultants across England, Scotland and Wales.

I read *Understanding Disability: From Theory to Practice* because I was interested in it as an activist but perhaps more significant was that I was preparing for a university assignment. I was using it to progress my own intellectual status. This fact led me to question to what extent the work of disability theorists is relevant to and supportive of the wider disabled people's movement. Does its usefulness to disabled people extend simply to challenging the institution of academia and the empowerment of disabled people who are on the road to academia themselves?

Inevitably disability theorists are open to accusations of elitism, concerned only with feathering their own nests and crafting their own career. It is a sad reflection that such accusations are prevalent within the disabled people's movement as well as outside the movement. As an activist who has been at the core of the local movement, I too am accused of elitism. My comrades and I have been described locally as those with the 'loudest voices and sharpest elbows' and 'a self appointed elite'. Clearly these tactics are designed to discredit and disempower, and are part of the oppression disabled people face. Politicized black people, lesbians, gay men and heterosexual women have been treated in the same way. Such accusations also reflect fear of change and our sad human nature which does not want to celebrate other people's success.

In my view this is to seriously miss the point and simply serves to undermine the individual and collective struggle. None of us is motivated by altruism. We are in this struggle because ultimately we benefit. It is both unreasonable and naive to expect that we will not be concerned with our own liberation: to the contrary, our own experience of oppression is an *essential* motivating force.

This is not to say that there are not dangers. The women's movement provides us with evidence that academia can become an end in itself rather than a part of a political movement:

> the relation between feminist theoretical work and political practice has become more problematic as time has passed; less has been written about it; earlier hopes for a fairly direct political input have a starry-eyed and naive ring to our ears today and have given way to

more general notions of empowerment. (Glucksmann, 1994, p. 149)

Whilst the going is good it is appropriate that the disabled people's movement engages in a meaningful dialogue about the relationship between theorists and the political activists with some urgency. The debate, then, is not about hierarchy and elitism, it is about our ability as a movement to expose ourselves to questions, where we openly and honestly consider our work, whose interest it serves and how far it contributes to the liberation of disabled people. Disability theorists need to open themselves up to 'critical' friends (Barton, 1996).

How far disability theorists contribute constructively to the struggle will depend on how they define their work in relation to the movement and take their lead from the movement. This is not only about a shared philosophical position but about coming together to write the research agenda. Whilst activists are agreed on the need for theoretical explanations and analysis to enrich our lives and contribute to the struggle, it is not at any cost. If research is to be useful and meaningful it must be able to be used by the activists: 'feminism outside of the academic mode has insisted on the crucial need for useful knowledge, theory and research as practice, on committed understanding as a form of praxis ("understand the world and then change it"), and also an unalienated knowledge' (Stanley, 1990b, p. 12). Disability theorists are not neutral or external to the disabled people's movement but a necessary part of a struggle for change. If all aspects of the movement are to work effectively on a common agenda there must be meaningful debate from which to identify the priorities and issues which would benefit from being the focus of research and study.

Whilst the body of enquiry available to us as activists is growing and contributes to the new knowledge we so desperately need, there is only one major example of academic research coming directly from the movement: *Disabled People in Britain and Discrimination: A Case for Anti-Discrimination Legislation* by Colin Barnes (1991b). This book was written for BCODP as a direct response to the government view that there was no evidence of discrimination against disabled people. We have now got the evidence written in a format which is credible and has the status to achieve the desired aim. It is a book which provides useful material for training disabled and non-disabled people, for backing up reports and setting the context for a new project and providing evidence in funding applications.

Similarly, Jenny Morris's work on community care and independent living (1993a; 1993c) contributed to the body of evidence required to argue for a shift in community care services towards independent living schemes. *The Politics of Disablement* (Oliver, 1990) provided the explanation and the theory needed to back up the work of the Avon Coalition with the former Avon County Council on developing a Disability Equality Policy during 1990/91. Clearly these are examples of the work of disability theorists being of direct use to activists at a local level and have been politically useful in bringing about change and providing important references for presentations, seminars and training.

Accessibility

The extent to which academic writing and research is accessible has been discussed within the context of the debate for emancipatory research (Barnes, 1996b; Shakespeare, 1996d) but this has not, thus far, been informed by activists. In fact in researching for this chapter I found very little written by activists about the work of disability theorists *per se*. How books are written, the language and terminology used, the style and the underlying assumptions will be different if they are written with disabled people in mind and if they are written for academic purposes. 'Writing about gender inequality obviously has a different quality and impact when it is orientated towards a politically active movement rather than towards a primarily academic audience' (Glucksmann, 1994, p. 149). Writing orientated to academics will read differently and will be based on a different set of assumptions to that which is written for disabled people. Jenny Morris suggests that researchers need to have addressed this from the outset by asking themselves the following: 'Who do I want this research to influence? Who do I want to be aware of this research? Who do I want to relate to this research?' (1992, pp. 201–2).

Ironically, I struggled to understand parts of *Understanding Disability*, and asked myself on numerous occasions why 'hegemony' and 'epistemology' had anything to do with campaigning for better services from the local authorities, supporting local disabled people to have a greater say over their lives or working for inclusive education. Had I not had some foundation in sociology I do not think I would have persevered. I am, however, very glad I did and I believe that Mike Oliver's book provides a comprehensive and readable overview of disability as a social, economic and political concern and offers important insight into the development of disability theory. It is an important book for students and organic intellectuals (Gramsci, 1971) who want to feel more confident about their ability to debate and analyse. In parts of the book Oliver picks up and responds to current debates and challenges from some activists and, like the final chapter, these parts appear to be written to comrades in the movement. The audience, however, is not clearly defined. Had these debates appeared in *Coalition* it would have been a clear statement about who was the intended readership.

It has been argued that theory cannot be oversimplified, and to attempt to do so distorts the discourse. However, if the work of academics is to be relevant to activists it has to be made relevant. In my work for example, I have had to find ways of translating academic discourse so that it relates and speaks to a wider group of disabled people. It is contradictory to promote empowerment and emancipatory approaches when the findings are inevitably inaccessible to an audience of disabled activists.

Likewise it is contradictory to be exploring the meaning of emancipatory approaches to research without actively engaging with organizations of disabled people to find out how they think research should be conducted if it is to be empowering. It is important that theorists do not confuse the dialogue they are having within the academic institution with dialogue and debate in the movement. *Exploring the Divide: Illness and Disability* (Barnes and Mercer, 1996) presents an academic debate across academic disciplines rather than the concerns of the movement although it draws on some perspectives in the movement.

Until such debates are taking place within the movement the academic environment will provide the only opportunity for some organic intellectuals to develop their work. The inevitable outcome will be two parallel debates and resulting literature rather than one which is enriched and strengthened by the considerable knowledge, expertise and perspectives available to us. The position of academics is a complex one: many endeavour to be part of the movement, as individuals *are* part of the movement, but as professionals they move between being the academics of the disabled people's movement and disability theorists within the academic institution.

Disability theorists have two strategic concerns – to challenge and to change the institution they work within and contribute to the liberation of disabled people. Each will require a different strategy in the same way that we, as paid activists, will work in different ways with officers in the local authority and with disabled people.

Setting the agenda

It is important that there should be a clear distinction between what is being done in the name of the movement and work which borrows on the movement agenda to inform the academic debate:

> Feminist theories are concerned to analyse how women can trans-
> form society so that they are no longer subordinated, by
> understanding how patriarchal relations control and constrict
> them. Consequently the adequacy of feminist theories is tested at
> least in part by their usefulness: that is, the extent to which they
> provide useful and useable knowledge for women. (Abbott and
> Wallace, 1997, p. 284)

The debate about engaging with disabled people and the movement has centred around emancipatory approaches (Barnes, 1996b; Oliver, 1996; Barton, 1996; French, 1994), where empowerment is part of the research process. Whilst Shakespeare (1996d) questions the ability of emancipatory research to bring about any real change, there are clearly aspirations associated with it which can only enhance the relationship between the academic and the activists. Len Barton, for example, sets the scene for the book *Disability and Society: Emerging Issues and Insights* (1996) by discussing an 'emancipatory' approach to sociological enquiry, stating that 'An emancipatory approach to the study of disability entails engaging with several key issues. For example, establishing relationships with disabled people, listening to their voice' (1996, p. 4).

The notion of emancipatory research is important as it encourages disability theorists to consider carefully their relationship to disabled people and what is motivating them. Emancipatory approaches also require researchers to consider how the findings can provide solutions and practical strategies: 'Black feminist research ... not only analyses the interface of racism, sexism, heterosexism and class oppression in women's lives but offers solutions to our situation' (Marshall, 1984, p. 121).

The experience of the women's movement demonstrates what is likely to happen if the work of disability theorists becomes disassociated from the disabled people's movement:

> In our cynical moments we ponder whether the masculinist hierarchy between theory and practice is being reproduced within academic feminism – demonstrated by the fact that the 'new' books which excite and exercise feminists are no longer held in common, that a language/discourse has developed which increasingly separates women inside and outside the academy. (Kelly *et al.*, 1994, p. 27)

If disability intellectuals locate themselves outside of the movement then there is a danger that disability studies will become at best irrelevant to the experience, and at worst will take over the agenda. With this in mind the recent work by Campbell and Oliver (1996) has one major omission: whilst this is a legitimate and very welcome text on the development of the movement, it fails to consider the role of disability theorists themselves.

Two recent texts – *The Sexual Politics of Disability* (Shakespeare *et al.*, 1996) and *Disability Politics: Understanding Our Past, Changing our Future* (Campbell and Oliver, 1996) – reflect what can be achieved through collaborative projects by activist and disability theorists. Such projects provide a useful relationship to the movement. By working with activists to produce texts and carry out research, they are sharing their access to the world of literature and opening up opportunities to more disabled people. Such collaboration will also provide a forum for sharing skills, experience and knowledge. Both books also draw on the real-life experience of disabled people within the movement and read as books written by and about disabled activists. Writing about *Disability Politics*, 'Rich' writes: 'It inspired this piece, got me back in touch with my strong self, my peers, our shared politics. This book's a contribution to my liberation. Just when I needed it, least expected it, it changed my life' (*DAIL*, issue 119, December 1996). An academic review of *Disability Politics* in *Disability and Society* reads: 'This book makes a welcome addition to the current paucity of critical literature on disability studies in Britain' (Johnstone and Corbett, 1997, p. 319). This demonstrates that a book can be meaningful to disabled people as well as being academically useful.

Conclusion

It would seem that thus far the academic and research agenda and how far it is useful to activists has been to a large degree left to chance and the personal integrity of the individuals concerned. Consequently channels of communication and accountability remain ambiguous and unexplored. There is a need to develop a meaningful structure for debate and analysis which brings together academics and activists, which reflects a wide range of perspectives and which is open and accountable to the wider movement. Inevitably this will involve us in discussions about *how* we facilitate debate which is encouraging and supportive whilst also providing opportunity to develop, to learn, to challenge and to disagree. This will mean creating different fora and using different media and engaging in sustained development work.

If disability theorists are to continue producing relevant and useful work it must be informed by the work of disabled people's organizations. It is not enough to be 'the researched', providing the evidence and material for academic study. All of us working in the struggle for disabled people's liberation ultimately have a very high investment in the relationship between academics and activists working effectively towards our common goal.

Note

I have been privileged to work with activists across the disabled people's movement who have helped me develop my understanding of the issues. I owe a particular debt of gratitude to my comrades at the West of England Coalition and CIL who have debated with me, argued with me and encouraged me: without their contribution I would not have been able to contribute to this book.

Further reading

Kelly, L., Burton, S. and Regan, L. (1994) Researching women's lives or studying women's oppression? Reflections on what constitutes feminist research, in M. Maynard and P. Purvis (eds) *Researching Women's Lives from a Feminist Perspective*. London: Taylor & Francis.

Oliver, M. (1996) *Understanding Disability: From Theory to Practice*. Basingstoke: Macmillan.

Afterword

These are exciting times to be working in disability studies. As the field becomes more established, so it becomes clearer how much work there is to be done. Given that women's studies and gay and lesbian studies are accepted parts of the curriculum, so disability equally deserves its place in the academy. The lacunae that exist around gender, sexuality or 'race' are paralleled by the massive absence of work on disability.

For example, we are only just beginning to develop historical understandings of the meaning of impairment and disability in the past. New readings of familiar cultural and literary texts are required, and philosophy needs urgently to embrace the challenge of the human being with impairment. Equally, more contemporary and practical issues demand exploration: the impact of genetics and other new medical and information technologies; the possibility of designing and building an inclusive world; the relationship between disability and globalization, and the meaning of disability in developing countries; the potential for civil-rights strategies to transform the lives of disabled people. In each area scholars are only just starting the research.

Within the disability movement, and within the academic disability community, there are debates about the role and direction of disability studies. There is a fear of departing from the clear principles of the social model, and leaving the practical political imperatives of disability equality behind. There is a lack of clarity as to the meaning of emancipatory research, and a confusion as to the role of non-disabled researchers. There is a threat that disability studies may lose its connections with the everyday experience of disabled people, and become just another recondite and meaningless academic exercise.

In my view a pluralism within the field is beneficial and important. There are different tasks – political, intellectual, personal – to be performed through research. There is so much to be learned, and so much to be re-thought. This highlights the essential principle which must underlie all the various approaches: disability offers a challenge to established ways of thinking which is not confined to issues of disabled people themselves. Rather than being of minority interest, the insights of disability studies have the potential to influence many other areas of human life, and force society to reassess questions about normality, independence, the physical body and the social environment, suffering and mortality.

These conclusions return to the perspectives developed by Paul Hunt thirty years ago. Disability is a major philosophical and ethical problem, as well as a pressing political and social issue. It affects non-disabled people, as well as disabled people. Disability studies is concerned with general matters of principle, meaning and value, as well as particular substantive problems, and it can influence broader debates about power and meaning, which form the central topic of social science.

Disability studies, therefore, must continue to draw on a range of disciplines, avoiding the intellectual pigeonhole which Vic Finkelstein fears. And, most importantly, it must avoid being ghettoized as a field of concern only to that proportion of the population experiencing impairment. Having successfully escaped from the category of medical science, disability studies must claim a right to relevant exploration of the central questions of human social experience.

Bibliography

Abberley, P. (1987) The concept of oppression and the development of a social theory of disability, *Disability, Handicap and Society*, vol. 2, no. 1, pp. 5–21.

Abberley, P. (1991) The significance of the OPCS disability surveys, in M. Oliver (ed.) *Social Work: Disabled People and Disabling Environments*. London: Jessica Kingsley Publishers.

Abberley, P. (1992a) *Three Theories of Abnormality*, Occasional Papers in Sociology. Bristol: Bristol Polytechnic.

Abberley, P. (1992b) Counting us out: a discussion of the OPCS disability surveys, *Disability, Handicap and Society*, vol. 7, no. 2, pp. 139–56.

Abberley, P. (1993) Disabled people and normality, in J. Swain, V. Finkelstein, S. French and M. Oliver (eds) *Disabling Barriers – Enabling Environments*. London: Sage and Open University Press.

Abberley, P. (1996) Work, utopia and impairment, in L. Barton (ed.) *Disability and Society: Emerging Issues and Insights*. Harlow: Longman.

Abbott, P. and Wallace, C. (1997) *An Introduction to Sociology: Feminist Perspectives*, 2nd edn. London: Routledge.

Adams, M. L. (1994) There's no place like home: on the place of identity in feminist politics, in M. Evans (ed.) *The Woman Question*. London: Sage.

Ainley, S., Becker, G. and Coleman, L. (eds) (1986) *The Dilemma of Difference: A Multidisciplinary View of Stigma*. London: Plenum Press.

Aitkin. K. and Rollings, J. (1993) *Community Care in a Multi-racial Britain: A Critical Review of the Literature*. London: HMSO.

Albrecht, G. L. (ed.) (1976) *The Sociology of Physical Disability and Rehabilitation*. Pittsburgh: University of Pittsburgh Press.

Albrecht, G. L. (ed.) (1981) *Cross National Rehabilitation Policies*. London: Sage.

Albrecht, G. L. (1992) *The Disability Business: Rehabilitation in America*. London: Sage.

Alcoff, L. (1988) Cultural feminism versus post-structuralism: the identity crisis in feminist theory, *Signs*, vol. 13, no. 3, pp. 405–36.

Altman, R. (1987) *The American Film Musical*. Bloomington: Indiana University Press.

Anderson, E. (1973) *The Disabled Schoolchild*. London: Methuen.

Anderson, E. M., Clarke, L. and Swain, B. (1982) *Disability in Adolescence*. London: Methuen.

Anderson, R. and Bury, M. (eds) (1988) *Living with Chronic Illness*. London: Unwin Hyman.

Anon. (1990) Sexual harassment in the disabled community, *Disability Arts in London*, June, pp. 14–15.

Anspach, R. (1979) From stigma to identity politics, *Social Science and Medicine*, vol. 134, pp. 765–73.

Appleby, Y. (1993) Disability and 'compulsory heterosexuality', in C. Kitzinger and S. Wilkinson (eds) *Heterosexuality*. London: Sage.

Appleby, Y. (1994) Out in the margins, *Disability and Society*, vol. 9, no. 1, pp. 19–32.

Ariès, P. (1973) *Centuries of Childhood*. London: Routledge & Kegan Paul.

Armstrong, D. (1983) *Political Anatomy of the Body*. Cambridge: Cambridge University Press.

Arnbrough, A. and Kinrade, D. (1995) *Directory for Disabled People*. London: Prentice Hall, Harvester Wheatsheaf.

Ashok, H., Hall, J. and Huws, U. (1985) *Home Sweet Workstation: Homeworking and the Employment Needs of People with Severe Impairments*. London: GLC Equal Opportunities Unit.

Atkin, K. (1991) Health, illness, disability and black minorities: a speculative critique of present day discourse, *Disability, Handicap and Society*, vol. 6, no. 1, pp. 37–49.

Atkin, K. and Rollings, J. (1993) *Community Care in a Multi-racial Britain: A Critical Review of the Literature*. London: HMSO.

Atkinson, D. and Williams, F. (1990) *Know Me As I Am: An Anthology of Poetry, Prose and Art by People with Learning Difficulties*. London: Hodder & Stoughton and Open University Press.

Audit Commission (1992a) *The Community Revolution: Personal Social Services and Community Care*. London: HMSO.

Audit Commission (1992b) *Getting in on the Act: Provision for Pupils with Special Educational Needs, the National Picture*. London: HMSO.

Australian Institute of Health and Welfare (1993) *Australia's Welfare 1993: Services and Assistance*. Canberra: Australian Government Publishing Service.

Bailey, D. and Hall, S. (eds) (1992) The vertigo of displacement: shifts within black documentary practices, in *Critical Decade: Black British Photography in the 80's*. London: Ten-8.

Bailey, R. (1996) Prenatal testing and the prevention of impairment: a woman's right to choose?, in J. Morris (ed.) *Encounters with Strangers: Feminism and Disability*. London: Women's Press.

Baird, J. and Workman, D. (eds) (1986) *Towards Solomon's Mountain: The Experience of Disability in Poetry*. Philadelphia: Temple University Press.

Baker-Shenk, C. and Kyle, J. G. (1990) Research with Deaf people: issues and conflicts, *Disability, Handicap and Society*, vol. 5, no. 1, pp. 66–75.

Bakhtin, M. M. (1984) *Rabelais and His World*. Bloomington: Indiana University Press.

Baldwin, S. (1986) *The Cost of Caring*. London: Routledge & Kegan Paul.

Baldwin, S. and Lunt, N. (1996) *Charging Ahead: Local Authority Charging Policies for Community Care*. York: Joseph Rowntree and Policy Press.

Ball, D. (1972) Self and identity in the context of deviance: the case of criminal abortion, in R. Scott and J. Douglas (eds) *Theoretical Perspectives on Deviance*. New York: Basic Books.

Ball, S. J. (1994) *Education Reform: A Critical and Post-structural Approach*. Buckingham: Open University Press.

Ballard, K. (1995) Inclusion, paradigms, power and participation, in C. Clark, A. Dyson and A. Millard (eds) *Towards Inclusive Schools?* London: David Fulton Publishers.

Bannerman Foster, S. (1989) *The Politics of Caring*. Lewes: Falmer Press.

Barnes, C. (1990) *Cabbage Syndrome: The Social Construction of Dependence*. Lewes: Falmer Press.

Barnes, C. (1991a) Discrimination, disability benefits and the 1980s, *Benefits*, vol. 1, no. 3.

Barnes, C. (1991b) *Disabled People in Britain and Discrimination: A Case for Anti-discrimination Legislation*. London: Hurst and Co. and BCODP.

Barnes, C. (1992a) *Disabling Imagery: An Exploration of Media Portrayals of Disabled People*. Derby: British Council of Organisations of Disabled People.

Barnes, C. (1992b) Qualitative research: valuable or irrelevant, *Disability, Handicap and Society*, vol. 7, no. 2, pp. 115–24.

Barnes, C. (ed.) (1993) *Making Our Own Choices: Independent Living, Personal Assistance and Disabled People*. Derby: British Council of Organisations of Disabled People.

Barnes, C. (1996a) The social model of disability: myths and misrepresentations, *Coalition*, August, pp. 25–30.

Barnes, C. (1996b) Disability and the myth of the independent researcher, *Disability and Society*, vol. 11, no. 1, pp. 107–10.

Barnes, C. (1996c) Theories of disability and the origins of the oppression of disabled people in western societies, in L. Barton (ed.) *Disability and Society: Emerging Issues and Insights*. Harlow: Longman.

Barnes, C. (1996d) Foreword, in J. Campbell and M. Oliver, *Disability Politics: Understanding Our Past, Changing Our Future*. London: Routledge.

Barnes, C., Mason, M. and Mercer, M. (eds) (1997) *In from the Cold*. Leeds: The Disability Press.

Barnes, C. and Mercer, G. (1995) Disability: emancipation, community participation and disabled people, in M. Mayo and G. Craig (eds) *Community Empowerment: A Reader in Participation and Development*. London: Zed Books.

Barnes, C. and Mercer, G. (eds) (1996) *Exploring the Divide: Illness and Disability*. Leeds: The Disability Press.

Barnes, C. and Oliver, M. (1995) Disability rights: rhetoric and reality in the UK, *Disability and Society*, vol. 10, no. 1, pp. 111–16.

Barrett, J. (1995) Multiple sclerosis: the experience of a disease, *Women's Studies International Forum*, vol. 18, no. 2, pp. 159–71.

Barton, L. (ed.) (1988) *The Politics of Special Educational Needs*. Lewes: Falmer Press.

Barton, L. (ed.) (1989) *Disability and Dependence*. Lewes: Falmer Press.

Barton, L. (1995) Segregated special education: some critical observations, in G. Zarb (ed.) *Removing Disabling Barriers*. London: Policy Studies Institute.

Barton, L. (ed.) (1996) *Disability and Society: Emerging Issues and Insights*. Harlow: Longman.

Barton, L. and Tomlinson, S. (eds) (1984) *Special Education and Social Interests*. London: Croom Helm.

Batchelor, R. (1994) *Henry Ford: Mass Production, Modernism, and Design*. Manchester: Manchester University Press.

Bauman, Z. (1992) *Mortality, Immortality and Other Life Strategies*. Cambridge: Polity Press.

Baxter, C., Ward, L., Poonia, K. and Nadirshaw, Z. (1990) *Double Discrimination: Issues and Services for People with Learning Difficulties from Black and Ethnic Minority Communities*. London: King's Fund and Commission for Racial Equality.

Baxter, D. (1989) Parallels between the social role perception of people with learning difficulties and Black and ethnic minority people, in A. Brechin and J. Walmsley (eds) *Making Connections: Reflecting on the Lives and Experiences of People with Learning Difficulties*. London: Hodder & Stoughton.

Bayley, M. (1991) Normalization or 'social role valorization': an adequate philosophy?, in S. Baldwin and J. Hattersley (eds) *Mental Handicap: Social Science Perspectives*. London: Tavistock Routledge.

Beardshaw, V. (1988) *Last on the List*. London: King's Fund Centre.

Beauvoir, S. de (1949) *The Second Sex*. London: Jonathan Cape.

Beazeley, S. and Moore, M. (1995) *Deaf Children, Their Families and Professionals*. London: David Fulton Publishers.

Becker, G. (1964) *Human Capital*. New York: Columbia University Press.

Becker, H. (1963) *Outsiders*. New York: Free Press.

Begum, N. (1990) *Burden of Gratitude: Women with Disabilities Receiving Personal Care*. Warwick: Social Care Practice Centre, Department of Applied Social Studies, University of Warwick.

Begum, N. (1992a) Disabled women and the feminist agenda, *Feminist Review*, vol. 40, pp. 70–84.

Begum, N. (1992b) *Something to Be Proud of . . . : The Lives of Asian Disabled People and Carers in Waltham Forest*. London: Waltham Forest Race Relations Unit.

Begum, N. (1994a) Mirror, mirror on the wall, in N. Begum, M. Hill and A. Stevens (eds) *Reflections: The Views of Black Disabled People on Their Lives and Community Care*. London: CCETSW.

Begum, N. (1994b) Optimism, pessimism and care management: the impact of community care policies, in N. Begum, M. Hill and A. Stevens (eds) *Reflections: The Views of Black Disabled People on Their Lives and Community Care*. London: CCETSW.

Begum, N., Hill, M. and Stevens, A. (eds) (1994) *Reflections: The Views of Black Disabled People on Their Lives and Community Care*. London: CCETSW.

Bell, D. (1974) *The Coming of Post-Industrial Society*. London: Heinemann.

Beresford, B. (1994) *Positively Parents: Caring for a Severely Disabled Child*. London: HMSO.

Beresford, P. (1994) *Changing the Culture: Involving Service Users in Social Work Education*. London: CCETSW.

Beresford, P. and Campbell, J. (1994) Disabled people, service users, user involvement and representation, *Disability and Society*, vol. 9, no. 3, pp. 315–26.

Beresford, P. and Harding, T. (1993) *A Challenge to Change: Practical Experience of Building User-led Services*. London: National Institute for Social Work.

Berger, P. (1979) *Facing up to Modernity*. Harmondsworth: Penguin.

Berkowitz, E. D. (1979) *Disability Policies and Government Programs*. New York: Praeger.

Berkowitz, E. D. (1987) *Disabled Policy: America's Program for the Handicapped*. Cambridge: Cambridge University Press.

Berthoud, R., Lakey, J. and McKay, S. (1993) *The Economic Problems of Disabled People*. London: Policy Studies Institute.

Bewley, C. and Glendinning, C. (1994) Representing the views of disabled people in community care planning, *Disability and Society*, vol. 9, no. 3, pp. 301–14.

Beynon, H. (1973) *Working for Ford*. Harmondsworth: Penguin.

Bhavnani, K.-K. and Coulson, M. (1986) Transforming socialist-feminism: the challenge of racism, in M. Evans (ed.) *The Woman Question*. London: Sage.

Bickenbach, J. E. (1993) *Physical Disability and Social Policy*. Toronto: University of Toronto Press.

Biegel, D., Sales, E. and Schulz, R. (1991) *Family Care Giving in Chronic Illness*. London: Sage.

Biklen, D. and Bailey, L. (eds) (1981) *Rudely Stamp'd: Imaginal Disability and Prejudice*. Washington, DC: University Press of America.

Blackford, K. A. (1993) Erasing mothers with disabilities through Canadian family-related policy, *Disability, Handicap and Society*, vol. 8, no. 3, pp. 281–94.

Blackwell-Stratten, M., Bestin, M. L., Mayerson, A. B. and Bailey, S. (1988) Smashing icons, in M. Fine and A. Asch (eds) *Women with Disabilities: Essays in Psychology, Culture and Politics*. Philadelphia: Temple University Press.

Blaxter, M. (1975) 'Disability' and rehabilitation: some questions of definition, in C. Cox and A. Mead (eds) *A Sociology of Medical Practice*. London: Collier Macmillan.

Blaxter, M. (1976) *The Meaning of Disability*. London: Heinemann.

Blaxter, M. (1984) Letter in response to Williams, *Social Science and Medicine*, vol. 17, no. 15, p. 1014.

Boddy, D. and Buchanan, D. A. (1986) *Managing New Technology*. Oxford: Blackwell.

Bogdan, R. (1987) The exhibition of humans with differences for amusement and profit, *Policy Studies Journal*, vol. 15, no. 3, March, pp. 537–50.

Bogdan, R. and Taylor, S. J. (1989) Relationships with severely disabled people: the social construction of humanness, *Social Problems*, vol. 36, pp. 135–48.

Bogle, J. E. and Shaul, S. L. (1981) Body image and the woman with a disability, in D. Bullard and S. Knight (eds) *Sexuality and Physical Disability: Personal Perspectives*. St Louis: C. V. Mosby Co.

Booth, T. (1987) Labels and their consequences, in D. Lane and B. Stratford (eds) *Current Approaches to Down's Syndrome*. London: Cassell.

Booth, T. (1996) Sounds of still voices: issues in the use of narrative methods with people who have learning difficulties, in L. Barton (ed.) *Disability and Society*. London: Longmans.

Booth, T. and Booth, W. (1994) *Parenting Under Pressure: Mothers and Fathers with Learning Difficulties*. Buckingham: Open University Press.

Bordo, S. (1993) *Unbearable Weight: Feminism, Western Culture and the Body*. Berkeley: University of California Press.

Bordwell, D. and Thompson, K. (1993) *Film Art: An Introduction*. New York: McGraw-Hill.

Bornat, J., Pereira, C., Pilgrim, D. and Williams, F. (1993) *Community Care: A Reader*. Basingstoke: Macmillan and Open University Press.

Borsay, A. (1986a) Personal trouble or public issue? Towards a model of policy for people with physical and mental disabilities, *Disability, Handicap and Society*, vol. 1, no. 2, pp. 179–96.

Borsay, A. (1986b) *Disabled People in the Community: A Study of Housing, Health and Welfare Services*. London: Bedford Square Press, NCVO.

Borsay, A. (1990) Disability and attitudes to family care in Britain: towards a sociological perspective, *Disability, Handicap and Society*, vol. 5, no. 2, pp. 107–23.

Bourdieu, P. (1984) *Distinction: A Social Critique of Judgement and Taste*. London: Routledge.

Bourne, J. (1980) Cheerleaders and ombudsmen: a sociology of race relations in Britain, *Race and Class*, vol. XXI, no. 4, pp. 331–52.

Bowe, F. (1990) Disabled and elderly people in the First, Second and Third World, *International Journal of Rehabilitation Research*, vol. 13, pp. 1–14.

Boylan, A. (1991) *Women and Disability*. London: Zed Books.

Braidotti, R. (1996) Signs of wonder and traces of doubt: on teratology and embodied difference, in N. Lykke and R. Braidotti (eds) *Between Monsters, Goddesses and Cyborgs: Feminist Confrontations with Science, Medicine and Cyberspace*. London: Zed Books.

Braithwaite, V. (1990) *Bound to Care*. Sydney: Allen & Unwin.

Braverman, H. (1974) *Labour and Monopoly Capitalism: The Degradation of Work in the Twentieth Century*. New York: Monthly Review Press.

Brechin, A. and Liddiard, P. (1983) *Look at It This Way*, 4th impression. Milton Keynes: Hodder & Stoughton in association with the Open University.

Brechin, A., Liddiard, P. and Swain, J. (eds) (1981) *Handicap in a Social World*. Sevenoaks: Hodder & Stoughton and Open University Press.

Brechin, A. and Walmsley, J. (1989) *Making Connections: Reflecting on the Lives and Experiences of People with Learning Difficulties*. London: Hodder & Stoughton.

Briggs, A. and Oliver, J. (1985) *Caring: Experiences of Looking After Disabled Relatives*. London: Routledge & Kegan Paul.

Brisenden, S. (1986) Independent living and the medical model of disability, *Disability, Handicap and Society*, vol. 1, no. 2, pp. 173–8. (See Chapter 2 above.)

Brisenden, S. (1989) Young, gifted and disabled: entering the employment market, *Disability, Handicap and Society*, vol. 4, no. 3, pp. 217–20.

Brisenden, S. (1992) Independent living: a case of human rights, in R. Rieser and M. Mason (eds) *Disability Equality in the Classroom: A Human Rights Issue*, 2nd edn. London: Disability Equality in the Classroom.

British Council of Organisations of Disabled People (1996a) *Update*, no. 14, January.

British Council of Organisations of Disabled People (1996b) *Directory of Organisations*. Derby: British Council of Organisations of Disabled People.

British Sociological Association (1997) Catching up with Peter Worsley (interview), *Network* (Newsletter of the British Sociological Assocation), vol. 67, March, pp. 7–8.

Brittan, A. and Maynard, M. (1984) *Sexism, Racism and Oppression*. Oxford: Blackwell.

Brown, H. (1994) 'An ordinary sexual life?': a review of the normalization principle as it applies to the sexual options of people with learning disabilities, *Disability and Society*, vol. 9, no. 2, pp. 123–44.

Brown, H. and Smith, H. (1989) Whose 'ordinary life' is it anyway?, *Disability, Handicap and Society*, vol. 4, no. 2, pp. 105–19.

Brown, H. and Smith, H. (1992) Defending community care: can normalization do the job?, *British Journal of Social Work*, vol. 22, no. 6, pp. 685–93.

Brown, P. and Scase, R. (1991) *Poor Work: Disadvantage and the Division of Labour*. Milton Keynes: Open University Press.

Browne, S., Connors, D. and Stern, N. (1985) *With the Power of Each Breath: A Disabled Woman's Anthology*. Pittsburgh: Cleis Press.

Bryman, A. (1988) *Quantity and Quality in Social Research*. London: Unwin Hyman.

Bullard, D. and Knight, S. (eds) (1981) *Sexuality and Physical Disability*. St Louis: C. V. Mosby & Co.

Burkhauser, R. V. and Haveman, R. H. (1982) *Disability and Work*. Baltimore: Johns Hopkins University Press.

Burleigh, M. (1994) *Death and Deliverance: Euthanasia in Germany 1900–1945*. Cambridge: Cambridge University Press.

Burr, V. (1995) *An Introduction to Social Constructionism*. London: Routledge.

Bury, M. B. (1979) Disablement in society, *International Journal of Rehabilitation Research*, vol. 2, pp. 34–40.

Bury, M. B. (1982) Chronic illness as biographical disruption, *Sociology of Health and Illness*, vol. 4, no. 2, pp. 167–92.

Bury, M. B. (1991) The sociology of chronic illness: a review of research and prospects, *Sociology of Health and Illness*, vol. 13, no. 4, pp. 451–68.

Bury, M. B. (1992) Medical sociology and chronic illness: a comment on the panel discussion, *Medical Sociology News*, vol. 18, no. 1, pp. 29–33.

Bury, M. B. (1996) Defining and researching disability: challenges and responses, in C. Barnes and G. Mercer (eds) *Exploring the Divide: Illness and Disability*. Leeds: The Disability Press.

Bury, M. B. and Gabe, J. (1994) Television and medicine: medical dominance or trial by media, in J. Gabe, D. Kelleher and G. Williams (eds) *Challenging Medicine*. London: Routledge.

Busby, G. (1990) Technology support (leader article), *Journal of the British Computer Society's Disabled People and IT Support Group*, summer. Warwick: BCS.

Bynoe, I. (1991) The case for anti-discrimination legislation, in I. Bynoe, C. Barnes and M. Oliver (eds) *Equal Rights for Disabled People*. London: Institute of Public Policy Research, pp. 17–61.

Campaign for People with a Mental Handicap (1981) *The Principle of Normalization: A Foundation for Effective Services*. London: CMH.

Campbell, J. and Oliver, M. (1996) *Disability Politics: Understanding Our Past, Changing Our Future*. London: Routledge.

Campion, M. J. (1990) *The Baby Challenge*. London: Tavistock and Routledge.

Campling, J. (1979) *Better Lives for Disabled Women*. London: Virago.

Campling, J. (1981) *Images of Ourselves: Women with Disabilities Talking*. London: Routledge & Kegan Paul.

Canguilhem, G. (1989) *The Normal and the Pathological*. New York: Zone Books.

Carby, H. (1982) White woman listen! Black feminism and the boundaries of sisterhood, in Centre for Contemporary Cultural Studies (eds) *The Empire Strikes Back: Race and Racism in 70's Britain*. London: Hutchinson.

Carew, J. and West, R. (1989) *Career Development for Visually Handicapped People Using IT*, Report by the Central Communication and Telecommunications Agency, no. 38. Peterborough: CCTA.

Carlin, M. F., Lauglin, J. L. and Saniga, R. D. (1991) *Understanding Abilities, Disabilities and Capabilities: A Guide to Children's Literature*. Englewood, CO: Libraries Unlimited.

Carnegie Council Review (1988) *After Attenborough: Arts and Disabled People*. London: Bedford Square Press.

Carnegie United Kingdom Trust (1985) *Arts and Disabled People: The Attenborough Report*. London: Bedford Square Press.

Carson, S. (1992) Normalization, needs and schools, *Educational Psychology in Practice*, vol. 1, no. 4, pp. 216–22.

Carver, V. and Rodda, M. (1978) *Disability and the Environment*. London: Elek Books.

Casling, D. (1993) Cobblers and songbirds: the language and imagery of disability, *Disability, Handicap and Society*, vol. 8, no. 2, pp. 203–10.

Casling, D. (1994) Art for whose sake, *Disability and Society*, vol. 9, no. 3, pp. 383–94.

Central Statistical Office (1996) *Social Trends*. London: Central Statistical Office.

Chadwick, A. (1996) Knowledge, power and the Disability Discrimination Bill, *Disability and Society*, vol. 11, no. 1, pp. 25–40.

Chamot, D. (1989) *Technology and Employment of Persons with Disabilities*, Switzer Monograph, 13th edn. Virginia: National Rehabilitation Association.

Chapkis, W. (1986) *Beauty Secrets: Women and the Politics of Appearance*. London: Women's Press.

Chappell, A. L. (1992) Towards a sociological critique of the normalization principle, *Disability, Handicap and Society*, vol. 7, no. 1, pp. 35–51.

Chappell, A. L. (1994a) A question of friendship: community care and the relationships of people with learning difficulties, *Disability, Handicap and Society*, vol. 9, no. 4, pp. 419–34.

Chappell, A. L. (1994b) Disability, discrimination and the criminal justice system, *Critical Social Policy*, vol. 14, no. 3, pp. 19–33.

Charmaz, K. (1983) Loss of self: a fundamental form of suffering in the chronically ill, *Sociology of Health and Illness*, vol. 5, no. 2, pp. 168–95.

Charmaz, K. (1991) *Good Days, Bad Days: The Self in Chronic Illness and Time*. New Brunswick: Rutgers University Press.

Chouinard, V. and Grant, A. (1996) On being not even anywhere near 'The Project', in N. Duncan (ed.) *Body Space*. London: Routledge.

Christensen, C. and Rizvi, F. (eds) (1996) *Disability and the Dilemmas of Education and Justice*. Buckingham: Open University Press.

Christie, N. (1992) Six ways to deal with stigma, in S. R. Baron and J. D. Haldane (eds) *Community, Normality and Difference*. Aberdeen: Aberdeen University Press.

Church, C. and Glennen, S. (1992) *Handbook of Assistive Technologies*. Oxford: Blackwell.

Clough, P. and Barton, L. (eds) (1995) *Making Difficulties: Research and the Construction of SEN*. London: Paul Chapman.

Cockburn, C. (1983) *Brothers: Male Domination and Technological Change*. London: Pluto.

Cockburn, C. (1985) *Machinery of Dominance*. London: Pluto.

Coffield, F., Borrill, C. and Marshall, S. (1986) *Growing Up at the Margins*. Milton Keynes: Open University Press.

Cohan, S. and Hark, I. R. (eds) (1993) *Screening the Male: Exploring Masculinities in Hollywood Cinema*. Basingstoke: Macmillan.

Cole, S. and Lejeune, R. (1972) Illness and the legitimation of failure, *American Sociological Review*, vol. 37, June, pp. 347–56.

Coleman, J. S. (1990) *Foundations of Social Theory*. London: Harvard University Press.

Coleman, J. S., Campbell, E., Hobson, C., McPartland, J., Mood, A., Weinfeld, F. and York, R. (1966) *Equality of Educational Opportunity*. Washington, DC: National Center for Educational Statistics.

Coleridge, P. (1993) *Disability, Liberation and Development*. Oxford: Oxfam Publications.

Comfort, A. (1978) *Sexual Consequences of Disability*. Philadelphia: Stickley.

Compton, T. (1992) *The Brief History of Disability (or The World Has Always Had Cripples)*. Berkeley: Hillegas.

Confederation of Indian Organizations (1984) *Double Bind: To Be Disabled and Asian*. London: CIO.

Connell, J. (1984) *Hard Earned Lives*. London: Tavistock.

Connolly, N. (1990) *Raising Voices: Social Services Departments and People with Disabilities*. London: Policy Studies Institute.

Connors, J. L. and Donnellan, A. M. (1993) Citizenship and culture: the role of disabled people in Navajo society, *Disability, Handicap and Society*, vol. 8, no. 3, pp. 265–80.

Coopers & Lybrand (1992) *Within Reach: Access for Disabled Children to Mainstream Education*. London: Coopers & Lybrand, National Union of Teachers and Spastics Society.

Corbett, J. (1994) A proud label: exploring the relationship between disability politics and Gay Pride, *Disability and Society*, vol. 9, no. 2, pp. 343–58.

Corbett, J. (1996) *Bad Mouthing: The Language of Special Education*. London: Falmer Press.

Corbett, J., Jones, E. and Ralph, S. (1993) A shared presentation: two disabled women on video, *Disability, Handicap and Society*, vol. 8, no. 2, pp. 172–86.

Corker, M. (1997) *Deaf and Disabled or Deafness Disabled: Towards a Human Rights Perspective*. Buckingham: Open University Press.

Cornes, P. (1984) *The Future of Work for People with Disabilities*. New York: World Rehabilitation Fund.

Cornes, P. (1987) *Impact of New Technology on the Employment of Persons with Disabilities in Great Britain*. Brussels: Rehabilitation International and European Community.

Cornes, P. (1989) *Effects of New Technology on the Employment of People with Severe Sensory or Physical Disabilities: Selected Cases from Ireland, Scotland and Sweden*. Paris: OECD.

Cornes, P. (1990) New technology training programmes for people with disabilities in Great Britain, *Rehabilitation International*, November.

Craft, M. and Craft, A. (1978) *Sex and the Mentally Handicapped*. London: Routledge & Kegan Paul.

Crawford, M. (1992) Can architects be socially responsible? in D. Ghirardo (ed.) *Out of Site: A Social Criticism of Architecture*. Seattle: Bay Press.

Crawford, R. (1994) The boundaries of the self and the unhealthy other: reflections on health, culture and AIDS, *Social Sciences and Medicine*, vol. 38, pp. 1347–65.

Crewe, N. and Zola, I. (eds) (1983) *Independent Living for Physically Disabled People*. San Francisco: Jossey Bass.

Crompton, R. and Sanderson, K. (1990) *Gendered Jobs and Social Change*. London: Unwin Hyman.

Cross, M. (1994) Abuse, in L. Keith (ed.) *Mustn't Grumble*. London: Women's Press.

Crow, L. (1992) Renewing the social model of disability, *Coalition*, July, pp. 5–9.

Crow, L. (1996) Including all of our lives: renewing the social model of disability, in J. Morris (ed.) *Encounters with Strangers: Feminism and Disability*. London: Women's Press.

Culyer, A. J. (1974) Economics, social policy and disability, in D. Lees and S. Shaw, *Impairment, Disability and Handicap*. London: Heinemann.

Cumberbatch, G. and Negrine, R. (1992) *Images of Disability on Television*. London: Routledge.

Custen, G. (1992) *Bio/Pics*. New Brunswick, NJ: Rutgers University Press.

Cutrona, C. E. and Suhr, J. E. (1994) Social support communication in the context of marriage: an analysis of couples' supportive interactions, in B. R. Burleson, T. L. Albrecht and I. G. Sarason (eds) *Communication of Social Support: Messages, Interactions, Relationships and Community*. London: Sage.

D'Aboville, E. (1991) Social work in an organization of disabled people, in M. Oliver, *Social Work: Disabled People and Disabling Environments*. London: Jessica Kingsley.

D'Aboville, E. (1994) *Promoting User Involvement: Ideas into Action*. London: King's Fund.

Dalley, G. (ed.) (1991) *Disability and Social Policy*. London: Policy Studies Institute.

Danek, M. (1992) The status of women with disabilities revisited, *Journal of Applied Rehabilitation Counseling*, vol. 23, no. 4, pp. 7–13.

Darke, P. (1994) The Elephant Man (David Lynch EMI Films): an analysis from a disabled perspective, *Disability and Society*, vol. 9, no. 3, pp. 327–42.

Dartington, T., Miller, E. J. and Gwynne, G. V. (1981) *A Life Together*. London: Tavistock.

Daunt, P. (1991) *Meeting Disability: A European Perspective*. London: Cassell Education.

Davidson, F. W. K., Woodill, G. and Bredberg, B. (1994) Images of disability in 19th century British children's literature, *Disability and Society*, vol. 9, no. 1, pp. 33–47.

Davies, C. (ed.) (1993) *Life Times: A Mutual Biography of Disabled People*. Farnham: Understanding Disability.

Davies, C. and Lifchez, R. (1987) An open letter to architects, in R. Lifchez (ed.) *Rethinking Architecture*. Berkeley: University of California Press, pp. 35–50.

Davis, A. (1989) *From Where I Sit: Living with Disability in an Able-bodied World*. London: Triangle.

Davis, F. (1964) Deviance disavowal and the visibly handicapped, in H. Becker (ed.) *The Other Side*. New York: Free Press.

Davis, Kathy (1997) *Embodied Practices: Feminist Perspectives on the Body*. London: Sage.

Davis, Ken (1981) 28–38 Grove Road: accommodation and care in a community setting, in A. Brechin, P. Liddiard and J. Swain (eds) *Handicap in a Social World*. Sevenoaks: Hodder & Stoughton and Open University Press.

Davis, Ken (1986a) Pressed to death, *Coalition News*, vol. 1, no. 4.

Davis, Ken (1986b) *Developing Our Own Definitions – Draft for Discussion*. London: British Council of Organisations of Disabled People.

Davis, Ken (1993) On the movement, in J. Swain, V. Finkelstein, S. French and M. Oliver (eds) *Disabling Barriers – Enabling Environments*. London: Sage and Open University Press.

Davis, Ken and Mullender, A. (1993) *Ten Turbulent Years: A Review of the Work of the Derbyshire Coalition of Disabled People*. Nottingham: University of Nottingham Centre for Social Action.

Davis, Ken and Mullender, A. (eds) (1994) Key issues in disability: rights or charity, the future of welfare, social action, *Journal of the Centre for Social Action*, vol. 2, no. 1.

Davis, L. D. (1995) *Enforcing Normalcy: Disability, Deafness and the Body*. London: Verso.

Deegan, M. J. (1987) *Physically Disabled Women and New Directions in Public Policy*. Monticello, IL: Vance.

Deegan, M. J. and Brooks, N. A. (eds) (1985) *Women and Disability: The Double Handicap*. New Brunswick, NJ: Transaction Books.

Degener, T. (1992) The right to be different: implications for child protection, *Child Abuse Review*, vol. 1, pp. 151–5.

De Jong, G. (1979) Independent living: from social movement to analytic paradigm, *Archives of Physical Medicine and Rehabilitation*, vol. 60, pp. 435–46.

De Jong, G. (1983a) Defining and implementing the independent living concept, in N. M. Crewe and I. K. Zola (eds) *Independent Living for Physically Disabled People*. San Francisco: Jossey Bass.

De Jong, G. (1983b) The movement for independent living: origins, ideology and implications for disability research, in A. Brechin, P. Liddiard and J. Swain (eds) *Handicap in a Social World*. Sevenoaks: Hodder & Stoughton and Open University Press.

Department of Health and Social Security (1971) *Better Services for the Mentally Handicapped*, Cmnd 4683. London: HMSO.

Department of Health and Social Security (1992) Guide-lines for funding applications to undertake disability research, *Disability, Handicap and Society*, vol. 7, no. 3, pp. 278–89.

Department of Social Security (1990) *Benefits for Disabled People*. London: HMSO.

Department of Social Security (1994) *A Consultation on Government Measures to Tackle Discrimination Against Disabled People*. Bristol: Department of Social Security and Enable.

Derrida, J. (1974) *Of Grammatology*. Baltimore: Johns Hopkins University Press.

Derrida, J. (1978) *Writing and Difference*. Chicago: University of Chicago Press.

Derrida, J. (1981) *Dissemination*. Chicago: University of Chicago Press.

Despouv, L. (1991) *Human Rights and Disability*. New York: United Nations Economic and Social Council.

Diamond, M. (1984) Sexuality and the handicapped, in R. P. Marinelli and A. dell Orto (eds) *The Psychological and Social Impact of Physical Disability*. New York: Springer Publishing.

Dicken, P. (1980) Social science and design theory, *Environment and Planning B: Planning and Design*, vol. 6, pp. 105–17.

Dimmock, A. F. (1993) *Cruel Legacy: An Introduction to the Record of Deaf People in History*. Edinburgh: Scottish Workshop Publications.

Disability Alliance (1975) *Poverty and Disability*. London: Disability Alliance.

Disability Alliance (1987) *Poverty and Disability, Breaking the Link: The Case for a Comprehensive Disability Income*. London: Disability Alliance.

Disability Alliance (1988) *Briefing on the First Report of the OPCS Surveys of Disability*. London: Disability Alliance.

Disability Awareness in Action (1995) *Overcoming Obstacles to the Integration of Disabled People*. London: Disability Awareness in Action.

Disability, Handicap and Society (1992) Special Issue: Researching Disability, vol. 7, no. 2.

Disability, Handicap and Society (1993) Special Issue: Citizens of the State? The Experience of Disabled People, vol. 8, no. 3.

Disabled Peoples' International (1993) *Proceedings of the 3rd World Congress of Disabled Peoples' International.* Winnipeg: Disabled Peoples' International.

Disabled Persons Transport Advisory Committee (1988) *Public Transport and the Missing Six Millions: What Can Be Learned?* London: Disabled Persons Transport Advisory Committee.

Disablement Income Group (1988) *Not the OPCS Survey: Being Disabled Cost More Than They Said.* London: Disablement Income Group.

Disablement Income Group (1990) *Short Changed by Disability.* London: Disablement Income Group.

Doddington, K., Jones, R. S. P. and Miller, B. Y. (1994) Are attitudes to people with learning difficulties negatively influenced by charity advertising: an experimental analysis, *Disability and Society*, vol. 9, no. 2, pp. 207–22.

Douglas, M. (1966) *Purity and Danger.* London: Routledge & Kegan Paul.

Doyal, L. (1979) *The Political Economy of Health.* London: Pluto Press.

Doyle, B. (1993) Employment rights, equal opportunities and disabled persons: the ingredients of reform, *Industrial Law Journal*, vol. 22, no. 2, pp. 89–103.

Doyle, B. (1995) *Disability Discrimination and Equal Opportunities: A Comparative Study of the Employment Rights of Disabled Persons.* London: Mansell.

Doyle, B. (1996) *Disability Discrimination: The New Law.* London: Jordans.

Drake, R. F. (1996) Charities, authority and disabled people: a qualitative study, *Disability and Society*, vol. 11, no. 1, pp. 5–24.

Driedger, D. (1989) *The Last Civil Rights Movement.* London: C. Hurst and Co.

Driedger, D. and Gray, S. (eds) (1994) *Imprinting Our Image: An International Anthology by Women with Disabilities.* Charlottetown, Prince Edward Island: Gynergy.

Dubrow, H. (1982) *Genre.* London: Methuen.

Duckworth, D. (1983), *The Classification and Measurement of Disablement.* London: HMSO.

Dumbleton, P. (1994) The other end of the rainbow, *Times Educational Supplement*, 19 March, p. 3.

Duncan, M. (1994) The politics of women's body images and practices:

Foucault, the Panopticon, and Shape magazine, *Journal of Sport and Social Issues*, vol. 18, no. 1, February, pp. 48–65.

Duncan, N. (1996) *Body Space*. London: Routledge.

Dunn, P. A. (1990) The impact of the housing environment upon the ability of disabled people to live independently, *Disability, Handicap and Society*, vol. 5, no. 1, pp. 37–53.

Durkheim, E. (1964) *The Division of Labour in Society*. Glencoe, IL: Free Press.

Durkheim, E. (1971) Individualism and the intellectuals (trans. S. and J. Lukes), *Political Studies*, vol. XVII, pp. 14–30.

Dyer, R. (1992) *Only Entertainment*. London: Routledge.

Dyer, R. (1993) *The Matter of Images*. London: Routledge.

Edgerton, R. B. (1967) *The Cloak of Competence: Stigma in the Lives of the Mentally Retarded*. Berkeley: University of California Press.

Ehrenreich, B. and English, D. (1976) *Complaints and Disorders: The Sexual Politics of Sickness*. London: Writers and Readers.

Elliot, D. and Elliot, R. (1976) *The Control of Technology*. London: Wyeham.

Ellis, K. (1993) *Squaring the Circle: User and Carer Participation in Needs Assessment*. York: Joseph Rowntree Foundation.

Engels, F. (1969) *The Condition of the Working Class in England*. St Albans: Granada Publishing.

Enticott, J. and Graham, P. (1992) *Polls Apart: Disabled People and the 1992 General Election*. London: The Spastics Society.

Equality Studies Centre (1994) *Equality, Status and Disability*. Dublin: University College Dublin.

Evers, A., Piji, M. and Ungerson, C. (eds) (1995) *Payments for Care: A Comparative Overview*. Aldershot: Avebury.

Falk, P. (1994) *The Consuming Body*. London: Sage.

Feeney, R. J. and Galer, M. D. (1981) Designing for the disabled, in A. Brechin, P. Liddiard and J. Swain (eds) *Handicap in a Social World*. Sevenoaks: Hodder & Stoughton and Open University Press.

Fiedler, B. (1988) *Living Options Lottery*. London: Prince of Wales Advisory Group on Disability.

Fiedler, B. (1991) Housing and independence, in M. Oliver (ed.) *Social Work: Disabled People and Disabling Environments*. London: Jessica Kingsley.

Fiedler, B. and Twitchin, D. (1992) *Achieving User Participation*. London: Living Options in Practice.

Fiedler, L. (1978) *Freaks: Myths and Images of the Secret Self*. New York: Simon & Schuster.

Fielding, N. G. and Fielding, J. (1986) *Linking Data*. Thousand Oaks, CA: Sage.

Fine, M. and Asch, A. (1985) Disabled women: sexism without the pedestal, in M. J. Deegan and N. A. Brooks (eds) *Women and Disability: The Double Handicap*. New Brunswick, NJ: Transaction Books.

Fine, M. and Asch, A. (1988a) *Women with Disabilities: Essays in Psychology, Culture and Politics*. Philadelphia: Temple University Press.

Fine, M. and Asch, A. (1988b) Disability beyond stigma: social interaction, discrimination and activism, *Journal of Social Issues*, vol. 44, no. 1, pp. 3–21.

Finger, A. (1991) *Past Due: A Story of Disability, Pregnancy and Birth*. London: Women's Press.

Finger, A. (1992) Forbidden fruit, *New Internationalist*, vol. 233, pp. 8–10.

Finkelstein, V. (1980) *Attitudes and Disabled People: Issues for Discussion*. New York: World Rehabilitation Fund.

Finkelstein, V. (1981a) To deny or not to deny disability, in A. Brechin, P. Liddiard and J. Swain (eds) *Handicap in a Social World*. Sevenoaks: Hodder & Stoughton and Open University Press.

Finkelstein, V. (1981b) Disability and the helper/helped relationship: an historical view, in A. Brechin, P. Liddiard and J. Swain (eds) *Handicap in a Social World*. Sevenoaks: Hodder & Stoughton and Open University Press.

Finkelstein, V. (1991) Disability: an administrative challenge?, in M. Oliver (ed.) *Social Work: Disabled People and Disabling Environments*. London: Jessica Kingsley.

Finkelstein, V. (1993a) The commonality of disability, in J. Swain, V. Finkelstein, S. French and M. Oliver (eds) *Disabling Barriers – Enabling Environments*. London: Sage and Open University Press.

Finkelstein, V. (1993b) Disability: A social challenge or an administrative responsibility, in J. Swain, V. Finkelstein, S. French and M. Oliver (eds) *Disabling Barriers – Enabling Environments*. London: Sage and Open University Press, pp. 34–44.

Finkelstein, V. (1994) *Workbook 1: Being Disabled*. Milton Keynes: Open University (K665 *The Disabling Society*).

Finkelstein, V. and French, S. (1993) Towards a psychology of disability, in J. Swain, V. Finkelstein, S. French and M. Oliver (eds) *Disabling Barriers – Enabling Environments*. London: Sage and Open University Press.

Finkelstein, V. and Stuart, O. (1996) Developing new services, in G. Hales (ed.) *Beyond Disability: Towards an Enabling Society*. London: Sage and Open University Press.

Finlay, B. (1978) *Housing and Disability: A Report on the Housing Needs of Physically Handicapped People in Rochdale*. Rochdale: Rochdale Voluntary Action.

Finnegan, R., Salaman, G. and Thompson, K. (eds) (1987) *Information Technology: Social Issues*. Milton Keynes: Open University Press.

Fish, J. (1986) *Young People with Handicaps: The Road to Adulthood*. Paris: OECD.

Flemming, M. and Manvell, R. (1985) *Images of Madness*. London: Associated University Press.

Floyd, M. and North, K. (eds) (1985) *Information Technology and the Employment of Disabled People*, Anglo-German Foundation Conference Paper. London: City University.

Ford, J. *et al.* (1982) *Special Education and Social Control*. London: Routledge & Kegan Paul.

Forester, T. (1989) *Computers in the Human Context: Information Technology, Productivity and People*. Oxford: Blackwell.

Forgacs, D. (ed.) (1988) *A Gramsci Reader: Selected Writings 1916–1935*. London: Lawrence & Wishart.

Foucault, M. (1972) *The Archaeology of Knowledge*. London: Tavistock.

Foucault, M. (1977) *Discipline and Punish: The Birth of the Prison*. London: Penguin.

Fowkes, A., Oxley, P. and Heiser, B. (1994) *Cross Sector Benefits of Accessible Public Transport*. London: Cranfield University.

Francis, A. (1986) *New Technology at Work*. Oxford: Clarendon.

Franey, R. (1983) *Hard Times: The Tories and Disability*. London: Disability Alliance.

Frank, A. (1991) For a sociology of the body: an analytical review, in M. Featherstone, M. Hepworth and B. S. Turner, *The Body: Social Process and Cultural Theory*. London: Sage.

Frank, A. (1995) *The Wounded Storyteller: Body, Illness, and Ethics*. London: University of Chicago Press.

Frank, G. (1988) Beyond stigma: visibility and self-empowerment of persons with congenital limb deficiencies, *Journal of Social Issues*, vol. 44, no. 1, pp. 95–115.

Freidson, E. (1968) Disability as social deviance, in M. B. Sussman (ed.) *Sociology and Rehabilitation*. Washington, DC: American Sociological Association.

French, S. (1993a) Disability, impairment or something in between?, in J. Swain, V. Finkelstein, S. French and M. Oliver (eds) *Disabling Barriers – Enabling Environments*. London: Sage and Open University Press.

French, S. (1993b) Can you see the rainbow – the roots of denial, in J. Swain, V. Finkelstein, S. French and M. Oliver (eds) *Disabling Barriers – Enabling Environments*. London: Sage and Open University Press.

French, S. (ed.) (1994) *On Equal Terms: Working With Disabled People*. Oxford: Butterworth.

French, S. (1996) Out of sight, out of mind: the experience and effects of a 'special' residential school, in J. Morris (ed.) *Encounters with Strangers: Feminism and Disability*. London: Women's Press.

Friedberg, J. B. (1992) *Portraying Persons with Disabilities: An Annotated Bibliography of Non-fiction for Children and Teenagers*. New Providence, NJ: R. R. Bowker.

Fukuyama, F. (1992) *The End of History and the Last Man*. New York: Free Press.

Fukuyama, F. (1995) *Trust: The Social Virtues and the Creation of Prosperity*. London: Hamish Hamilton.

Fulcher, G. (1989) *Disabling Policies? A Comparative Approach to Education Policy and Disability*. Lewes: Falmer Press.

Gabe, J., Kelleher, D. and Williams, G. (1994) *Challenging Medicine*. London: Routledge.

Gallagher, H. G. (1989) *FDR's Splendid Deception*. New York: Dodd Mead.

Gallagher, H. G. (1990) *By Trust Betrayed: Patients and Physicians in the Third Reich*. London: Henry Holt.

Gallie, D. (1988) *Employment in Britain*. Oxford: Blackwell.

Gardiner, S. (1974) *Le Corbusier*. London: Fontana.

Gardner, C. (1980) Passing by: street remarks, address rights, and the urban female, *Sociological Inquiry*, vol. 50, nos 3–4, pp. 328–56.

Garland, R. (1995) *The Eye of the Beholder: Deformity and Disability in the Graeco-Roman World*. London: Duckworth.

Gartner, A. and Joe, T. (eds) (1987) *Images of the Disabled: Disabling Images*. New York: Praeger.

Gelb, S. A. (1987) Social deviance and the 'discovery' of the moron, *Disability, Handicap and Society*, vol. 2, no. 3, pp. 247–58.

George, V. and Wilding, P. (1994) *Welfare and Ideology*. London: Harvester Wheatsheaf.

Gerber, D. A. (1990) Listening to disabled people: the problem of voice and authority in Robert B. Edgerton's *The Cloak of Competence*, *Disability, Handicap and Society*, vol. 5, no. 1, pp. 3–25.

Gergen, K. J. (1989) Warranting voice and the elaboration of the self, in J. Shotter and K. J. Gergen (eds) *Texts of Identity*. London: Sage.

Gerhardt, U. E. (1989) *Ideas About Illness: An Intellectual and Political History of Medical Sociology*. Basingstoke: Macmillan Educational.

Gerschick, T. J. and Miller, A. S. (1995) Coming to terms, in D. Sabo and D. Gordon (eds) *Men's Health and Illness*. London: Sage, pp. 183–204.

Gertner, V. (1994) Interview with Rob Imrie. Berkeley, California, 3 April.

Ghirardo, D. (ed.) (1991) *Out of Site: A Social Criticism of Architecture*. Seattle: Bay Press.

Gibler, C. (1989) Rehabilitation, technology and industry's role, in Switzer Monograph no. 13. Alexandra, VA: National Rehabilitation Association.

Giddens, A. (1986) *Sociology: A Brief Critical Introduction*, 2nd edn. Basingstoke: Macmillan.

Giddens, A. (1989) *Sociology*. Cambridge: Polity Press.

Giddens, A. (1991) *Modernity and Self-Identity: Self and Security in the Late Modern Age*. Cambridge: Polity Press.

Gill, C. (1985) *Work, Unemployment, and New Technology*. London: Polity.

Gillespie-Sells, K. (1994) Getting things right, *Community Care Inside*, 31 March.

Gillespie-Sells, K. and Ruebain, D. (n.d.) *Double the Trouble, Twice the Fun*. London: Channel 4.

Gilman, S. L. (1985) *Pathology and Difference*. Ithaca, NY: Cornell University Press.

Gilman, S. L. (1988) *Disease and Representation*. Ithaca, NY: Cornell University Press.

Gilman, S. L. (1991) *Inscribing the Other*. Lincoln: Nebraska University Press.

Gilman, S. L. (1995) *Health and Illness: Images of Difference*. London: Reaktion.

Glaser, B. and Strauss, A. (1975) *Chronic Illness and the Quality of Life*. St Louis: C. V. Mosby & Co.

Gleeson, B. J. (1991) Notes towards a materialist history of disability. Occasional Paper, University of Bristol Department of Geography, July.

Gleeson, B. J. (1997) Disability studies: a historical materialist view, *Disability and Society*, vol. 12, no. 2, pp. 179–202.

Glendinning, C. (1986) *A Single Door: Social Work With Families of Disabled Children*. London: Allen & Unwin.

Glendinning, C. (1991) Losing ground: social policy and disabled people in Great Britain, 1980–1990, *Disability, Handicap and Society*, vol. 6, no. 1, pp. 3–19.

Glendinning, C. (1992a) No way ahead? Social policy and disability, in N. Manning and R. Page (eds) *Social Policy 1991/92*. London: Longman.

Glendinning, C. (1992b) *The Costs of Informal Care: Looking Inside the Household*. London: HMSO.

Glendinning, C. and Bewley, C. (1993) *Involving Disabled People in Community Care Planning: The First Report*. University of Manchester, Department of Social Policy.

Glucksmann, M. (1994) The work of knowledge and the knowledge of women's work, in M. Maynard and P. Purvis (eds) *Researching Women's Lives from a Feminist Perspective*. London: Taylor & Francis.

Goffman, E. (1968a) *Asylums*. Harmondsworth: Penguin.

Goffman, E. (1968b) *Stigma*. Harmondsworth: Pelican.

Goode, D. (1994) *A World Without Words: The Social Construction of Children Born Deaf and Blind*. Philadelphia: Temple University Press.

Gooding, C. (1994) *Disabling Laws, Enabling Acts: Disability Rights in Britain and America*. London: Pluto.

Gooding, C. (1996) *Disability Discrimination Act 1995*. London: Blackstone Press.

Goodley, D. (1997) Locating self-advocacy in models of disability: understanding disability in the support of self-advocates with learning difficulties, *Disability and Society*, vol. 12, no. 3, pp. 367–80.

Gordon, G. (1966) *Role Theory and Illness: A Sociological Perspective*. New Haven: Connecticut College and University Press.

Gorz, A. (1982) *Farewell to the Working Class*. London: Pluto.

Gouldner, A. (1971) *The Coming Crisis in Western Sociology*. Brighton: Harvester Press.

Gouldner, A. (1975) *For Sociology: Renewal and Critique in Sociology Today*. Harmondsworth: Pelican.

Gowman, A. G. (1956) Blindness and the role of companion, *Social Problems*, vol. 4, no. 1, pp. 68–75.

Graham, H. (1993) Social divisions in caring, *Women's International Studies Forum*, vol. 16, no. 5, pp. 461– 70.

Graham, P., Jordon, A. and Lamb, B. (1990) *An Equal Chance or No Chance?* London: Spastics Society.

Graham, P. and Oehlschlaeger, F. H. (1992) *Articulating the Elephant Man*. Baltimore: Johns Hopkins Press.

Gramsci, A. (1971) *Selections from the Prison Notebooks*. London: Lawrence & Wishart.

Grant, B. K. (ed.) (1986) *Film Genre Reader*. Austin: University of Texas.

Grant, L. (1995) *Disability and Debt: The Experience of Disabled People in Debt*. Sheffield: Sheffield Citizens Advice Bureau Debt Support Unit.

Greaves, M. and Massie, B. (1977) *Work and Disability*. London: Disabled Living Foundation.

Greengross, W. (1976) *Entitled to Love: The Sexual and Emotional Needs of the Handicapped*. London: Malaby Press.

Gregory, S. and Hartley, G. (eds) (1990) *Constructing Deafness*. London: Pinter and The Open University.

Griffiths, E. (compiler) (1975) Sexual dysfunctions associated with physical disabilities, *Archives of Physical Medicine and Rehabilitation*, vol. 56, pp. 8–13.

Groce, N. E. (1985) *Everyone Here Spoke Sign Language*. Cambridge, MA: Harvard University Press.

Grossberg, L., Nelson, C. and Treichler, P. (eds) (1992) *Cultural Studies*. New York: Routledge.

Grosz, E. (1994) *Volatile Bodies: Towards a Corporeal Feminism*. St Leonards: Allen & Unwin.

Grover, R. and Gladstone, F. (1981) *Disabled People – A Right To Work*. London: Bedford Square Press.

Guthrie, D. (1981) *Disability: Legislation and Practice*. London: Macmillan.

Haber, L. D. and Smith, R. T. (1971) Disability and deviance: normative adaptations of role behaviour, *American Sociological Review*, vol. 36, pp. 87–97.

Hafferty, F. E. and Foster, S. (1994) Deconstructing disability in the crime mystery genre: the case of the invisible handicap, *Disability and Society*, vol. 9, no. 2.

Hahn, H. (1986) Disability and the urban environment: a perspective on Los Angeles, *Environment and Planning D: Society and Space*, 4, pp. 273–88.

Hahn, H. (1988) The politics of physical differences: disability and discrimination, *Journal of Social Issues*, vol. 44, no. 1, pp. 39–47.

Hahn, H. (1989) Disability and the reproduction of bodily images: the dynamics of human appearances, in J. Wolch and M. Dear (eds) *The Power of Geography: How Territory Shapes Social Life*. Boston: Homan.

Hales, G. (ed.) (1996) *Beyond Disability: Towards an Enabling Society*. London: Open University Press and Sage.

Hall, S. (1996) Introduction: who needs identity? in S. Hall and P. Du Gay (eds) *Questions of Cultural Identity*. London: Sage.

Halsey, A. H. (1995) *Change in British Society: From 1900 to the Present Day*, 4th edn. Oxford: Oxford University Press.

Hammersley, M. (1992) On feminist methodology, *Sociology*, vol. 26, no. 2, pp. 187–206.

Hamnett, C., McDowell, L. and Sarre, P. (1989) *The Changing Social Structure*. Milton Keynes: Open University Press.

Hanks, J. and Hanks, L. (1980) The physically handicapped in certain non-occidental societies, in W. Philips and J. Rosenberg (eds) *Social Scientists and the Physically Handicapped*. London: Arno Press.

Hanna, A. J. and Rogovsky, B. (1991) Women with disabilities: two handicaps plus, *Disability, Handicap and Society*, vol. 6, no. 1, pp. 49–63.

Hannington, W. (1937) *The Problem of the Distressed Areas*. London: Gollancz and Left Book Club.

Haraway, D. (1990) Manifesto for cyborgs: science, technology, and socialist feminism in the 1980s, in L. Nicholson (ed.) *Feminism/Postmodernism*. London: Routledge.

Haraway, D. (1992) The promise of monsters: a regenerative politics for inappropriate/d Others, in L. Grossberg, C. Nelson and P. Treichler (eds) *Cultural Studies*. New York: Routledge.

Hardikker, P. (1994) Thinking and practising otherwise: disability and child abuse, *Disability and Society*, vol. 9, no. 2, pp. 257–63.

Hargreaves, A. (1994) *Changing Teachers, Changing Times: Teachers' Work and Culture in the Postmodern Age*. London: Cassell.

Harré, R. (1981) The positivist-empiricist approach and its alternative, in P. Reason and J. Rowan (eds) *Human Inquiry: A Sourcebook of New Paradigm Research*. Chichester: John Wiley and Sons.

Harris, A. (1971) *Handicapped and Impaired in Great Britain*. London: HMSO.

Harris, J. (1995) *The Cultural Meaning of Deafness*. Aldershot: Avebury.

Harrison, J. (1989) *Severe Physical Disability: Responses to the Challenge of Care*. London: Cassell.

Harrison, J. (1993) Medical responsibilities to disabled people, in J. Swain, V. Finkelstein, S. French and M. Oliver (eds) *Disabling Barriers – Enabling Environments*. London: Sage and Open University Press.

Harvey, D. (1982) *The Limits to Capital*. Oxford: Blackwell.

Harvey, D. (1989) *The Condition of Postmodernity*. Oxford: Blackwell.

Hasler, F. (1993) Developments in the disabled people's movement, in J. Swain, V. Finkelstein, S. French and M. Oliver (eds) *Disabling Barriers – Enabling Environments*. London: Sage and Open University Press.

Hayden, D. (1981) What would a non sexist city be like: speculations on housing, urban design, and human work, in C. Stimpson (ed.) *Women and the American City*. Chicago: Signs.

Hazan, P. (1981) Computing and the handicapped, *Computing*, vol. 14, no. 1.

Hearn, K. (1988a) A woman's right to cruise, in C. McEwen and S. O'Sullivan (eds) *Out the Other Side: Contemporary Lesbian Writing*. London: Virago.

Hearn, K. (1988b) Oi! What about us, in B. Cant and S. Hemmings (eds) *Radical Records: 30 Years of Lesbian and Gay History*. London: Routledge.

Hearn, K. (1991) Disabled lesbians and gays are here to stay, in T. Kaufmann and P. Lincoln, *High Risk Lives: Lesbian and Gay Politics After the Clause*. Bridport: Prism Press.

Heath, J. (1987) *Disability in the Pacific Islands*. Oaklands Park: McDonald-Heath.

Heiser, B. (1995) The nature and causes of transport disability in Britain and how to overcome it, in G. Zarb (ed.) *Removing Disabling Barriers*. London: Policy Studies Institute.

Helander, E. (1993) *Prejudice and Dignity: An Introduction to Community Based Rehabilitation*. Geneva: World Health Organisation.

Helen House (1990) *Zimbabwe: Steps Ahead – Community Rehabilitation and People with Disabilities*. London: Catholic Institute for International Relations.

Henderson, M. G. (1992) Speaking in tongues: dialogics, dialectics and the Black woman writer's literary tradition, in J. Butler and J. Scott (eds) *Feminists Theorise the Political*. London: Routledge.

Henderson, P. (1974) *Disability in Childhood and Youth*. London: Oxford University Press.

Herd, D. and Stalker, K. (1996) *Involving Disabled People in Services: A Document Describing Good Practice for Planners, Purchasers and Providers*. Edinburgh: Social Work Services Inspectorate for Scotland.

Herndl, D. P. (1993) *Invalid Women: Figuring Feminine Illness in American Fiction and Culture 1840–1940*. Chapel Hill: University of North Carolina Press.

Herrnstein, R. and Murray, C. (1994) *The Bell Curve: Intelligence and Class Structure in American Life*. New York: Free Press.

Herzlich, C. (1973) *Health and Illness: A Social Psychological Analysis*. London: Academic Press.

Herzlich, C. and Pierret, J. (1987) *Illness and Self in Society*. Baltimore: Johns Hopkins University Press.

Hevey, D. (1991) From self love to the picket line, in S. Lees (ed.) *Disability Arts and Culture Papers*. London: Shape Publications.

Hevey, D. (1992) *The Creatures Time Forgot: Photography and Disability Imagery*. London: Routledge.

Hevey, D. (1993) The tragedy principle: strategies for change in the representation of disabled people, in J. Swain, V. Finkelstein, S. French and M. Oliver (eds) *Disabling Barriers – Enabling Environments*. London: Sage and Open University Press.

Hey, S. C., Kiger, G. and Seidel, J. (eds) (1984) *Social Aspects of Chronic Illness, Impairment and Disability*. Salem, OR: Willamette University Press.

Higgins, P. (1980) *Outsiders in a Hearing World*. Beverly Hills: Sage.

Higgins, P. C. (1992) *Making Disability: Exploring the Human Transformation of Human Variation*. Springfield, IL: Charles C. Thomas.

Hill, J. (1986) *Sex, Class and Realism*. London: BFI Publications.

Hill, M. (1994a) Getting things right, *Community Care Inside*, 31 March.

Hill, M. (1994b) 'They are not our brothers': the disability movement and the black disability movement, in N. Begum, N. Hill and A. Stevens (eds) *Reflections: The Views of Black Disabled People on Their Lives and Community Care*. London: CCETSW.

Hill, M. (1994c) Burn and rage: black voluntary organizations as a source of social change, in N. Begum, N. Hill and A. Stevens (eds) *Reflections: The Views of Black Disabled People on Their Lives and Community Care*. London: CCETSW.

Hill-Collins, P. (1990) *Black Feminist Thought: Knowledge, Consciousness and the Politics of Empowerment*. London: Unwin Hyman.

Hills, J. (1993) *The Future of Welfare: A Guide to the Debate*. York: Joseph Rowntree Foundation.

Hillyer, B. (1993) *Feminism and Disability*. Norman: University of Oklahoma Press.

Hirst, M. and Baldwin, S. (1994) *Unequal Opportunities: Growing Up Disabled*. York: Social Policy Research Unit.

HMSO (1989) *Caring for People: Community Care in the Next Decade and Beyond*. London: HMSO.

Hockey, J. and James, A. (1993) *Growing Up and Growing Old: Ageing and Dependency in the Life Course*. London: Sage.

Holden, L. (1991) *Forms of Deformity*. Sheffield: JSOT Press.

Honey, S., Meagar, N. and Williams, M. (1993) *Employers' Attitudes Towards People with Disabilities*. University of Sussex, Manpower Studies Institute.

hooks, b. (1989) *Talking Back: Thinking Feminist, Thinking Black*. Boston: South End Press.

Hornby, G. (1992) A review of fathers' accounts of their experience of parenting children with disabilities, *Disability, Handicap and Society*, vol. 7, no. 4, pp. 363–74.

House of Commons Social Security Committee (1990) *Community Care: Social Security for Disabled People* (9th Report). London: HMSO.

Houston, S., Percival, B. and Epperley, R. E. (eds) (1994) *The More We Get Together*. Charlottetown, Prince Edward Island: Gynergy.

Howard, M. and Thompson, P. (1995) *There May Be Trouble Ahead*. London: Disability Alliance and Disability Incomes Group.

Huet, M. (1993) *Monstrous Imagination*. London: Harvard University Press.

Hughes, B. and Paterson, K. (1997) The social model of disability and the disappearing body: towards a sociology of impairment, *Disability and Society*, vol. 12, no. 3, pp. 325–40.

Hughes, J. (1990) *The Philosophy of Social Research*. London: Longman.

Hull, R. (1992) *Disability, Unfreedom & Injustice*. Stoke-on-Trent: Staffordshire Papers in Politics and International Relations, no. 5.

Humphries, S. and Gordon, P. (1992) *Out of Sight: The Experience of Disability 1900–1950*. Plymouth: Channel Four and Northcote House.

Hunt, P. (ed.) (1966a) *Stigma: The Experience of Disability*. London: Geoffrey Chapman.

Hunt, P. (1966b) A critical condition, in P. Hunt (ed.) *Stigma: The Experience of Disability*. London: Geoffrey Chapman. (See Chapter 1 above.)

Hunt, P. (1981) Settling accounts with the parasite people, *Disability Challenge*, no. 2, pp. 37–50.

Hutson, S. and Jenkins, R. (1989) *Taking the Strain: Families, Unemployment and Transition to Adulthood*. Milton Keynes: Open University Press.

Illich, I. (1975) *Medical Nemesis*. London: Boyars.

Illich, I., Zola, I. K., McKnight, J., Caplan, J. and Shaiken, H. (1977) *Disabling Professions*. London: Boyars.

Imrie, R. (1996) *Disability and the City: International Perspectives*. London: Paul Chapman Publishing.

Ingelby, D. (1983) Mental health and social order, in S. Cohen and A. Scull (eds) *Social Control and the State*. London: Blackwell.

Ingstad, B. and Reynolds-Whyte, S. (1995) *Disability and Culture*. Berkeley: University of California Press.

Jencks, C. (1987) *Le Corbusier and the Tragic View of Architecture*. Harmondsworth: Penguin.

Jenkins, P. (1991) Disability and social stratification, *British Journal of Sociology*, vol. 42, no. 4, pp. 557–80.

Jobling, R. (1992) Psoriasis and its treatment in psycho-social perspective, *Reviews in Contemporary Pharmacotherapy*, vol. 7, no. 3, pp. 339–45.

Joe, J. and Miller, D. L. (1987) *American Indian Perspectives on Disability*. Tucson, AZ: Native American Research and Training Center.

Johnson, M. and Dikins, S. (eds) (1989) *Reporting on Disability: Approaches and Issues*. Louisville, KY: Avocado Press.

Johnson, R. A. (1983) Mobilizing the disabled, in J. Freeman (ed.) *Social Movements of the Sixties and Seventies*. New York: Longman.

Johnstone, D. and Corbett, J. (1997) Review of *Disability Politics*, *Disability and Society*, vol. 12, no. 2, pp. 317–19.

Jones, G. (1986) *Social Hygiene in 20th Century Britain*. London: Croom Helm.

Jones, G. (1997) Barriers to adulthood: dependency and resistance in youth, paper presented to the Third Annual Colloquium of the International Social Sciences Institute, 'Families and the State: Conflicts and Contradictions', University of Edinburgh, 23–24 May.

Jones, L., Kyle, J. and Wood, P. (1987) *Words Apart*. London: Tavistock.

Jordan, R. and Powell, S. (1992) Stop the reforms, Calvin wants to get off, *Disability, Handicap and Society*, vol. 7, no. 1, pp. 85–8.

Jupp, K. (1992) *Everyone Belongs.* London: Souvenir.

Karpf, A. (1988) *Doctoring the Media.* London: Routledge.

Kassebaum, G. G. and Bauman, B. O. (1965) Dimensions of the sick role in chronic illness, *Journal of Health and Human Behaviour*, vol. 6, pp. 16–27.

Katz, I. (1996) *The Construction of Racial Identity in Children of Mixed Parentage.* London: Jessica Kingsley Publishers.

Keith, L. (1992) Who cares wins? Women, caring and disability, *Disability, Handicap and Society*, vol. 7, no. 2, pp. 167–75.

Keith, L. (ed.) (1994) *Mustn't Grumble.* London: Women's Press.

Keith, L. (1996) Encounters with strangers: the public's response to disabled women and how this effects our sense of self, in J. Morris (ed.) *Encounters with Strangers: Feminism and Disability.* London: Women's Press.

Keith, L. and Morris, J. (1996) Easy targets: a disability rights perspective on the 'children as carers' debate, in J. Morris (ed.) *Encounters with Strangers: Feminism and Disability.* London: Women's Press.

Kelly, L. (1992) The connections between disability and child abuse: a review of the research evidence, *Child Abuse Review*, vol. 1, pp. 157–67.

Kelly, L., Burton, S. and Regan, L. (1994) Researching women's lives or studying women's oppression? Reflections on what constitutes feminist research, in M. Maynard and P. Purvis (eds) *Researching Women's Lives from a Feminist Perspective.* London: Taylor & Francis.

Kelly, M. (1992) *Colitis.* London: Tavistock, Routledge.

Kennedy, M. (1996) Sexual abuse and disabled children, in J. Morris (ed.) *Encounters with Strangers: Feminism and Disability.* London: Women's Press.

Kent, D. (1987) Disabled women: portraits in fiction and drama, in A. Gartner and T. Joe (eds) *Images of the Disabled, Disabling Images.* New York: Praeger.

Kestenbaum, A. (1993a) *Making Community Care a Reality.* Nottingham: Independent Living Fund.

Kestenbaum, A. (1993b) *Taking Care in the Market.* Nottingham: Independent Living Fund.

Kestenbaum, A. (1995) *An Opportunity Lost? Social Services Use of the Independent Living Transfer.* London: Disablement Income Group.

Kestenbaum, A. (1996) *Independent Living: A Review.* York: YPS and Joseph Rowntree Foundation.

Kevles, D. J. (1986) *In the Name of Eugenics.* Harmondsworth: Penguin.

Killin, D. (1993) Independent living, personal assistance, disabled lesbians and disabled gay men, in C. Barnes (ed.) *Making Our Own Choices.* Derby: British Council of Organisations of Disabled People.

Kilsby, M. and Beyer, S. (1997) Comparing support, *Llais*, Spring, pp. 9–12.

King, D. K. (1988) Multiple jeopardy, multiple consciousness: the context of a black feminist ideology, *Signs*, Autumn.

King Jordan, I. (1992) Language and change, in M. D. Garretson (ed.) *Viewpoints on Deafness: A Deaf American Monograph*, vol. 42.

Klobas, L. E. (1988) *Disability Drama in Television and Film*. Jefferson, NC: McFarland & Co. Inc.

Knesl, J. (1984) The powers of architecture, *Environment and Planning D: Society and Space*, vol. 2, pp. 3–22.

Knox, P. (1987) The social production of the built environment – architects, architecture, and the post modern city, *Progress in Human Geography*, vol. 11, no. 3, pp. 354–78.

Kriegel, L. (1987) The cripple in literature, in A. Gartner and T. Joe (eds) *Images of the Disabled, Disabling Images*. New York: Praeger.

Kristeva, J. (1982) *Powers of Horror*. New York: Columbia University Press.

Kuh, D., Lawrence, C., Tripp, J. and Treber, G. (1988) Work and work alternatives for disabled young people, *Disability, Handicap and Society*, vol. 3, no. 1, pp. 3–27.

Kuhn, T. (1961) *The Structure of Scientific Revolutions*. Chicago: Chicago University Press.

Kumar, K. (1978) *Prophecy and Progress: The Sociology of Industrial and Post-industrial Societies*. Harmondsworth: Pelican.

Kyle, J. G. (1991) *The Deaf Community*, Block 1, Unit 2, D251 'Issues in Deafness'. Milton Keynes: Open University.

Ladd, P. and John, M. (1991) *Deaf People As a Minority Group: The Political Process*, Block 3, Unit 9, D251 'Issues in Deafness'. Milton Keynes: Open University.

Lakey, J. (1994) *Caring About Independence: Disabled People and the Independent Living Fund*. London: Policy Studies Institute.

Lakey, J. and Simpkins, R. (1994) *Employment Rehabilitation for Disabled People*. London: Policy Studies Institute.

Lamb, B. and Layzell, S. (1994) *Disabled in Britain: A World Apart*. London: Scope.

Lamb, B. and Layzell, S. (1995) *Disabled in Britain: Counting on Community Care*. London: Scope.

Lancaster-Gaye, D. (ed.) (1972) *Personal Relationships, the Handicapped and the Community*. London: Routledge & Kegan Paul.

Lane, H. (1988) *When the Mind Hears: A History of the Deaf*. London: Penguin.

Lane, H. (1992) *The Mask of Benevolence*. New York: Alfred A. Knopf.

Lane, H. (1995) Constructions of deafness, *Disability and Society*, vol. 10, no. 2, pp. 171–90.

Large, P. (1991) Paying for the additional costs, in G. Dalley (ed.) *Disability and Social Policy*. London: Policy Studies Institute.

Lash, S. (1994) Structure, aesthetics, community, in U. Beck, A. Giddens and S. Lash (eds) *Reflexive Modernisation: Politics, Tradition and Aesthetics in the Modern Social Order*. Cambridge: Polity Press.

Lash, S. and Urry, J. (1987) *The End of Organized Capitalism*. Cambridge: Polity Press.

Lash, S. and Urry, J. (1993) *Economies of Signs and Space*. London: Sage.

Lather, P. (1991) *Getting Smart: Feminist Research and Pedagogy With/In the Postmodern*. London: Routledge.

Laura, R. S. (1980) *Problems of Handicap*. Melbourne: Macmillan.

Laurie, L. (ed.) (1992) *Building Our Lives: Housing, Independent Living and Disabled People*. London: Shelter.

Law Society (1992) *Disability, Discrimination and Employment Law: A Report on the Law Society's Employment Law Committee*. London: Law Society.

Laws, G. (1994) Oppression, knowledge, and the built environment, *Political Geography*, vol. 13, no. 1, pp. 7–32.

Le Corbusier (1927) *Towards a New Architecture*, trans. by F. Etchells. London: Architectural Press.

Lecouturier, J. and Jacoby, A. (1995) *Study of User Satisfaction with Wheelchair Provision in Newcastle*. Newcastle upon Tyne: University of Newcastle, Centre for Health Services Research.

Lee, G. and Loveridge, R. (eds) (1987) *The Manufacture of Disadvantage*. Milton Keynes: Open University Press.

Lees, D. and Shaw, S. (1974) *Impairment, Disability and Handicap*. London: Heinemann.

Leonard, A. (1992) *A Hard Act to Follow: A Study of the Experience of Parents and Children Under the 1981 Education Act*. London: The Spastics Society.

Leonard, A. (1994) *Right from the Start*. London: Scope.

Levitas, R. (1990) *The Concept of Utopia*. Hemel Hempstead: Philip Allen.

Lewis, A. (1995) *Children's Understanding of Disability*. London: Routledge.

Lewis, D. (1990) Tungaru conjugal jealousy and sexual mutilation, *Pacific Studies*, vol. 13, no. 3 (July), pp. 115–26.

Lifchez, R. and Winslow, B. (1979) *Design for Independent Living*. Berkeley, CA: University of California Press.

Lifton, R. J. (1986) *The Nazi Doctors*. New York: Basic Books.

Liggett, H. (1988) Stars are not born: an interpretive approach to the politics of disability, *Disability, Handicap and Society*, vol. 3, no. 3, pp. 263–76.

Lindlow, V. and Morris, J. (1995) *Service User Involvement: Synthesis of*

Findings and Experience in the Field of Community Care. York: Joseph Rowntree Foundation.

Linton, S., Mello, S. and O'Neill, J. (1995) Disability studies: expanding the parameters of diversity, *Radical Teacher*, vol. 47, pp. 4–10.

Lister, R. (1991) *The Exclusive Society: Citizenship and the Poor.* London: Child Poverty Action Group.

Litman, T. J. (1962) Self conception and physical rehabilitation, in A. M. Rose (ed.) *Human Behaviour and Social Processes.* London: Routledge & Kegan Paul.

Littler, C. (1984) *The Experience of Work.* Aldershot: Gower.

Lloyd, M. (1992) Does she boil eggs? Towards a feminist model of disability, *Disability, Handicap and Society*, vol. 7, no. 3 (October), pp. 207–21.

Locker, D. (1983) *Disability and Disadvantage.* London: Tavistock.

Lofland, J. and Lofland, L. H. (1995) *Analysing Social Settings.* Belmont, CA: Wadsworth.

Longmore, P. (1987) Screening stereotypes: images of disabled people in television and motion pictures, in A. Gartner and T. Joe (eds) *Images of the Disabled, Disabling Images.* New York: Praeger, pp. 65–78.

Lonsdale, S. (1986) *Work and Inequality.* Harlow: Longman.

Lonsdale, S. (1990) *Women and Disability: The Experience of Physical Disability Among Women.* Basingstoke: Macmillan.

Lorber, J. (1967) Deviance as performance: the case of illness, *Social Problems*, vol. 14, no. 3, pp. 302–10.

Lukes, S. (1979) Power and authority, in T. Bottomore and R. Nisbet (eds) *A History of Sociological Analysis.* London: Heinemann.

Lumby, C. (1996) Sexism in the eye of the beholder, *Sydney Morning Herald*, 24 October.

Lunt, N. and Thornton, P. (1993) *Employment Policies for Disabled People: A Review of Legislation and Services in Fifteen Different Countries.* Sheffield: Employment Department.

Lunt, N. and Thornton, P. (1994) Disability and employment: towards an understanding of discourse and policy, *Disability and Society*, vol. 9, no. 2, pp. 223–38.

Lykke, N. and Braidotti, R. (1996) *Between Monsters, Goddesses and Cyborgs: Feminist Confrontations with Science, Medicine and Cyberspace.* London: Zed Press.

Lynch, B. and Perry, R. (1992) *Experiences of Community Care.* London: Longman.

Lyon, D. (1988) *The Information Society.* Oxford: Blackwell.

McCagg, W. O. and Siegelbaum, L. (1989) *The Disabled in the Soviet Union: Past and Present, Theory and Practice.* Pittsburgh: University of Pittsburgh Press.

Macdonald, P. (1991) Double discrimination must be faced now, *Disability Now*, March.

MacFarlane, A. (1994) On becoming an older disabled woman, *Disability and Society*, vol. 9, no. 2.

MacFarlane, A. (1996) Aspects of intervention: consultation, care, help and support, in G. Hales (ed.) *Beyond Disability*. London: Sage.

MacFarlane, K. (1990) Skills of the disabled: a vital resource, *Information Technology and Public Policy*, vol. 8, no. 3.

McGlynn, S. and Murrain, P. (1994) The politics of urban design, *Planning Practice and Research*, vol. 9, no. 3, pp. 311–20.

Macheray, P. (1978) *A Theory of Literary Production*. London: Routledge.

McKee, A. (1982) The feminization of poverty, *Graduate Woman*, vol. 76, no. 4, pp. 34–6.

McKenzie, D. and Wajcman, J. (eds) *The Social Shaping of Technology*. Milton Keynes: Open University Press.

Maclean, M. and Jefferys, M. (1974) Disability and deprivation, in D. Wedderburn (ed.) *Poverty, Inequality and Class Structure*. Cambridge: Cambridge University Press.

McLoughlin, J. and Clarke, J. (1988) *Technological Change at Work*. Milton Keynes: Open University Press.

McNamara, J. (1997) Review of *The Sexual Politics of Disability: Untold Desires*, *Disability Arts in London*, vol. 124, May 1997.

Mairs, N. (1992) On being a cripple, in L. McDowell and R. Pringle (eds) *Defining Women*. Cambridge: Polity Press, pp. 56–66.

Malin, N. (1994) *Implementing Community Care*. Buckingham: Open University Press.

Malin, N. (1995) *Services for People with Learning Difficulties*. London: Routledge.

Mannion, R. (1994) *Disabling Transport: Mobility, Deprivation and Social Policy*. Aldershot: Avebury.

Marcuse, H. (1955) *Eros and Civilization*. New York: Vintage Books.

Marinelli, R. P. and dell Orto, A. (1984) *The Psychological and Social Impact of Physical Disability*. New York: Springer Publishing.

Marshall, A. (1984) Sensuous sapphires: a study of the social construction of Black female sexuality, in M. Maynard and J. Purvis (eds) *Researching Women's Lives from a Feminist Perspective*. London: Taylor & Francis.

Marshall, T. H. (1952) *Citizenship and Social Class*. Cambridge: Cambridge University Press.

Martin, J., Meltzer, H. and Elliot, D. (1988) *OPCS Surveys of Disability in Great Britain: Report 1 – The Prevalence of Disability among Adults*. London: HMSO.

Martin, J. and White, A. (1988) *The Financial Circumstances of Disabled Adults Living in Private Households*. London: HMSO.

Martin, J., White, A. and Meltzer, H. (1989) *Disabled Adults: Services, Transport and Employment*. London: HMSO.

Marx, K. (1913) *A Contribution to the Critique of Political Economy*. Chicago: Chicago University Press.

Marx, K. (1969) Wage-labour and capital, in *Marx–Engels Selected Works*, vol. 1. Moscow: Progress Publishers.

Marx, K. (1973) *Grundrisse*. Harmondsworth: Penguin.

Marx, K. (1974a) *Capital*, vol. 1. London: Lawrence & Wishart.

Marx, K. (1974b) Critique of the Gotha Programme, in *The First International and After: Political Writings*, vol. 3. Harmondsworth: Penguin.

Mascia-Lees, F. and Sharpe, P. (eds) (1992) *Tattoo, Torture, Mutilation and Adornment: The Denaturalization of the Body in Culture and Text*. Albany: State University of New York Press.

Mason, P. (1992) The representation of disabled people: a Hampshire Centre for Independent Living discussion paper, *Disability, Handicap and Society*, vol. 7, no. 1, pp. 79–85.

Matrix (1984) *Making Space: Women and the Man-made Environment*. London: Pluto Press.

Matthews, A. and Truscott, P. (1990) *Disability, Household Income and Expenditure*. London: HMSO.

Mayall, B. (1996) *Children, Health and the Social Order*. Buckingham: Open University Press.

Mead, G. (1934) *Mind, Self and Society*. Chicago: Chicago University Press.

Mechanic, D. (1959) Illness and social disability: some problems of analysis, *Pacific Sociological Review*, vol. 2, pp. 37–41.

Media Information Australia (1994) Body's Image (Special Issue), vol. 72.

Meekosha, H. (1986) Eggshell personalities strike back – a response to the bosses' doctors on RSI, *Refractory Girl*, May (29), pp. 2–6.

Meekosha, H. (1990) Is feminism able bodied? Reflections from between the trenches, *Refractory Girl*, August.

Meekosha, H. and Dowse, L. (1997) Distorting images, invisible images: gender, disability and the media, *Media International Australia*, February.

Meekosha, H. and Jakubowicz, A. (1991) RSI: The rise and fall of an Australian disease, *Critical Social Policy*, vol. 11, no. 1 (31), Summer, pp. 18–37.

Meekosha, H. and Jakubowicz, A. (1996) Disability, participation, representation and social justice, in C. Christensen and F. Rizvi (eds) *Disability and the Dilemmas of Education and Social Justice*. Milton Keynes: Open University Press.

Merton, R. (1968) *Social Theory and Social Structure*. New York: Free Press.

Mezey, S. G. (1988) *No Longer Disabled: The Federal Courts and the Politics of Social Security Disability*. New York: Greenwood.

Middleton, L. (1992) *Children First: Working with Children and Disability*. London: Venture Press.

Middleton, L. (1996) *This Far and No Further: Towards Ending the Abuse of Disabled Children*. London: Venture Press.

Milam, L. W. (1984) *The Cripple Liberation Front Marching Band Blues*. San Diego: Mho and Mho Works.

Miles, M. (1990) Disability and Afghan reconstruction, *Disability, Handicap and Society*, vol. 5, no. 3, pp. 257–69.

Miles, R. (1989) *Racism*. London: Routledge.

Miller, E. J. and Gwynne, G. V. (1972) *A Life Apart*. London: Tavistock.

Mills, C. W. (1970) *The Sociological Imagination*. Harmondsworth: Penguin.

Ming, G. (1993) Demographic features of people with disabilities in China, *Disability, Handicap and Society*, vol. 8, no. 2, pp. 211–14.

Monks, J. and Frankenberg, R. (1995) Being ill and being me: self, body and time in Multiple Sclerosis narratives, in B. Ingstad and S. R. Whyte (eds) *Disability and Culture*. Berkeley: University of California Press.

Moore, C. and Bloomer, K. (1977) *Body, Memory, and Architecture*. New Haven, CT: Yale University Press.

Moore, N. (1995) *Access to Information: A Survey of the Provision of Disability Information*. London: Policy Studies Institute.

Morgan, K. (1991) Women and the knife: cosmetic surgery and the colonization of women's bodies, *Hypatia*, vol. 6, no. 3, pp. 25–53.

Morrell, J. (1990) *The Employment of People with Disabilities: Research into the Policies and Practices of Employers*. Sheffield: Employment Services.

Morris, A. and Butler, A. (1972) *No Feet to Drag*. London: Sidgwick & Jackson.

Morris, J. (1989) *Able Lives*. London: Women's Press.

Morris, J. (1990a) *Freedom to Lose: Housing Policy and People with Disabilities*. London: Shelter.

Morris, J. (1990b) *Our Homes, Our Rights: Housing, Independent Living and Physically Disabled People*. London: Shelter.

Morris, J. (1991) *Pride Against Prejudice: Transforming Attitudes to Disability*. London: Women's Press.

Morris, J. (1992) Personal and political: a feminist perspective on researching physical disability, *Disability, Handicap and Society*, vol. 7, no. 2, pp. 157–66.

Morris, J. (1993a) Feminism and disability, *Feminist Review*, no. 43, pp. 57–70.

Morris, J. (1993b) *Community Care or Independent Living*. York: Joseph Rowntree Foundation.

Morris, J. (1993c) *Independent Lives: Community Care and Disabled People*. Basingstoke: Macmillan.

Morris, J. (1993d) Gender and disability, in J. Swain, V. Finkelstein, S. French and M. Oliver (eds) *Disabling Barriers – Enabling Environments*. London: Sage and Open University Press.

Morris, J. (1994a) *The Shape of Things to Come: User-led Social Services*. London: National Institute for Social Work.

Morris, J. (1994b) Rights muddle, *Community Care*, 21–27 July, pp. 22–3.

Morris, J. (1995) *Gone Missing*. London: Who Cares Trust.

Morris, J. (ed.) (1996) *Encounters with Strangers: Feminism and Disability*. London: Women's Press.

Morrison, E. and Finkelstein, V. (1993) Broken arts and cultural repair: the role of culture in the empowerment of disabled people, in J. Swain, V. Finkelstein, S. French and M. Oliver (eds) *Disabling Barriers – Enabling Environments*. London: Sage and Open University Press.

Morrow, R. with Brown, D. (1994) *Critical Theory and Methodology*. London: Sage.

Moses, J. F. (1988) Preparing for a brave new workplace: the impact of new technology on the employment of people with disabilities, *International Rehabilitation Review*, vol. 7, no. 10.

Mouzelis, N. (1995) *Sociological Theory: What Went Wrong*. London: Routledge.

Murphy, R. (1987) *The Body Silent*. New York: Henry Holt.

Murphy, R., Scheer, J., Murphy, Y. and Mack, R. (1988) Physical disability and social liminality: a study of the rituals of adversity, *Social Science and Medicine*, vol. 26, pp. 235–42.

Murray, B. and Kenny, S. (1990) Teleworking as an employment option for people with disabilities, *International Journal of Rehabilitation Research*, vol. 13.

National Union of the Deaf (1992) *Deaf Liberation*. London: National Union of the Deaf.

Neale, S. (1987) *Genre*. London: BFI Publications.

Nevins, D. (1981) From eclecticism to doubt, *Heresies*, vol. 11, no. 3, pp. 71–2.

New Internationalist (1992) Disabled lives: difference and defiance, *New Internationalist*, vol. 233, July.

Newell, C. (1995) Consumer reflections on the Disability Discrimination Act, *Australian Disability Review*, vol. 2, pp. 60–5.

Nicholson, L. (1990) *Feminism/Postmodernism*. London: Routledge.

Norden, M. (1994) *The Cinema of Isolation*. New Brunswick, NJ: Rutgers University Press.

Northern Officers Group (1996) *The Disability Discrimination Act: A Policy and Practice Guide for Local Government and Disabled People*. Sheffield: Northern Officers Group.

Norwich, B. (1994) *Segregation and Inclusion: English LEA Statistics 1988–92*. Bristol: Centre for Studies on Inclusive Education.

Oakes, J., Haslem, S. A. and Turner, J. C. (1994) *Stereotyping and Social Reality*. Oxford: Blackwell.

Oakley, A. (1972) *Sex, Gender and Society*. London: Maurice Temple Smith.

Oldman, C. (1993) *Moving in Old Age: New Directions in Housing Policy*. York: Social Policy Research Unit.

Oliver, M. (1985) The integration/segregation debate: some sociological considerations, *British Journal of Sociology of Education*, vol. 6, no. 1.

Oliver, M. (1986) Social policy and disability: some theoretical issues, *Disability, Handicap and Society*, vol. 1, no. 1, pp. 5–18.

Oliver, M. (1987a) Re-defining disability: a challenge to research, *Research, Policy and Planning*, vol. 5, no. 1, pp. 9–13.

Oliver, M. (1987b) *Social Work with Disabled People*. Basingstoke: Macmillan.

Oliver, M. (1989) Disability and dependency: a creation of industrial societies?, in L. Barton (ed.) *Disability and Dependency*. Lewes: Falmer Press.

Oliver, M. (1990) *The Politics of Disablement*. Basingstoke: Macmillan.

Oliver, M. (1991a) Multi-specialist and multi-disciplinary – a recipe for confusion? Too many cooks spoil the broth, *Disability, Handicap and Society*, vol. 6, no. 1, pp. 65–8.

Oliver, M. (ed.) (1991b) *Social Work: Disabled People and Disabling Environments*. London: Jessica Kingsley.

Oliver, M. (1991c) Speaking out: disabled people and social welfare, in G. Dalley (ed.) *Disability and Social Policy*. London: Policy Studies Institute.

Oliver, M. (1992a) Intellectual masturbation: a rejoinder to Soder and Booth, *European Journal of Special Needs Education*, vol. 7, no. 1.

Oliver, M. (1992b) Changing the social relations of research production, *Disability, Handicap and Society*, vol. 7, no. 2, pp. 101–14.

Oliver, M. (1992c) *Disability, Citizenship and Empowerment*, K665 'The Disabling Society'. Milton Keynes: Open University.

Oliver, M. (1993a) Re-defining disability: a challenge to research, in J. Swain, V. Finkelstein, S. French and M. Oliver (eds) *Disabling Barriers – Enabling Environments*. London: Sage and Open University Press.

Oliver, M. (1993b) *Workbook 2. Disability, Citizenship and Empowerment.* K665 'The Disabling Society'. Milton Keynes: Open University Press.

Oliver, M. (1994) *Capitalism, Disability and Ideology: A Materialist Critique of the Normalization Principle*, paper presented at the conference '25 Years of Normalization, Social Role Valorization and Social Integration: A Retrospective and Prospective View', University of Ottawa, 10–13 May.

Oliver, M. (1996) *Understanding Disability: From Theory to Practice.* Basingstoke: Macmillan.

Oliver, M. (1997) Emancipatory research: realistic goal or impossible dream, unpublished paper.

Oliver, M. and Barnes, C. (1991) Discrimination, disability and welfare: from needs to rights, in I. Bynoe, M. Oliver and C. Barnes, *Equal Rights for Disabled People.* London: Institute of Public Policy Research.

Oliver, M. and Hasler, F. (1987) Disability and self-help: a case study of the Spinal Injuries Association, *Disability, Handicap and Society*, vol. 2, no. 2, pp. 113–25.

Oliver, M. and Zarb, G. (1989) The politics of disability: a new approach, *Disability, Handicap and Society*, vol. 4, no. 3, pp. 221–41.

Oliver, M. and Zarb, G. (1993) *Ageing with a Disability.* London: University of Greenwich.

Oliver, M., Zarb, G., Silver, J., Moore, M. and Salisbury, V. (1988) *Walking into Darkness: The Experience of Spinal Cord Injury.* London: Macmillan.

Olsen, R. (1996) Young carers: challenging the facts and politics of research into children and caring, *Disability and Society*, vol. 11, no. 1, pp. 41–54.

O'Neil, J. (1995) *The Poverty of Postmodernism.* London: Routledge.

Orlowska, D. (1991) Residential care for people with learning difficulties in Poland: a view from a visitor, *Disability, Handicap and Society*, vol. 6, no. 2, pp. 129–38.

Owens, P. (1987) *Community Care and Severe Physical Disability.* London: Bedford Square Press and NCVO.

Padden, C. and Humphries, T. (1988) *Deaf in America: Voices from a Culture.* Cambridge, MA: Harvard University Press.

Pagel, M. (1988) *On Our Own Behalf: An Introduction to the Self Organisation of Disabled People.* Manchester: Greater Manchester Coalition of Disabled People Publications.

Palmer, J. (1978) *Genesis and the Structure of Popular Genre.* London: Edward Arnold.

Parker, G. (1993) *With This Body: Caring and Disability in Marriage.* Buckingham: Open University Press.

Parker, G. and Lawton, D. (1994) *Different Types of Care, Different Types of Carer.* London: HMSO.

Parsons, T. (1951) *The Social System.* New York: Free Press.

Patrick, D. L. and Peach, H. (eds) (1989) *Disablement in the Community*. Oxford: Oxford University Press.

Payne, M. (1995) *Social Work and Community Care*. Basingstoke: Macmillan.

Pearl, A. (1997) Democratic education as an alternative to deficit thinking, in R. Valencia (ed.) *The Evolution of Thinking: Educational Thought and Practice*. London: Falmer Press.

Percy, S. L. (1989) *Disability, Civil Rights and Public Policy: The Politics of Implementation*. Tuscaloosa and London: University of Alabama Press.

Perlman, L. G. and Hansen, C. E. (eds) (1989) *Technology and the Employment of Persons with Disabilities*, Switzer Monograph. Alexandra, VA: National Rehabilitation Association.

Pettman, J. (1996) *Worlding Women: A Feminist International Politics*. Sydney: Allen & Unwin.

Pfeiffer, D. (1990) Public transit access for disabled persons in the United States, *Disability, Handicap and Society*, vol. 5, no. 2, pp. 153–66.

Pfeiffer, D. (1991) The influence of socio-economic characteristics of disabled people on their employment status and income, *Disability, Handicap and Society*, vol. 6, no. 2, pp. 103–14.

Phaure, S. (1991) *Who Really Cares: Models of Voluntary Sector Community Care and Black Communities*. London: London Voluntary Service Council.

Phelan, P. and Cole, S. (1991) Social work in a traditional setting, in M. Oliver (ed.) *Social Work: Disabled People and Disabling Environments*. London: Jessica Kingsley, pp. 55–64.

Phillips, M. J. (1990) Damaged goods: oral narratives of the experiences of disability in American culture, *Social Science and Medicine*, vol. 30, no. 8, pp. 857–9.

Philp, M. and Duckworth, D. (1982) *Children with Disabilities and Their Families: A Review of the Literature*. Windsor: NFER-Nelson.

Philpot, T. and Ward, L. (eds) (1995) *Values and Visions: Changing Ideas in Services for People with Learning Difficulties*. London: Butterworth–Heinemann.

Pinder, R. (1996) Sick-but-fit or fit-but-sick? Ambiguity and identity at the workplace, in C. Barnes and G. Mercer (eds) *Exploring the Divide*. Leeds: The Disability Press.

Pinet, G. (1990) *Is the Law Fair to the Disabled?* Copenhagen: World Health Organization Regional Office for Europe.

Plummer, K. (1995) *Telling Sexual Stories*. London: Routledge.

Pointon, A. with Davies, C. (1997) *Framed: A Disability Media Reader*. London: BFI Publications.

Potts, M. and Fido, R. (1991) *A Fit Person to Be Removed: Personal Accounts of Life in a Mental Deficiency Institution*. Plymouth: Northcote House.

The Powerhouse (1996) Power in the house: women with learning difficulties organising against abuse, in J. Morris (ed.) *Encounters with Strangers: Feminism and Disability*. London: Women's Press.

Prak, N. (1984) *Architects: The Noted and the Ignored*. Chichester: Wiley.

Prescott-Clarke, P. (1990) *Employment and Handicap*. London: Social and Community Planning Research.

Priestley, M. (1994) *Organising for Change*. Leeds: Leeds City Council Health Unit.

Pring, R. and Walford, G. (eds) (1997) *Affirming the Comprehensive Ideal*. London: Falmer Press.

Quicke, J. (1985) *Disability in Modern Children's Fiction*. London: Croom Helm.

Racino, J. A., Walker, S., O'Connor, S. and Taylor, S. J. (1993) *Housing, Support and Community: Choices and Strategies for Adults with Disabilities*. Philadelphia: Temple University Press.

Radley, A. (ed.) (1993) *Worlds of Illness: Biographical and Cultural Perspectives on Health and Disease*. London: Routledge.

Rajan, A. (1985) *Information Technology and Disabled Young Workers*. Brighton: OECD and Institute for Manpower Studies.

Ranson, S. (1994) *Towards the Learning Society*. London: Cassell.

Read, J. (1988) *The Equal Opportunities Book*. London: Interchange Books.

Reason, P. (ed.) (1988) *Human Inquiry in Action: Developments in New Paradigm Research*. London: Sage.

Reid, C. (1994) Voice-over training needed, *British Deaf News*, Letters page, February issue, p. 19.

Renteria, D. (1993) Rejection, in R. Luczak (ed.) *Eyes of Desire: A Deaf Gay & Lesbian Reader*. New York: Alyson Publications.

'Rich' (1996) Explaining the politics of disability, *Disability Arts in London (DAIL)*, issue 119, December.

Riddell, S. (1996) Theorising special educational needs in a changing climate, in L. Barton (ed.) *Disability and Society*. Harlow: Longman.

Riddell, S. (forthcoming) Transitions to adulthood for young disabled people – the dynamic of transition, in C. and K. Robinson (eds) *Growing Up with Disability*. London: Jessica Kingsley.

Riddell, S., Baron, S., Stalker, K. and Wilkinson, H. (1997) The concept of the learning society for adults with learning difficulties: human and social capital perspectives, *Journal of Education Policy*.

Riddell, S. and Brown, S. (eds) (1991) *School Effectiveness Research: Its Messages for School Improvement*. Edinburgh: HMSO.

Riddell, S., Ward, K. and Thomson, G. O. B. (1993) The significance of employment as a goal for young people with special educational needs, *British Journal of Education and Work*, vol. 6, no. 2, pp. 57–72.

Rieser, R. and Mason, M. (1992) *Disability Equality in the Classroom: A Human Rights Issue*, 2nd edn. London: Disability Equality in the Classroom.

Rioux, M. H. and Bach, M. (eds) (1994) *Disability Is Not Measles*. North York, Ontario: Roeher.

Ritzer, G. (1995) *The McDonaldization of Society*. New York: Sage.

Roberts, H. (ed.) (1981) *Doing Feminist Research*. London: Routledge & Kegan Paul.

Robinault, I. (1978) *Sex, Society and the Disabled*. Hagerstown, MD: Harper & Row.

Robinson, I. (1988) *Multiple Sclerosis*. London: Routledge.

Rose, G. (1990) The struggle for political democracy: emancipation, gender, and geography, *Society and Space*, vol. 8, no. 4, pp. 395–408.

Rose, G. (1995) *Love's Work*. London: Chatto & Windus.

Rose, N. (1996) *Inventing Ourselves: Psychology, Power and Personhood*. Cambridge: Cambridge University Press.

Rosenberg, C. E. and Golden, J. (eds) (1992) *Framing Disease: Studies in Cultural History*. New Brunswick, NJ: Rutgers University Press.

Roth, M. and Kroll, J. (1986) *The Reality of Mental Illness*. Cambridge: Cambridge University Press.

Roth, W. (1981) *The Handicapped Speak*. Jefferson, NC: McFarland.

Rowan, J. (1981) A dialectical paradigm for research, in P. Reason and J. Rowan (eds) *Human Inquiry: A Source Book of New Paradigm Research*. Chichester: John Wiley & Son.

Rowe, A. (ed.) (1990) *Lifetime Homes: Flexible Housing for Successive Generations*. London: Helen Hamlyn Foundation.

Russell, W. (revised 1980; first published 1963) *New Lives for Old: The Story of the Cheshire Homes*. London: Victor Gollancz Ltd.

Ryan, J. and Thomas, F. (1980) *The Politics of Mental Handicap*. London: Free Association Books.

Safilios-Rothschild, C. (1970) *The Sociology and Social Psychology of Disability and Rehabilitation*. New York: Random House.

Safilios-Rothschild, C. (1976) Disabled persons' self-definitions and their implications for rehabilitation, in G. L. Albrecht (ed.) *The Sociology of Physical Disability and Rehabilitation*. Pittsburgh: University of Pittsburgh Press.

Sainsbury, S. (1970) *Registered as Disabled*, Social Administration Research Trust Occasional Papers on Social Administration, no. 35. London: Social Administration Research Trust.

Sandhu, J. (1987) Information technology and the employment of disabled people, *Employment Gazette*, December. London: Employment Department.

Sandow, S. (1995) *Whose Special Need: Some Perspectives of Special Educational Needs*. London: Paul Chapman.

Sapey, B. and Hewitt, N. (1991) The changing context of social work practice, in M. Oliver (ed.) *Social Work: Disabled People and Disabling Environments*. London: Jessica Kingsley.

Sartre, J.-P. (1963) *Search for a Method*. New York: Braziller.

Saussure, F. de (1974) *Course in General Linguistics*. London: Fontana.

Saxton, M. (1988) *Prenatal Screening and Discriminatory Attitudes About Disability*. New York: Harrington Park Press.

Saxton, M. and Howe, F. (1988) *With Wings: An Anthology of Literature by Women with Disabilities*. London: Virago.

Scambler, G. (1989) *Epilepsy*. London: Routledge.

Scheer, J. and Groce, N. (1988) Impairment as a human constant: cross-cultural and historical perspectives on variation, *Journal of Social Issues*, vol. 44, no. 1, pp. 23–37.

Schneider, J. W. (1988) Disability as moral experience: epilepsy and self in routine relationships, *Journal of Social Issues*, vol. 44, no. 1, pp. 63–78.

Schofield, J. M. (1981) *Microcomputer Based Aids for the Disabled*, British Computer Society Monograph. Chichester: Heyden.

Schuchmann, J. (1988) *Hollywood Speaks: Deafness and the Film Entertainment Industry*. Chicago: University of Illinois Press.

Schutz, A. (1974) The stranger, in M. Natanson (ed.) *The Collected Works of Alfred Schutz*. The Hague: Martinus Nijhoff.

Schwartz, D. B. (1992) *Crossing the River: Creating a Conceptual Revolution in Community and Disability*. Boston: Brookline Books.

Schweickart, P. (1983) What if . . . science and technology in feminist utopias, in J. Rothschild (ed.) *Machina ex Dea: Feminist Perspectives on Technology*. Oxford: Pergamon.

Schwier, K. M. (1994) *Couples with Intellectual Disability Talk About Living and Loving*. Rockville, MD: Woodbine House.

Scotch, R. K. (1984) *From Goodwill to Civil Rights: Transforming Federal Disability Policy*. Philadelphia: Temple University Press.

Scotch, R. K. (1988) Disability as the basis for a social movement: advocacy and the politics of definition, *Journal of Social Issues*, vol. 44, no. 1, pp. 159–72.

Scotch, R. K. (1989) Politics and policy in the history of the disability rights movement, *The Milbank Quarterly*, vol. 67, suppl. 2, part 2, pp. 380–401.

Scott, C., Lefley, H. and Hicks, D. (1993) Potential risk factors for rape in three ethnic groups, *Community Mental Health Journal*, vol. 29, no. 2, April, pp. 133–41.

Scott, R. A. (1969) *The Making of Blind Men*. New York: Russell Sage Foundation.

Scott Parker, S. (1989) *They Aren't in the Brief*. London: King's Fund Centre.

Scull, A. (1982) *Museums of Madness: The Social Organisation of Insanity in Nineteenth-Century England*. Harmondsworth: Penguin.

Scull, A. (1984) *Decarceration*, 2nd edn. London: Polity Press.

Scull, A. (1993) *The Most Solitary of Afflictions: Madness and Society in Britain*. London: Yale University Press.

Secretaries of State for Health, Social Services (1989) *Caring for People: Community Care in the Next Decade and Beyond*. London: HMSO.

Sennett, R. (1990) *The Conscience of the Eye: The Design and Social Life of Cities*. London: Faber & Faber.

Shakespeare, T. (1993) Disabled people's self-organization: a new social movement?, *Disability and Society*, vol. 8, no. 3, pp. 249–64.

Shakespeare, T. (1994a) Conceptualising disability: impairment in sociological perspective, unpublished PhD thesis, University of Cambridge.

Shakespeare, T. (1994b) Disabled by prejudice, *The Pink Paper*, 1 April, p. 13.

Shakespeare, T. (1994c) Cultural representation of disabled people: dustbins for disavowal?, *Disability and Society*, vol. 9, no. 3, pp. 283–99.

Shakespeare, T. (1995a) Back to the future: new genetics and disabled people, *Critical Social Policy*, vol. 44/5.

Shakespeare, T. (1995b) Redefining the disability problem, *Critical Public Health*, vol. 6, no. 2.

Shakespeare, T. (1996a) Power and prejudice: issues of gender, sexuality and disability, in L. Barton (ed.) *Disability and Society: Emerging Issues and Insights*. Harlow: Longman.

Shakespeare, T. (1996b) chapter in Bob Cant (ed.) *Invented Identities*. London: Cassell.

Shakespeare, T. (1996c) Disability, identity and difference, in C. Barnes and G. Mercer (eds) *Exploring the Divide: Illness and Disability*. Leeds: The Disability Press.

Shakespeare, T. (1996d) Rules of engagement: doing disability research, *Disability and Society*, vol. 10, no. 4, pp. 115–20.

Shakespeare, T. (1998) Social constructionism as a political strategy, in I. Velody and R. Williams (eds) *The Politics of Social Constructionism*. London: Sage.

Shakespeare, T., Gillespie-Sells, K. and Davies, D. (1996) *The Sexual Politics of Disability: Untold Desires*. London: Cassell.

Shakespeare, T. and Watson, N. (1997) Defending the social model, *Disability and Society*, vol. 12, no. 2, pp. 293–300.

Shapiro, J. (1993) *No Pity: People with Disabilities Forging a New Civil Rights Movement*. New York: Times Books and Random House.

Sharma, A. and Love, D. (1991) *A Change in Approach: A Report on the Experience of Deaf People from Black and Ethnic Minority Communities*. London: The Royal Association in Aid of Deaf People.

Shearer, A. (1981a) A framework for independent living, in A. Walker with P. Townsend, *Disability in Britain*. Oxford: Martin Robertson.

Shearer, A. (1981b), *Disability, Whose Handicap?* Oxford: Blackwell.

Sieglar, M. and Osmond, M. (1974) *Models of Madness: Models of Medicine*. London: Collier Macmillan.

Silver, R. and Wortman, C. (1980) Coping with undesirable life events, in J. Gerber and M. Seligman (eds) *Learned Helplessness, Theory and Applications*. London: Academic Press.

Silvers, A. (1995) Reconciling equality to difference: caring (f)or justice for people with disabilities, *Hypatia*, vol. 10, no. 1, pp. 30–55.

Simon, W. (1996) *Postmodern Sexualities*. London: Routledge.

Sinason, V. (1992) *Mental Handicap and the Human Condition: New Approaches from the Tavistock*. London: Free Association Books.

SJAC (1979) *Can Disabled People Go Where You Go? Silver Jubilee Access Report*. London: Department of Health and Social Security.

Skrtic, T. (1995) *Disability and Democracy: Reconstructing (Special) Education for Post Modernity*. London: Teachers College Press.

Slee, R. (1995) *Changing Theories and Practices of Discipline*. London: Falmer Press.

Smith, B., Floyd, M. and Provall, M. (1991) *Managing Disability at Work*. London: Jessica Kingsley.

Smith, N. (1980) Physical handicap, disability and welfare, in R. S. Laura (ed.) *Problems of Handicap*. Melbourne: Macmillan.

Smith, S. (1992) *Wasted Opportunities: The Practice of Training and Enterprise Councils As Viewed by Training Providers and Advocates for Disabled People*. London: The Spastics Society.

Smith, S. and Jordan, A. (1991) *What the Papers Say and Don't Say About Disability*. London: The Spastics Society.

Sobsey, D. (1991) *Disability, Sexuality and Abuse: An Annotated Bibliography*. Baltimore: P. H. Brooks.

Sobsey, D. and Doe, T. (1991) Patterns of sexual abuse and assault, *Sexuality and Disability*, vol. 9, no. 3, pp. 243–59.

Social Services Inspectorate (1995) *Growing Up and Moving On: Report on SSI Project on Transitional Services for Disabled Young People*. Bristol: Social Services Inspectorate, Department of Health.

Soder, M. (1991) Theory, ideology and research: a response to Tony Booth, *European Journal of Special Needs Education*, vol. 6, no. 1, pp. 17–23.

Sontag, S. (1991) *Illness As Metaphor* and *AIDS and Its Metaphors*. London: Pelican.

Spinal Injuries Association (no date) *Sexuality and Spinal Cord Injury*. London: Spinal Injuries Association.

Stanley, L. (ed.) (1990a) *Feminist Praxis: Research, Theory and Epistemology in Feminist Sociology*. London: Routledge.

Stanley, L. (1990b) Feminist praxis and the academic mode of production: an editorial introduction, in L. Stanley (ed.) *Feminist Praxis: Research Theory and Epistemology in Feminist Sociology*. London: Routledge.

Steinberger, P. (1985) *Ideology and the Urban Crisis*. Albany: New York State University Press.

Stevens, A. (1991) *Disability Issues: Developing Anti-discriminatory Practice*. London: CCETSW.

Stevenson, J. and Sutton, D. C. (1983) Employment opportunities for physically disabled people in computing in Britain, *International Journal of Rehabilitation Research*, vol. 6, no. 4.

Stevenson, O. and Parsloe, P. (1993) *Community Care and Empowerment*. York: Joseph Rowntree Foundation.

Stone, D. A. (1985) *The Disabled State*. Macmillan: Basingstoke.

Stronach, I. (1988) Vocationalism and educational recovery: the case against witchcraft, in S. Brown and R. Wake (eds) *Education in Transition: What Role for Research?* Edinburgh: Scottish Council for Research in Education.

Stuart, O. (1993) Double oppression: an appropriate starting point? in J. Swain, V. Finkelstein, S. French and M. Oliver (eds) *Disabling Barriers – Enabling Environments*. London: Sage and Open University Press.

Stuart, O. W. (1992) Race and disability: just a double oppression? *Disability, Handicap and Society*, vol. 7, no. 2, pp. 177–88.

Stuart, O. W. (1994) Journey from the margin: black disabled people and the anti-racist debate, in N. Begum, M. Hill and A. Stevens (eds) *Reflections: The Views of Black Disabled People on their Lives and Community Care*. London: CCETSW.

Sullivan, L. (1947) *Kindergarten Chats and Other Writings*. New York: Witterborn Schultz.

Sutherland, A. T. (1981) *Disabled We Stand*. London: Souvenir Press.

Swain, J., Finkelstein, V., French, S. and Oliver, M. (eds) (1993) *Disabling Barriers – Enabling Environments*. London: Sage in association with the Open University Press.

Swann, W. (1992) *Segregation Statistics: English LEAs 1988–91*. London: Centre for Studies on Integration in Education.

Szasz, T. (1970) *The Manufacture of Madness*. New York: Harper & Row.

Tajfel, H. (1978) *The Social Psychology of Minorities*, Report no. 38. London: Minority Rights Group.

Taylor, C. (1989) *Sources of the Self: The Making of the Modern Identity*. Cambridge: Cambridge University Press.

Taylor, D. (1989) Citizenship and social power, *Critical Social Policy*, vol. 26.

Taylor, F. W. (1947) *The Principles of Scientific Management*. New York: Harper & Row.

Taylor, G. and Bishop, J. (eds) (1991) *Being Deaf: The Experience of Deafness*. London: Pinter Publishers.

Taylor, S. J. and Bogden, R. (1989) On accepting relationships between people with mental retardation and non-disabled people: towards an understanding of acceptance, *Disability, Handicap and Society*, vol. 4, no. 1, pp. 21–36.

Taylor-Gooby, P. and Dale, J. (1981) *Social Theory and Social Welfare*. London: Edward Arnold.

Thomas, A. P., Bax, M. C. O. and Smyth, D. P. L. (1989) *The Health and Social Needs of Young Adults with Physical Disabilities*. Oxford: Blackwell Scientific Publications.

Thomas, D. (1978) *The Social Psychology of Childhood Disability*. London: Methuen.

Thomas, D. (1982) *The Experience of Handicap*. London: Methuen.

Thomas, E. J. (1966) Problems of disability from the perspective of role theory, *Journal of Health and Human Behaviour*, vol. VII, pp. 2–13.

Thompson, D. (1994) Men with learning disabilities' sex with men in public toilets: taking responsibility, BSA Conference paper.

Thompson, K. and Andrzejewski, J. (1988) *Why Can't Sharon Kowalski Come Home*. San Francisco: Spinsters.

Thompson, P. (1983) *The Nature of Work*. London: Macmillan.

Thompson, P., Lavery, N. and Curtice, J. (1990) *Short Changed by Disability*. London: Disablement Income Group.

Thomson, R. G. (1994) Redrawing the boundaries of feminist disability studies, *Feminist Studies*, vol. 20, nos 3, 4, pp. 583–95.

Thomson, R. G. (1997) *Extraordinary Bodies: Figuring Physical Disability in American Culture and Literature*. New York: Columbia University Press.

Thornton, P. and Lunt, N. (1995) *Employment for Disabled People: Social Obligation or Individual Responsibility*. York: Social Policy Research Unit, University of York.

Toffler, A. (1980) *The Third Wave*. New York: William Manow.

Tonnies, F. (1957) *Community and Society*, (ed. and trans. C. P. Loomis). New York: Harper & Row (first published 1887).

Topliss, E. (1982) *Social Responses to Handicap*. Harlow: Longman.

Topliss, E. and Gould, B. (1979) *Provision for the Disabled*. Oxford: Blackwell and Martin Robertson.

Townsend, P. (1979) *Poverty in the United Kingdom*. Harmondsworth: Penguin.

Turner, B. (1986) *Citizenship and Capitalism*. London: Allen & Unwin.

Turner, B. (1996) *The Body and Society*. London: Sage.

Turner, G. H. (1994) How is deaf culture?, *Sign Language Studies*, vol. 83, Summer, pp. 103–25.

Turow, J. (1989) *Playing Doctor: Television Storytelling and Medical Power*. New York: Oxford University Press.

Twaddle, A. (1969) Health decisions and sick role variations, *Journal of Health and Social Behaviour*, vol. 10, pp. 195–215.

UPIAS (1975) *Policy Statement*. London: Union of Physically Impaired Against Segregation.

UPIAS (1976) *Fundamental Principles of Disability*. London: Union of Physically Impaired Against Segregation.

Vasey, S. (1995) The experience of care, in G. Hales (ed.) *Beyond Disability*. London: Sage.

Vaughan, C. E. (1991) The social basis of conflict between blind people and agents of rehabilitation, *Disability, Handicap and Society*, vol. 6, no. 3, pp. 203–18.

Vernon, A. (1995) Understanding simultaneous oppression, in Conference Report, 'Disability Rights: A Symposium of the European Regions', October, Southampton.

Vernon, A. (1996a) A stranger in many camps: the experiences of disabled black and ethnic minority women, in J. Morris (ed.) *Encounters with Strangers*. London: Women's Press.

Vernon, A. (1996b) Fighting two different battles: unity is preferable to enmity, *Disability and Society*, vol. 11, no. 2, pp. 285–90.

Vernon, A. (1996c) Deafness, disability and simultaneous oppression, paper presented to the PSI/ADSUP conference 'Deaf and Disabled People: Towards a New Understanding', December.

Vernon, A. (1997a) Multiple oppression: a minority interest or a majority experience?, paper presented at ESRC seminar at City University, 29 January.

Vernon, A. (1997b) The social model under attack?, *Coalition*, March.

Vernon, G. (1995) Truly, madly, deeply, *Disability Now*, February, p. 22.

Vlachou, A. (1997) *Struggles for Inclusive Education: An Ethnographic Study*. Buckingham: Open University Press.

Voysey, M. (1975) *A Constant Burden*. London: Routledge & Kegan Paul.

Wade, B. and Moore, M. (1993) *Experiencing Special Education: What Young*

People with Special Education Needs Can Tell Us. Buckingham: Open University Press.

Walker, A. (1982) *Unqualified and Underemployed*. London: Macmillan and National Children's Bureau.

Walker, A. (1995) Universal access and the built environment – or from glacier to garden gate, in G. Zarb (ed.) *Removing Disabling Barriers*. London: Policy Studies Institute.

Walker, A. and Parmar, P. (1993) *Warrior Marks: Female Genital Mutilation and the Sexual Blinding of Women*. New York: Harcourt Brace & Co.

Walker, A. and Townsend, P. (1981) *Disability Britain*. Oxford: Martin Robertson.

Walmsley, J. (1991) Talking to top people: some issues relating to the citizenship of people with learning difficulties, *Disability, Handicap and Society*, vol. 6, no. 3, pp. 219–32.

Walmsley, J. (1993) Contradictions in caring: reciprocity and interdependence, *Disability, Handicap and Society*, vol. 8, no. 2, pp. 129–41.

Warburton, W. (1990) *Developing Services for Disabled People*. London: Department of Health.

Ward, L. (1987) *Talking Points: The Right to Vote*. London: Values Into Action (formerly CMH).

Warnock Report (1978) *Special Educational Needs: Report of the Committee of Enquiry into the Education of Children and Young People*. London: HMSO.

Weber, M. (1949) *The Methodology of the Social Sciences*. Glencoe, IL: Free Press.

Weisman, L. (1992) *Discrimination by Design*. Chicago: University of Illinois Press.

Welch, C. (1996) Key issues in support, in G. Hales (ed.) *Beyond Disability*. London: Sage.

Wendell, S. (1989) Toward a feminist theory of disability, *Hypatia*, vol. 4, no. 2, pp. 104–23.

Wendell, S. (1996) *The Rejected Body: Feminist Philosophical Reflections on Disability*. London: Routledge.

Wertheimer, A. (1988) *According to the Papers: Press Reporting on People with Learning Difficulties*. London: Values Into Action.

West, J. (1991) *The Americans with Disabilities Act: From Policy to Practice*. New York: Milbank Memorial Fund.

West, P. (1985) Becoming disabled: perspectives on the labelling approach, in U. E. Gerhardt and M. J. Wadsworth (eds) *Stress and Stigma: Explanation and Evidence in the Sociology of Crime and Illness*. Basingstoke: Macmillan.

Westcott, H. (1993) *Abuse of Children and Adults with Disabilities*. London: National Society for the Prevention of Cruelty to Children.

Westcott, H. and Cross, M. (1996) *This Far and No Further: Towards the Ending of the Abuse of Disabled Children*. Birmingham: Venture Press.

Wickham-Searl, P. (1992) Careers in caring: mothers of children with disabilities, *Disability, Handicap and Society*, vol. 7, no. 1, pp. 5–18.

Wilding, P. (1982) *Professional Power and Social Welfare*. London: Routledge & Kegan Paul.

Williams, C. (1993) Vulnerable victims? A current awareness of the victimization of people with learning disabilities, *Disability, Handicap and Society*, vol. 8, no. 2, pp. 161–72.

Williams, C. (1995) *Invisible Victims: Crime and Abuse Against People with Learning Difficulties*. London: Jessica Kingsley.

Williams, F. (1989) *Social Policy: A Critical Introduction*. London: Polity Press.

Williams, F. (1995) Race/ethnicity, gender, and class in welfare states: a framework for comparative analysis, *Social Politics*, Summer, pp. 127–59. Chicago: University of Illinois.

Williams, G. and Wood, P. H. N. (1988) Coming to terms with chronic illness: the negotiation of autonomy in rheumatoid arthritis, *International Disability Studies*, vol. 10, pp. 128–32.

Williams, G. H. (1984) The movement for Independent Living: an evaluation and critique, *Social Science and Medicine*, vol. 17, no. 15, pp. 1000–12.

Williams, G. H. (1991) Disablement and the ideological crisis in health care, *Social Science and Medicine*, vol. 32, pp. 517–24.

Williams, G. H. (1996) Representing disability: some questions of phenomenology and politics, in C. Barnes and G. Mercer (eds) *Exploring the Divide: Illness and Disability*. Leeds: The Disability Press.

Williams, P. and Shoultz, B. (1992) *We Can Speak for Ourselves*. London: Souvenir Press.

Willis, G. (1993) *Barriers to Employment of Disabled People*. London: Excel Employment.

Willis, P. (1977) *Learning to Labour*. Farnborough: Saxon House.

Willis, P. (1984) Youth unemployment: thinking the unthinkable, *Youth and Policy*, vol. 2, no. 4, pp. 17–24 and 33–6.

Wilson, G. (1995) *Community Care: Asking the Users*. London: Chapman & Hall.

Wilson, J. (1983) *Disability Prevention: The Global Challenge*. Oxford: Oxford University Press.

Wiltshire, S. (1991) *Floating Cities*. London: Michael Joseph.

Wolfe, T. (1981) *From Bauhaus to Our House*. New York: Farrar, Straus, Giroux.

Wolfensberger, W. (1970) The principle of normalization and its implications for psychiatric services, *American Journal of Psychiatry*, vol. 127, pp. 291–7.

Wolfensberger, W. (1972) *The Principle of Normalisation in Human Services*. Toronto: National Institute on Mental Retardation.

Wolfensberger, W. (1989) Human service policies: the rhetoric versus the reality, in L. Barton (ed.) *Disability and Dependency*. Lewes: Falmer Press.

Wolfensberger, W. (1993) A reflection on the life of Alfred Hoche, the ideological godfather of the German euthanasia programme, *Disability, Handicap and Society*, vol. 8, no. 3, pp. 311–17.

Wolfensberger, W. (1994) The growing threat to the lives of handicapped people in the context of modernistic values, *Disability and Society*, vol. 9, no. 3, pp. 395–413.

Wolfensberger, W. (1995) Social role valorization is too conservative. No, it is too radical, *Disability and Society*, vol. 10, no. 3, pp. 245–7.

Wolinsky, F. D. and Wolinsky, S. R. (1981) Expecting sick role legitimation and getting it, *Journal of Health and Social Behaviour*, vol. 22, pp. 229–42.

Wood, P. (1980) *International Classification of Impairments, Disabilities and Handicaps*. Geneva: World Health Organisation.

Wood, R. (1991) Care of disabled people, in G. Dalley (ed.) *Disability and Social Policy*. London: Policy Studies Institute.

World Health Organization (1980) *International Classification of Impairments, Disabilities and Handicaps*. Geneva: WHO.

Wright, D. and Digby, A. (eds) (1996) *From Idiocy to Mental Deficiency*. London: Routledge.

Younghusband, E., Birchall, D., Davie, R. and Kellmer Pringle, M. L. (1970) *Living with Handicap: The Report of a Working Party on Children with Special Needs*. London: National Children's Bureau.

Yuker, H. E. (ed.) (1988) *Attitudes Towards People with Disabilities*. New York: Springer.

Zarb, G. (1991) Creating a supportive environment: meeting the needs of people who are ageing with a disability, in M. Oliver (ed.) *Social Work: Disabled People and Disabling Environments*. London: Jessica Kingsley.

Zarb, G. (1992) On the road to Damascus: first steps towards changing the relations of disability research production, *Disability, Handicap and Society*, vol. 7, no. 2, pp. 125–38.

Zarb, G. (ed.) (1995) *Removing Disabling Barriers*. London: Policy Studies Institute.

Zarb, G. and Oliver, M. (1993) *Ageing with a Disability: What Do They Expect After All These Years*. London: University of Greenwich.

Zola, I. (1979) Helping one another: a speculative history of the self-help movement, *Archives of Physical Medicine and Rehabilitation*, vol. 60.

Zola, I. (1983) Developing new self-images and interdependence, in N. M. Crewe and I. K. Zola (eds) *Independent Living for Physically Disabled People*. San Francisco: Jossey Bass.

Zola, I. (1989) Towards the necessary universalising of a disability policy, *The Milbank Quarterly*, vol. 67, suppl. 2, part 2, pp. 401–28.

Zola, I. (1991) Bringing our bodies and ourselves back in: reflections on a past, present and future medical sociology, *Journal of Health and Social Behaviour*, vol. 32, pp. 1–16.

Zola, I. (1992) The politics of disability, *Disability Studies Quarterly*, vol. 12, no. 3.

Zola, I. (1994) Towards inclusion: the role of people with disabilities in policy and research in the United States – a historical and political analysis, in M. H. Rioux and M. Bach (eds) *Disability Is Not Measles: New Research Paradigms in Disability*. North York, Ontario: Roeher.

Index

Abberley, P.   58. 75, 217, 223
Albrecht, G.   71
Altman, R.   185, 189, 193ff.
Annie's Coming Out   185
Archigram   135
Aristotle   187
Asylum for the Industrious Blind   96
Australia   167, 170, 173
Avon Coalition of Disabled People   250

Bailey, D and Hall, S.   161
Baldwin, J.   14
Ballard, K.   62
Barnes, C.   1, 60, 130, 144, 181, 207, 214, 223, 249
Barton, L.   223, 252
Bauhaus   135, 140
Becker, H.   234
Bedlam   172
Bell Curve, The   61
Benton, P.   179
Berger, P.   235
The Best Years of Our Lives   185, 194
Beynon, H.   98
Blaxter, M.   238
Blink   195
Born on the Fourth of July   184, 185, 192, 193
Bradshaw, S.   36, 43
Breaking the Waves   185

Brisenden, S.   2
British Council of Organisations of Disabled People (BCODP)   65, 67, 79, 88
British Deaf Association (BDA)   67
Brown C.   194
Bury, M.   66, 149, 237ff.

Campbell, J. and Oliver, M.   206
Campling, J.   77
Carver, V.   40ff.
Castle, I.   185
Cavalier   117
Chappell, A. L.   100ff.
Charmaz, K.   149, 175
Cheshire Homes   37ff.
Children of a Lesser God   185
China   92
Christie, N.   100
Chronically Sick and Disabled Persons Act (1970)   36
Clough, P. and Barton, L.   62
Cobby, Anita   163
Coffield, F.   95
Coleman, J. S.   105ff.
Coming Home   192
Les Congrès Internationaux d'Architecture   137
Conservative Party   97
Corbett, J.   62, 224
Cornes, P.   115, 117
Crawford, M.   133ff., 145
Crawford, R.   159

Crow, L.   149, 216, 217
Cumberbatch, G. and Negrine,
   R.   182
Custen, G.   184
Cutter's Way   192
Czech Republic   96

Davies, C. and Lifchez, R.   132ff.,
   141, 145
Davis, K.   43, 247
Davis, L.   2, 182ff., 227
A Day in the Life of Joe Egg   194,
   195, 196
De Jong, G.   69ff.
Derrida, J.   227ff.
Disability Alliance (DA)   67
Disability and Society (book)   252
*Disability, Handicap and Society/
   Disability and Society* (journal)   3,
   246, 253
Disability Politics   253
Disability Studies Quarterly   3
*Disabled People in Britain and
   Discrimination*   249
Disabled Peoples'
   International   67, 79
Disablement Income Group   35ff.,
   67
Dr Kildare   186
Donaldson's School for the
   Deaf   96
Doyal, L.   83ff.
Duet for One   196
Dumb and Dumber   194
Dumbleton, P.   99ff.
Durkheim, E.   80ff.
Dyer, R.   190

Edinburgh   96, 156
Education (Scotland) Act
   (1906)   96
Egerton Commission   96
The Eighth Day   185
Ekistics   135
The Elephant Man   185, 193, 194,
   196

Engels, F.   82ff.
Evans, P.   57
Exploring the Divide   251
Extreme Measure   195

Fermat's Last Theorem   100
Finkelstein, V.   2, 72ff., 89, 257
Fokus   42
Fordism   101
Foucault, M.   171, 176, 226, 231,
   247
France   141
Freaks   185
French, S.   100, 217
Freud, S.   87, 223
Fry   187
Fukuyama, F.   106ff.

Garland Thompson, R.   2
Gelb, S. A.   215
Gerhardt, U.   149
Germany   105, 141, 144, 195
Gerschick, T. J. and Miller,
   A. S.   150
Gertner, V.   141–3
Ghirardo, D.   131
Gibson, L.   163
Giddens, A.   54, 160
Glaser, B. and Strauss, A.   238
Glasgow   97
Goddard   215
Goffman, E.   147, 237
The Good, the Bad and the Ugly   186
Gorz, A.   88
Gouldner, A.   88
Gramsci, A.   3, 69, 82, 190
Gray, E.   135
Greater Manchester Coalition of
   Disabled People (GMCDP)   75,
   246
Greaves, M.   35
Gropius, W.   137
Grosz, E.   173
Grove Road   43

Hahn, H.   130

Hanna, A. J. and Rogovsky,
  B. 204
Hannington, W. 83ff.
Harré, R. 228
Harvey, D. 98ff.
Hawking, S. 115
Hayden, D. 145
Hearn, K. 201
Henderson, M. G. 202
Herrnstein, R. and Murray, C. 61
Hevey, D. 214
Hill, M. 206
Hill Collins, P. 90, 203
Hillyer, B. 165
Hines, M. 43
Hollywood 185, 187, 192, 196
The Hunchback of Notre Dame 186
Hunt, P. 2, 44–5, 73
Hutson, S. and Jenkins, R. 95

I Don't Want To Be Born 186
International Classificiation of
  Impairments, Diseases,
  Handicaps (ICIDH) 66, 79ff.,
  236

Jencks, C. 134
Johnny Belinda 185
Johnny Got His Gun 185
Jones, G. 95

Keith, L. 217
Klobas, L. 181
Knesl, J. 144
Knox, P. 137, 139
Kriegel, L. 161
Kuhn, T. 69

Labour Party 97, 98
Ladd, P. 43, 229
Lambeth 43
Lane, H. 226, 227
Lash, S. and Urry, J. 99, 108
Le Corbusier 136ff.
Leaman, Dick 43

Leeds, University of 1
Lenin, V. 82
Lewis, D. 178
Liberation Network of People with
  Disabilities 74
Liggett, H. 228
Local Enterprise Companies
  (LECs) 94ff.
Longmore, P. 181
Lonsdale, S. 204
Los Angeles 130
Loury 105
Lumb, K. 43

Macdonald, P. 206
McDonald's 104
MacFarlane, A. 202
MacFarlane, K. 115
McGlynn, S. and Murrain,
  P. 131ff.
Madison, M. 90
Manchester 43
Marx, K. 69, 82ff., 223
Marxism 82ff., 98, 107
Matrix 132ff.
Mental Deficiency Act (1913) 215
Mexico 193
Micronesia 178
Midnight Cowboy 186
Miller, E. J. and Gwynne,
  G. V. 38, 42, 46, 67
Mills, C. W. 54
Moby Dick 185
Monkey Shines 186, 195
Moore, C. and Bloomer, K. 139
Morris, J. 1, 2, 58, 149, 150, 181,
  205ff., 212ff., 217, 250
Morris, W. 87
Mouzelis, N. 149
The Mummy 194
My Left Foot 184, 185, 187, 193,
  194

National League of the Blind
  (NLB) 67
Neale, S. 186, 189

Netherlands 151, 144
Night Song 195
Norden, M. 181ff.
NUD.IST 151

Oakes, J. *et al.* 188
Oakland, CA 141, 142
Oliver, M. 1, 2, 3, 45, 47, 75, 148, 213, 217, 219, 243, 246ff.
O'Neil, J. 137, 143
Open University 2, 31, 38ff.

Parsons, T. 66
Passion Fish 185
Pearl, A. 61
Piaget, J. 223
Pinder, R. 149
Politics of Disablement, The 246, 250
Pride of the Marines 185
Pring, R. and Walford, G. 64
The Proud One 194

The Raging Moon 185, 193
Rain Man 185
Renteria, D. 208
Riddell, S. 223
Riddell, S. and Brown, S. 96
Rose, G. 167, 175
Rose, N. 148
Royal Institution of British Architects (RIBA) 133
Ryan, J. and Thomas, F. 57

Sartre, J.-P. 82
Schuchmann, J. 181
Schweickart, P. 91
Scottish Enterprise 103
Sennett, R. 131ff.
Sexual Politics of Disability, The 253
Shakespeare, T. 216, 243, 252
Singapore 96
The Small Back Room 186
Spinal Injuries Association 36, 43

Stichting Architectin Research 141
Stone, D. 70
The Story of Alexander Graham Bell 184, 185
Straus, R. 236
Stuart, O. 202
Sullivan, L. 136
Sutherland, A. 74
Sweden 144

Taylor, C. 148
Taylor, F. W. 98, 107
The Tingler 186
Todorov, T. 187
Topliss, E. 81ff.
Torch Song 185
Townsend, P. 68
Tungaru 178

Understanding Disability 247ff., 250
Union of Physically Impaired Against Segregation (UPIAS) 56, 68, 73
United States 1, 144, 167, 170

Van der Rohe, M. 139
Venturi, R. 137

Warnock Report 97
The Waterdance 185, 195
Weisman, L. 140, 141, 145
Whose Life Is It Anyway? 185, 187, 194–5, 196
Williams, F. 215
Willis, P. 95, 102
Wolfe, T. 135, 137
Wolfensberger, W. 70ff., 176
World Health Organization 66, 79ff., 236
Worsley, P. 235

Zola, I. 166, 243ff.